Praise for *Crash Course*

"*Crash Course* is a compelling moment-by-moment recounting of a startling modern air disaster. But above all, it's a vital account of the bruising fight to make aviation safer and to hold a corporation accountable for its actions."

—Paul Collins, author of *Duel With the Devil*

"*Crash Course* is a masterful, true account of a forgotten commercial airline tragedy that forever changed aviation. It's a must-read for any aviation enthusiast—or anyone who flies."

—Chris Mendenhall
Air Traffic Controller and son of Flight Engineer
Forrest Mendenhall lost in the crash of United Flight 173

"The story of United Flight 173 stands at the intersection of power and justice, of profit and safety, and life and death."

—Greg Kafoury
Litigator and Civil Justice Activist
Kafoury & McDougal

"Human drama, aviation operations, corporate intrigue, government bureaucracy, legal machination are all here. If you are looking for a great read, you will enjoy *Crash Course*. I could not put it down when I read it—either time!"

—Tom Cordell
FAA Designated Pilot Examiner, Retired United Airlines Captain

"The public rarely gets to glimpse the personal ordeal and legal trajectory of a high-stakes case. So much of what gets decided in our halls of justice goes unpublished and unnoticed, even when the ripple effects reach us all. A captivating read, *Crash Course* peels back the lid on the astonishing aftermath and enduring legacy of an aviation disaster."

—Lori Osmundsen
Civil Litigator
Harvard Law

Accidents don't just happen...

Crash Course

Julie Whipple

Yamhill Canyon Press
Portland, Oregon

For

Stewart M. Whipple

and all who were aboard United Flight 173

Author's note: the following narrative is based on and rendered from cockpit voice recorder transcripts; trial depositions, testimony and discovery; NTSB investigation records; passenger, crew and witness recollections; news reports, interviews, and other research materials as noted in the text and bibliography. All photos are from trial exhibits or were taken by the author unless otherwise noted.

Foreword

The crash of United Flight 173 was a devastating event that ended ten lives and forever changed the lives of countless others—including yours. One book cannot tell all these important stories, but I hope this one gives a glimpse of how a disaster bursts into existence and then stretches out in ever-widening waves of connection and impact across communities and generations, forging tangible links between our past and present.

Lodged now in numberless hearts and memories, and in safety practices and civil protections that we must never take for granted, the many legacies of Flight 173—shared at dinner tables, in cockpits, boardrooms and courtrooms—are part of us in ways we might never really grasp. With deepest respect and humility, this story is offered as the record of one of these complex, far-reaching trajectories, and as a tribute to them all.

JW

Contents

Prologue

"Stories have to be told or they die, and when they die, we can't remember who we are or why we're here."

-- Sue Monk Kidd, author

My father sits across from me at his big oak desk, wearing his blue business suit and his favorite brown belt cinched to the last notch around his slender frame. The briefcase before him is full, as always, of news articles and copies of the latest Oregon Appeals and Supreme Court decisions. We are at his Macadam Avenue office where he has been practicing law for over half of his sixty-three-year legal career and is now the last surviving partner of his Portland law firm, Whipple, Johansen, McClain. From the case, he produces a certificate he has received in the mail from the Oregon Bar Association congratulating him, Stewart M. Whipple, on his fifty years of service.

"Apparently that's as high as they go," he says, with a smile.

His neatly-combed hair is pure white now and corn-silk thin, and he has to remind himself to stand up straighter sometimes, but you can still see the litigator in him. His soft-spoken ways are rarely ruffled, but the warrior is there just beneath the calm surface, competitive, controlled and very experienced. Now ninety-one, his courtroom days are past, thanks to declining hearing, but he's still lawyering—though down to thirty hours a week—advising and solving problems for clients, many of whom he's had for a lifetime, and for the descendants of several he has now outlived.

He remembers everything—every case, most of the names, the expert witnesses, the wins, the few losses. One stands out this afternoon: the *Elizabeth Andor v. United Airlines* case. He hasn't shredded the files from that trial yet—there's always something else to do. But he also has a hunch that someday folks might want to know about the case and the secrets it revealed. He points to it now as a possible pathway for a daughter's many overdue questions about his life's work and important moments.

As I soon discover, the archive holds a still-resonating tale of victory and injustice that's always been there for the asking, the records of a poorly-understood, life-and industry-changing airline disaster and lawsuit that for years have been stacked and curtained on steel shelves near his desk.

Inside eight cardboard banker's boxes, neatly labeled by his long-since-retired secretary, is the only collection that may yet exist of depositions, trial exhibits, transcripts, video tapes, engineering and maintenance reports, company documents, and photos from the groundbreaking case against a corporate giant. It's a trove of material that holds long-hidden truths about a famous plane crash, and sheds a rare light on our civil justice system both then and now.

And there's also a strangely evocative child's dark-blue oxford shoe, scuffed with wear and screwed to a pair of stout metal braces attached to a wide saddle-leather band that buckles just below the knee, as if from the polio era. The shoe-contraption, still marked with a little yellow "evidence" sticker, is heavy in my hands, and I imagine the child forced to wear it coming in from outside and hurriedly pulling it off, anxious to be rid of the awful thing.

Even though decades have passed since United Flight 173 ran out of fuel and crash-landed in a Portland neighborhood, the accident holds important lessons for us now. That's why my father still clips and saves any article he finds that concerns safety, training, and accountability in the airline industry, and the protection of the constitutional rights of the individual in the courts.

His vigilance is born of experience and alarm, since many of today's stories reflect aviation maintenance and operational factors similar to those that led to the needless loss of a passenger jet on a chill winter night in 1978. Other stories echo the issues of civil justice he fought for in the dramatic legal battle that followed—a battle that anyone who has been injured by a corporation's unsafe product or practice *still* faces, but now against even higher odds thanks to pro-business legislation, court secrecy, forced arbitration agreements, and other recent initiatives that favor corporations over the individual.

And it's also because of the little girl, Elizabeth, "Lisa," who was just three years old when she was pulled, barely breathing, from the wreckage. She captured his heart when he met her for the first time in the hospital, her body encased in a plaster cast, her light-brown hair hidden under bandages.

"It was a sad thing," he recalls, and I can see him mentally replay the images. "She had a little stuffed animal, and when she saw me she raised it up and said, 'He's going to get you!'" Dad smiles at the memory of her spirit, and as if to say that her story should not be forgotten.

His old office chair gives out a very familiar squeak as he leans forward and pushes a stack of files across his cluttered desk toward me. Among them is the thick 1981 deposition of the disgraced pilot, Captain Malburn Adair McBroom, along with the cockpit voice recorder transcript of his doomed aircraft; also, three DC-8 service bulletins from McDonnell Douglas sent out to its airline industry customers over the course of ten years before the crash, warning of a mechanical problem that needed to be fixed.

"Read these," he says. "It's a good place to start."

The Oregonian
Friday, December 29, 1978
United DC-8 Crashes at E. Burnside, 157th;
10 Killed, 175 Survive

==================================

At midnight, reporters were still frantically nailing down facts about the dead and survivors of a devastating air crash in a Portland suburb when the Sunrise Edition of The Oregonian had to go to press for morning delivery. It had been a chaotic scene around the carcass of the big jet, tucked among splintered trees and nearby homes, as stunned passengers, rescue workers, the media, neighbors and curious bystanders tried to comprehend what had just happened.

Six hours earlier. . .

Chapter 1

The End of Routine

Gabor Andor was by all accounts a happy man. He had done pretty well for himself in his new country. He'd been in the United States for only eight years, but, surrounded by his wife and three young daughters, flying into Portland first-class, Gabor could only have marveled at the change in his life since his escape from Hungary in 1968.

He checked his seat belt and glanced at his wife, perhaps giving way to a sense of wonder as he looked at Rosie's pretty round face. He'd never have dreamed that the work he found in a butcher shop in Vienna after his escape would lead him here. Memories of his time in the Austrian capital were still vivid. The city had been full of refugees from behind the Iron Curtain. That's where he'd befriended fellow Hungarian escapee Louie Csonaki. Like others who had managed to reach the West from the dictatorships in Poland, Hungary, Romania, East Germany, and Czechoslovakia, both young men hoped to get to the United States as political refugees. In 1970 Louie's visa came through, and shortly after that, he and his boss, a chainsaw distributor who needed warehouse labor, helped to sponsor Gabor into the United States.

In the beginning, Gabor had often been lonely here. The country was so big and unpredictable compared to the tightly controlled existence he'd grown up under, and, of course, he didn't speak the language. He missed his parents and the three brothers he'd left behind, but he soon found other jobs that kept him busy and his mind

7

occupied, and he had his friend Louie in Vancouver, Washington who'd given him a temporary home.

It wasn't that Gabor had gotten rich over the intervening years in America, but the six-foot, square-jawed immigrant with a stevedore's build knew how to work hard and make the most of opportunities. His time in the Hungarian army had taught him that much. And he had a stubborn streak, well-known among his friends, that tended to assert itself after a few drinks. To be sure, he was used to overcoming barriers. His determination showed through his strong foreign accent and may have tempted some to assume that the scar on the right side of his face where (as one story went) a horse had kicked him in his youth was instead the result of a more intentional incident.

Gabor's persistence paid off when he landed a position with United Airlines in the food service department, a good fit for someone who loved to cook and entertain. Then he hit the jackpot and everything changed when he met and married his beautiful Rosina, a petite hairdresser from Chicago who'd come to the United States with her parents from Italy when she was a teenager. The couple decided to settle and start their family not far from Louie in Vancouver.

Now, as 1978 was coming to a close, Gabor had recently moved his growing family from a duplex to a larger house in Vancouver. The mortgage interest rates were high—9.5 percent and rising—but Gabor and Rosina needed more space to accommodate their three little girls, Elizabeth (Lisa), Gabriella, and baby Rosina, and he saw it as an investment in the future. His work with the airline was steady, and he was coming up on his one-year anniversary as a full-fledged U.S. citizen. Truly, he was living the American Dream.

Still, with the recent deregulation of the airline industry, new uncertainties were rippling through conversations at work. There was talk that the in-flight meals, always a key area of competition between airlines, would be among the first costs to be cut once ticket prices were fully de-controlled. Gabor wasn't sure how that might affect his job in United's catering department in the coming year, but there was no use in worrying about that now. United was a big company. It would take care of them.

It had been a long day's travel from Chicago with the little ones after the holiday visit with Rosina's parents and her sister's family. Fortunately, it was Thursday, December 28, so they'd have the whole weekend and Monday, New Year's Day, to get resettled. Gabor was also looking forward to celebrating his thirty-ninth birthday on Saturday.

As a United employee, he had free travel perks that made it possible to afford family vacations like this trip to Illinois to visit his wife's relatives. They could even sit in first class on a space-available basis. They had changed planes in Denver, connecting with the last leg of United Flight 173 from New York to Portland. The flight was fairly full, but they'd been delighted to find that there were some open seats together in the first-class section so the family would have a little extra room.

An off-duty pilot, T. D. Garrett, was sitting behind them on his way to join an outbound flight crew in Portland. And Joan Wheeler, the lead flight attendant, was in charge of the section. She was under the weather but had been very sweet to them, offering extra pillows and United Airlines wing badges to the children.

Both flights had gone smoothly, but Gabor and Rosina were tired now and anxious to get home and put the girls to bed. It was 5:05 p.m., already dark, and Gabor could see the lights of Portland in the distance as he tucked away the latest issue of *Time Magazine* announcing President Carter's historic re-establishment of diplomatic ties with Communist China after thirty years of frost between the two powers. Growing up under the Hungarian Communist dictatorship left Gabor with a deep mistrust toward such governments. The United States would have to proceed very cautiously.

In the main cabin, seventeen-year-old Aimee Conner had only just barely made the flight in Denver after a late connection from Texas. She pushed her smooth brown hair from her face and apologized as she scrambled into her middle seat just behind the right wing next to a woman from Eugene named Nancy. Once in the air, the year's hit movie, *Animal House*, which had been filmed at the University of Oregon in Eugene, would have made a natural conversation starter for the friendly teenager as they settled in over a snack of ham salad served on the two-and-a-half-hour flight.

Aimee, her name spelled like the French word for "beloved," was headed to Portland for a brief stop on her way back to complete her senior year at a high school at the remote north end of Lake Chelan, Washington. She'd spent the Christmas holidays at a family gathering in Roswell, New Mexico, getting caught up with relations and new bands like the Police and the Blues Brothers. She was still dressed for warmer weather in a light polyester jacket. She planned to spend the night in Portland with friends and then catch a small commuter plane to Wenatchee, Washington on Cascade Airlines the fol-

10

lowing day. Then she'd take the lake ferry to get to tiny Holden Village, where a Lutheran retreat center and her school were located.

Though her family lived in Minnesota, and she'd only been in Holden for four months, since the start of fall term, Aimee already felt it was her spiritual home, her refuge from the stress that came from being the middle child of five. For this black sheep of the family, it was also a last chance to graduate with a high school diploma. It had been a particularly rough year. In the spring, she'd had enough of her public high school and dropped out. Not long after, her mother had nearly died from a cerebral aneurysm.

She still had a ways to go on her journey "home," but she was finally getting closer to the snow-covered cabins in the mountains where she could read and study and practice knitting. Her ears popped as the aircraft started its descent into Portland.

Sandy Bass slipped her rust-red uniform jacket back on over her matching polyester trousers and finished securing the middle galley for landing. The weather was chilly in Portland, so it was great that flight attendant uniforms finally included a pants option—heck, the airline had even just removed the ban on pregnancy. Big year for women's lib!

It was a typical after-Christmas trip with one 181 passengers on board. The autumn-gold seats, three abreast on either side of the blue-carpeted aisle, were filled with families returning home who'd been on the plane the week before, and were now laden with their holiday loot. The new digital-format watch was a hit, gracing many of the wrists on board, and some of the kids had happily occupied themselves with a bright red, plastic gadget called a Speak & Spell. One man had used the holiday to get a hair transplant, while another, a prisoner, was traveling back to jail with his armed escort.

Sandy had been on the route for the whole month, flying lead position while Joan was on vacation, and then out sick. Joan was back now, but still not well, so Sandy had checked in the passengers at the gate in Denver. Tonight was her last trip for December, a Portland turn, which meant they'd land, debark the passengers and then fly back to Denver where she'd catch a flight home to Dallas and relax for a few days before her next assignment.

She might have time to grab a quick bite with the crew at the airport before heading back out. Folks were still buzzing about the Jonestown mass suicide, and the huge Lufthansa heist in the New York airport just two weeks earlier. Maybe there was some new scuttlebutt going around among the New York based flight crews that would shed more detail on how the thieves had pulled off a robbery at the airport terminal that netted a whopping six million in cash.

She glanced at the faces down the length of the "stretch" DC-8. Many, without the distraction of children, were buried in the recent crop of best-selling novels: *Eye of the Needle;* the latest Michener door-stop *Chesapeake;* and the *Hobbit* prequel, *The Silmarillion.* Some of the women were reading *Wifey,* a surprisingly racy new novel for grown-ups by the famed children's book author, Judy Blume.

Sandy's well-trained instincts told her it was about time for the announcement for flight attendants to prepare for landing. She had already been through her section of the cabin checking seat belts and hand luggage. Everything was ready for arrival.

In his shirtsleeves in the cockpit, Captain Malburn "Buddy" McBroom was on an approach into Portland he'd already done twelve times that month—and countless other times before that. It was dark, and a winter-cold thirty degrees, but visibility was good for that time of year, sparkling clear. As the plane passed a snow-covered Mt. Hood, ghostly pale against the night sky, a few lighted ski runs twinkled on the slopes below like fireflies beaded on strings. McBroom got on the intercom.

"For you folks on the right side of the aircraft, there's a great view of the night skiing on the mountain out the window."

Having worked December and November with his younger co-pilot Rod Beebe, the fifty-two year-old McBroom had given the controls to him so he could get some more time hand-flying the Super 61 DC-8. Clearance had just come in from approach control at the Portland airport to descend from 10,000 feet.

McBroom, a veteran pilot, liked to have the arrival paperwork done before beginning descent, and Engineer Forrest "Frostie" Mendenhall, who'd also flown the route with McBroom all of the month of December, was a step ahead of him. He'd already prepared the landing card listing the wind, temperature, ceiling, approach speed, fuel on board, arrival time—all routine.

At the controls, Beebe called for flaps fifteen degrees to reduce speed for the lower altitude, and McBroom, acting as co-pilot, gave it to him. Over the radio, Portland approach called out air traffic five miles directly ahead of them. McBroom had already spotted the red lights of the aircraft and responded, "Roger, one seventy-three heavy, I have him."

Now at 7,000 feet, Beebe asked for landing gear down and McBroom leaned over and grasped a lever he'd pulled hundreds of times in his twenty-seven-year career, and knew by heart. Instinctively, his hand and ears expected the sequence: the change in the wind noise when the bay doors opened, and the vibrating rumble of the gear mechanism as the hydraulic system began to lower the nearly two-ton wheel assemblies on either side of the aircraft into landing-ready position.

But that's not what happened.

Chapter 2

A Bird Takes Wing

Long Beach, California—1965

Bagpipers were playing on the runway under a smoggy southern California sky in honor of Donald Douglas's Scottish heritage when his company, Douglas Aircraft, rolled out its gleaming new DC-8 Super Sixty series to the world in April 1965. Built at the company's Long Beach plant, the big four-engine passenger jet was a "stretched" model of its popular earlier DC-8s, and also a departure from Douglas' reluctance to adapt its fuselage design to match the desires of its airline customers.

But after years of brutal competition between Douglas and the more market-accommodating Boeing, coupled with the need to reduce rising congestion at airports by using higher-capacity aircraft, Douglas chose practicality over pride and added nearly thirty-seven feet to the cabin of its DC-8s, and the Super Sixties were born.

They were a game changer for the company—at least temporarily. For the next three years the stretch DC-8 would be refined, re-engined and modified until it was the largest single-aisle commercial jet in the world, with a longer range and a maximum capacity of 259 passengers, forty more than the largest version of its closest rival, the Boeing 707. It was a position that wouldn't be challenged until the wide-body Boeing 747 jumbo jet came on the scene in 1970.

It was still early days in the world of commercial jet transport, but virtually in the blink of an eye, travel and air freight transitioned away from the old piston-type propeller aircraft, largely fueled by growing demand for faster, longer-range travel. In 1935, it took seventeen hours to cross the U.S. in a prop-driven DC-3. In 1960, only twenty-four years later, it took a little over five hours to do the same in the first DC-8 passenger jets.

Built to last, with redundant systems throughout, the DC-8s came out of what might be called the something-to-prove-generation that developed the atomic bomb and put a man on the moon just two decades after ice boxes really used ice. They were the slide-rule-wielding designers and engineers who were out to demonstrate that new technology could do a lot more, and yet be just as sturdy, just as reliable as a set of wheels and four legs.

The all-metal DC-8 was engineered to be durable—along with everything else of the era, including appliances from Westinghouse and General Electric, and vehicles from General Motors and Chevrolet. And they're still out there, working and stylish: the 1940s vintage stoves, 1950s Cadillacs, even a few 1960s DC-8s.

But that's not to say the new jets didn't have problems as companies struggled to keep pace with rapid growth in demand—the number of passengers traveling by air in the U.S. tripled between 1959 and 1969, stretching the limits of industry safety and capability. The sixties and seventies, in particular, were a dangerous proving ground for the airlines. The decades are infamous for the highest number of air crashes worldwide of any decade before or since (except during World War II), with 1,799 and 2,993 accidents respectively. It lethally demonstrated the need for better air traffic control, regulatory oversight, pilot training, safety and maintenance protocols, and equipment improvements.

Aircraft manufacturers scrambled to prevent or respond to problems as they emerged by notifying their customers, and working with them to make improvements. Douglas Aircraft (soon to be known as McDonnell Douglas) issued fifty-nine service bulletins, along with suggested remedies, to its customers between 1960 and 1968 about its DC-8s regarding a range of maintenance and structural issues encountered with the wings, fuselage, flight controls and landing gear.

Aircraft manufacturers weren't the only ones trying to keep up with the headlong rush into the jet age. The Federal Aviation Administration (FAA), founded in 1958 as the first jets were rolling off the line, was charged with keeping the flying public safe in the air, but it could barely process the variety of dangers being encountered, much less stay ahead of them.

So the regulators developed a priority system that categorized some of the problem areas and service bulletins as critical enough to reinforce with mandatory Airworthiness Directives. An AD requires airlines to take time-certain action to fix such problems. But many other service bulletins were left to the airlines to handle as part of their routine maintenance schedules. Even so, in 1972, the FAA took stock of the DC-8, and gathered and published a complete list of service bulletins in an "Advisory Circular" prefaced with the following cautionary reminder:

> "It must be emphasized that the manufacturer has published several service bulletins concerning the inspection, repair and modification of McDonnell Douglas DC-8 series aircraft. Service bulletins highlight the importance of maintaining struc-

tural integrity on aircraft with particular reference to areas known to have experienced crack and corrosion damage."

Because of exposure to moisture, and the punishment associated with landings and take-offs, the landing gear was particularly susceptible to such crack and corrosion problems. Sixteen service bulletins were dedicated to this area alone, three of which, issued in 1966, 1967 and 1968, involved the piston rod end eyebolt on the main landing gear retraction cylinder, the mechanism that raised the gear for flight, or lowered it for landing. Metal engineers had discovered that the sharp, machine-cut threads on the eyebolt had a tendency to crack; they did not have the strength, durability and corrosion-resistance of bolts manufactured with rolled-type threads. Douglas changed to the stronger bolt in its later DC-8s and advised its airline customers three times to replace them on their existing fleets, and to inspect and re-seal the components regularly.

But not everybody did. The FAA didn't make the repair mandatory, even though they'd documented several reports from DC-8 owners of landing gear problems connected with broken retraction cylinder eyebolts. In one instance of such problems with the gear, "Flight crew reported a severe jolt when the landing gear was extended and did not get a down and locked indication. Inspection showed the left main landing gear was not down and locked due to broken retract and bungee cylinders," the latter touted as the back-up system for the landing gear mechanism. Both had failed.

United Airlines, the largest DC-8 operator of the time, knew all about this, having recorded five such failures on its own fleet. But instead of replacing the bolts on its DC-8s as McDonnell Douglas recommended in its service bulletins, the company began a cost and time-saving radioisotope imaging program in 1973 using gamma rays to inspect landing gear components without taking them apart. The idea was to detect if cracking or corrosion was indeed underway and actually necessitated the bolt replacement.

This strategy was in line with a new decision-based maintenance discipline called Reliability Centered Maintenance (RCM), which was developed and described in the mid 1970s in a study by two United employees, and sponsored by the Department of Defense. Its authors, F. Stanley Nowlan and Howard F. Heap, started with a euphemistic definition of failure as "an unsatisfactory condition," and then listed the consequences of failure from the point of view of safety and economics. They wrote that if imminent danger to property and personnel could be ruled out as a consequence of a given failure, then "In all other cases the consequences of failure are economic and the value of preventive maintenance must be measured in economic terms."

RCM made a lot of business sense as the costs of aircraft maintenance skyrocketed. Nowlan and Heap noted that much of this was due to "unexamined reasons" for many routine maintenance activities, and a lack of real data supporting the costs and benefits associated with them. They proposed a different approach:

"Each scheduled maintenance task in an RCM program is generated for an identifiable and explicit reason. The consequences of each failure possibility are evaluated, and the failures are then classified according to the severity of their consequences."

Once the failures were categorized, an airline maintenance department could use a rational, yes/no question-based flow chart the authors provided to determine when to correct problems. Stated matter-of-factly, they made their point: "Failures may well be tolerable in the sense that it is less expensive to correct them as they occur than to invest in the cost of preventing them."

Preventing eyebolt failure by replacing them on the entire United fleet would not have required significant time, cost, or service interruption. The new bolt itself was only $124, and the replacement process outlined in Douglas' service bulletin was well within the scope of United's nineteen Line Maintenance centers. Douglas estimated the job would take about eighteen hours for each airplane—a "loss of service" that the RCM authors said also had to be factored into the decision making:

"Whenever equipment is removed from service to correct a failure, the cost of failure includes that loss of service—a fact that must be taken into account in evaluating the benefit of preventative maintenance."

But according to two former United line mechanics, the fix could be accomplished within a normal graveyard shift. The plane could be back in the air in time for the next morning flights. In fact, as former United landing gear mechanic Tom Sanderson later pointed out, if just the eyebolt was replaced, it would take, "Maybe an hour and a half, two hours at the most."

Nevertheless, from 1973 to 1978, United relied on its gamma ray inspection program to deal with the eyebolt issue. A National Transportation Safety Board (NTSB) report indicates that during the first three years of the program, United was fairly aggressive in its inspections, examining most of its aircraft each year. This isn't too surprising, since United had experienced main landing gear retract rod end failures on four of its aircraft in those first three years.

But then the inspection program lost steam. In 1976 no aircraft were inspected even though another rod end eyebolt failure occurred on a United DC-8 that same year. In 1977 and 1978 only thirty-one aircraft were examined. The gamma ray program was then discontinued.

During the six years it lasted, the inspection program detected corrosion in eyebolts in over 170 landing gears. But it wouldn't be clear until much later how often these tests actually resulted in replacement or preventative maintenance, or who at United even knew about the findings.

In January 1974, the company added to its maintenance manual a *modification* procedure "to provide a repair for pistons with corroded or worn piston rod threads." Again, counter to manufacturer service bulletins recommending that airlines replace the existing machine-threaded bolt with a stronger rolled-thread bolt, the repair detailed an alternate machining process that would grind "a new thread section as a continuation of the existing threads" into the rod end of the piston. This called for a longer bolt that United could get more quickly and cheaply from a local manufacturer.

The repair was described in the Landing Gear Overhaul chapter of the company's maintenance manual, suggesting from its placement there that United viewed the urgency of the eyebolt problem differently than Douglas did, and that repairing any corroded eyebolts would coincide with, or be deferred to, an already scheduled landing gear overhaul, which was costly and infrequent.

Landing gear components are "timed equipment" or "life limited," which means they have to be replaced after a certain period of time in operation because of the wear and tear they receive. Of course a landing gear assembly has many different components, and they don't all wear out conveniently at the same time. The manufacturer, factoring in these differences, and hoping to capture the lion's share of problems before they became a safety issue, recommended gear overhaul on DC-8s when the aircraft had about 12,000 hours of flight time on it (approximately five years). But the procedure could be—and often was—extended with FAA cooperation.

United had little trouble extending time limits or changing maintenance procedures, since it was an air carrier with "Engineering Variance Authority." The company's extensive, in-house maintenance and engineering capabilities were authorized for major aircraft repairs and modifications—including engine replacement—which would otherwise require attention from the manufacturer. Indeed, with this designation, "United's engineering and self-approval authority was equal to that of the manufacturer," observed one former pilot and mechanic.

The FAA's role in overseeing United's maintenance and engineering practices might best be described as a paperwork partnership. If United wanted to change a procedure or extend a time limit, they produced a Change Order Authorization (COA) and advised the FAA office of it. According to Gene Lansing, who was the FAA Maintenance Inspector of Airworthiness assigned to United from 1970 to 1983, such modifications and extensions were a frequent occurrence:

"United's 'time extends' bring in quite a bit of work for us—when they decide to move the time limits on some article or part of the airplane or the whole airplane."

But, Lansing added, "The COAs, while they went across our desk, did not seek formal approval. We were aware, and if there was something objectionable in there we would take it up with them."

In practice, as long as United delivered the required paperwork to the FAA, most of the actions they wanted to take were virtually a done deal.

On May 22, 1968, Douglas delivered a brand new DC-8-61 to United Airlines where it entered service in the "Friendly Skies" as Mainliner #N8082U. When the aircraft had 15,931 flight hours on it, both main landing gears were overhauled, but the eyebolts were not changed. A gamma ray inspection, detected "moderate corrosion" on the eyebolts of the plane's landing gear, but nothing was done. After another inspection, United's eyebolt-piston rod repair modification was completed on the left main landing gear, but not on the right. The last gamma ray inspection was done on its landing gear at 27,064 aircraft hours. Corrosion was documented, but the repair was deferred again.

Chapter 3

Bumps in the Night

Over Portland—December 28, 1978

In the cockpit of Flight 173, McBroom felt the surprise running up his arm as he released the gear-down lever, and co-pilot Rod Beebe suddenly pulled hard on the yoke to compensate for two massive jolts. It was 5:09 pm and the airport was in sight.

"What the hell was that?" McBroom scanned out the windows. Had he missed seeing another aircraft? Had they hit something?

"She yawed pretty good to the right, Buddy," Beebe said.

Pulse quickening, McBroom checked his instrument panels, and turned to the flight engineer, Forrest "Frostie" Mendenhall.

"What's happening with the hydraulics, Frostie?" McBroom asked.

"Looks fine; pressure, fluid, all normal."

McBroom glanced at the fuel gauges on Mendenhall's panel. They had 12,000 pounds in the tanks—plenty to get the plane on the ground. He shifted his concern back to the landing gear. What could rock a giant airliner so hard, he wondered, except maybe one of the nearly two-ton landing gears in free fall? And if that was the case, what broke? What was the condition of the gear—or the underside of the plane for that matter?

The down-lock indicator lights would hopefully tell him what he needed to know: that the gear was down and safe. But they were dark.

"The landing gear warning circuit breaker just popped," said Mendenhall.

"Reset it, and let's see what we get."

The lights came back on showing the nose gear reading steady green. The left main gear was fainter green but steady. But the right main gear was blinking green, on and off. It was as if the landing gear was swinging free, McBroom thought, making contact and breaking contact with the electrical circuit. One thing was certain, there was a short circuit in the right main landing gear—if not something worse.

"Ok, let's get the books out."

"Portland approach is clearing us for a lower altitude," Beebe said, the plane still descending.

McBroom took the radio. "United one seventy three, Portland, negative, we'd like to stay at 5,000. We got a gear problem."

Approach control asked them to climb to 7,000 to avoid air traffic but McBroom was reluctant to expend the fuel needed to gain the extra 2,000 feet. The controller agreed, and gave him a triangular holding pattern fifteen to twenty miles south of the airport.

"United one seventy three heavy, turn left heading one zero, zero; I'll just orbit you out there 'til you get your problem fixed."

At 5:15 pm, McBroom lit a cigarette, his mind a mixture of curiosity and alarm, as his co-pilot turned the plane south away from the airport and the city lights.

The cabin intercom began to buzz just as he picked up the microphone to make an announcement. And Joan, the lead flight atten-

25

dant, was already at the cockpit door wanting to know what was go ing on. She was calm, an experienced crew member, but she'd neve had a serious in-flight emergency in her fourteen years flying. She' never felt jolts like that and wanted to know if she should be worried.

"We're not sure yet; the landing gear came down hard; w may have bent a strut," McBroom ventured. "I'm sending Frostie bac to check the landing gear wings tabs, to see if they're up. They'll shov if the gear is down and locked. Was just going to make an announce ment. Tell the girls to get their manuals out. I'll keep you informed."

In the mid-galley of the cabin a few moments earlier, Sand had just finished some last minute tidying up with her fellow crev member, Nancy King when they'd nearly been knocked off their fee as the aircraft jolted twice to the side. "What the fuck!" Sandy and Nancy locked eyes. Something was wrong. Instinctively, Sandy step ped to the closest window to check the wings—yep, still there—whil Nancy reached for her emergency procedures handbook.

"That must have been a heck of an air pocket we just hit, Sandy said, knowing it was something else.

The aircraft leveled steady and smooth again, but the passen gers were visibly shaken. A baby started to cry. Sandy buzzed th cockpit for an explanation and was waiting for an answer when Joa came toward them down the aisle, all business, with the flight engi neer right behind her, carrying a flashlight.

"I just spoke to Buddy..." But Joan was interrupted by the in tercom.

"This is the captain speaking. What you heard was the extension of the landing gear. It was not normal. We'll hold in the Portland area, check it out and let you know what we are going to do."

"He thinks we may have bent a strut," Joan said quietly to the two women, fighting her own alarm. "Let's go over our handbooks," she added over her shoulder, as she headed back to brief Dianne Woods and Martha (Marty) Fralick, the two flight attendants in the rear cabin. "I'll let you know more as soon as I hear."

It was as if the volume of air inside the passenger cabin suddenly shrank as the people on board took a simultaneous deep breath in at the announcement. Several passengers in the smoking section lit cigarettes to steady their nerves.

Mendenhall made his way to the seat row over the right wing where Aimee Conner was sitting next to the now very distressed woman beside her. For seventeen-year-old Aimee, the landing gear issue—though certainly alarming when it had occurred—was likely a minor technical issue that would soon be solved. However, it was clear that for her seat companion, the circumstances felt far more dire. She'd gone very quiet and tense. Instinctively, Aimee put her hand on the woman's and said, "I think we'll get through this."

"Sorry to bother you, ladies," Mendenhall interrupted pleasantly. "I just need to check something if you wouldn't mind." The two let him by so he could get close enough to peer through the window with his flashlight.

In the cockpit, McBroom flipped on the floodlights, illuminating the vast white surface of the wingspan against the black sky so the flight engineer could get a good view.

The down-and-locked indicator is not a big target to spot; it's a disk about the size of a hockey puck with a little indicator tab in the center of it nicknamed the "bottle cap." When the wheels are retracted in flight, the tab sits flush with the surface of the disk and wing. But when the wheels are extended, and are locked in place for landing, a metal rod attached to the landing gear assembly engages and pushes the tab up a few centimeters. If the electrical system and landing gear indicator lights are not functioning properly, this tab is a physical sign that the gear is, or is not, down and locked.

After a few moments, Mendenhall backed his slender, six foot two frame into the aisle where Joan was chatting reassuringly to Aimee and her seat-mate. At forty-one, "Frostie" was the youngest officer in the cockpit, a handsome father of two, known for his goofy sense of humor.

"Looks like the bottle caps are up, so our gear seems to be down," he said, with a warm smile that contradicted his nickname.

Mendenhall made his way back to the cockpit, pausing briefly in the first-class section to let off duty Captain Garrett in on his findings. In the next seat forward, Gabor Andor might have overheard and squeezed his wife's hand to reassure her as she busied herself with the baby in her lap and their other two increasingly impatient little girls.

Chapter 4

Cowboys and Errors

Honolulu, Hawaii — 2014

"The DC-8s were noisy, the last of the tanks," says former DC-8 captain Gary Estes. He laughs and adds that he's got an appointment to have his hearing checked later in the week. The aircraft's four Pratt & Whitney turbojet engines were indeed famously loud, described as starting with a breathy whine, going from bass to highs, then growing to a throaty roar.

"The hush kits they developed later weren't standard on DC-8s until after the Sixty-ones," Estes recalls.

Estes, a baby-faced pilot in his late fifties with prematurely white hair and matching mustache, flies Boeing 747 cargo jets now for Kalitta Air, but he learned his profession on the 'eights.'

"I started as a mechanic on the DC-8, then trained and flew as flight engineer, co-pilot and then pilot for ten years."

He says the robust DC-8 was easy to fly and hard to destroy. "You could lose hydraulics or the electrical system and still fly the plane because everything was cable driven." In fact, he says, you could opt to cable-fly the aircraft without the hydraulics. "It felt good; sometimes I even preferred it."

We've climbed a steep metal stairway on wheels into the cramped cockpit of a DC-8-62 combination freight/passenger jet #N799AL. With the giant business-end of the aircraft stretching out

29

behind us for half a city block, it's easy to imagine being inside a very big bird with a very small head.

This forty-five-year-old bird, fledged in 1966, began her storied life in 1968 with SAS (Scandinavian Airlines), later flying the globe with seven other national airlines including Air Marshall Islands where she got her nickname, "Little AMI."

Air Transport International (ATI) bought the jet in 1998 and eventually retired the aircraft from service, donating Little AMI to the Naval Air Museum Barbers Point in Hawaii. The airliner is now part of the museum's historic aircraft collection, and an example of an increasingly hard-to-find, intact DC-8. Only ten are listed as still in service globally. Most nowadays have been sent to indefinite storage at the desert aircraft grave yards in Mojave, California and Marana, Arizona, or scrapped for parts. This one, in almost mint condition and available to visit, is a very lucky find.

On this overcast tropical afternoon, punctuated by warm showers, the museum has arranged for Estes, who's on a flight layover, to show me through the aircraft. He admits to being happy to get the chance to poke around and indulge his own nostalgia.

Little AMI sits almost expectantly on the rain-glazed tarmac. Inside the battleship-grey cockpit, a pavé of analog gauges, switches and dials covers the walls and ceiling. The matching, no-nonsense grey-upholstered pilot and copilot seats are frayed at the shoulders where aviators have gripped them countless times for support as they maneuvered into position over the years. Estes does exactly that as he squeezes into the co-pilot's seat, and takes hold of the yoke like a kid pretending to drive a parked car. Then he points at the switches that would fire the start-up sequence.

"It's tempting," he smiles.

Oxygen masks still hang at the ready, aircraft manuals, quick reference cards and spiral notebooks fill the nooks and seat back pockets. It's as if the crew has just stepped out for a break between flights.

"The pilot's on the left and copilot on the right," Estes says. "The flight engineer sits here, behind the copilot."

There's hardly room to turn around in the tiny space, but everything is within reach and within sight. Still, it's easy to imagine how quickly the close quarters could change from cozy to claustrophobic under stressful conditions—in an emergency, or if communication issues exist between the officers on the flight deck. What would it be like to have to go on the equivalent of a multi-hour road trip every day in a space the size of a compact car with someone you don't get along with? I wonder aloud.

Estes nods and explains that pilots—especially the older generation that came out of the military and were accustomed to flying solo—have a well-deserved reputation for being alpha-type individuals who like things done a certain way: *their* way.

"Some pilots don't want their copilots to do anything but sit quietly with their hands in their laps."

There's no shortage of dictatorial pilot stories. His remark echoes a conversation I had a few months earlier with another pilot, Tom Cordell. He, too, described a captain who was so controlling, it made the multi-hour trips they flew together nearly unbearable.

"He didn't allow any talking in the cockpit. You did your job and kept your mouth shut," he said.

The solution to the problem came unexpectedly, though. One day, he recalled, a fly found its way into the cockpit, and became such a source of consternation for this pilot, he spent much of the flight trying to swat it. Cordell, who was his co-pilot at the time, said that fly took so much pressure off of him and the flight engineer, "The trip went great!" After that, he said with a laugh, "The flight engineer who lived on a farm, began smuggling flies on board in his flight bag, and sure enough, it kept that captain more occupied with the flies than with us."

It's a funny story, but just under the surface hides a dangerous situation. More than simply unpleasant, the top-down command structure has been blamed for many deadly accidents where a captain's flawed decisions or perceptions went unchallenged by subordinate crew members afraid to speak up.

Air accident statistics show that pilot error is the single leading cause of fatal crashes, responsible for more than half of the accidents in the decades since the 1950s. That's why NASA began research in the early 1970s on the role human error played in air transport crashes. Their studies determined that failures of interpersonal communications, decision-making, and leadership were the key factors involved in the majority of crashes caused by mistakes.

In a study published by the Department of Transportation and Federal Aviation Association, Richard Jensen and R. Benel refined the issue a step further. They analyzed fatal US aviation accidents from 1970 to 1974 where pilot error was involved, and classified the mistakes into three categories: procedural, perceptual-motor and decision-making.

Examples of procedural errors include retracting the landing gear instead of flaps, or overlooking checklist items and ignoring procedures. One of the most famous instances of this type of error happened in 1977 in Tenerife, Canary Islands when the pilot of a KLM 747 took off in dense fog without clearance and crashed into a Pan Am 747 taxiing on the runway. The accident killed 583 people.

Perceptual-motor errors include things like misjudging a glide-slope or stalling the aircraft. In June 1972, a British Airways flight crashed after taking off from Heathrow when the pilot reduced power and climbed too steeply, ignoring stall warnings, and killing all 118 aboard.

Decisional tasks include flight planning and in-flight hazard evaluation. Errors in this category include failing to delegate tasks in an emergency situation or choosing to continue flight into adverse weather. In 1972, the failure to delegate resulted in the crash of Eastern Flight 401, which plummeted into the Everglades while the entire crew was consumed with troubleshooting a landing gear light malfunction. Ninety-nine people died.

The findings of the Jensen and Benel study were significant, showing that the largest cause of error-based accidents was due to decision-making mistakes followed closely by perceptual-motor errors, and procedural errors a distant third.

This raised some obvious questions for the air transport industry: in a team environment involving highly-skilled crew members, how could so many deadly decision-making mistakes be happening? Wouldn't a poor choice be noticed and questioned on the flight deck? The numbers made it clear that bad decisions were not only the leading cause of accidents, *the decisions were not being challenged by the crew.* Whatever "right stuff" a pilot might possess in the captain's chair, plenty of "wrong stuff" was getting past everyone else in the other seats.

According to aviation "human factors" expert, Alan Diehl, a dangerous gap in pilot training existed in the area of decisional judgment or "headwork." Even though everyone agreed that strong cognitive and decision-making skills were vital to being a good pilot, Diehl noted that, "Such abilities were historically assumed to be a by-product of flying experience, or taught only informally." In other words, you just absorbed it over time, or maybe had a good mentor somewhere along the way. But the studies left little doubt that this model wasn't working.

The problem was exacerbated by a flight-deck culture that attracted and supported type-A personalities, often referred to as "cowboys," and at the same time discouraged subordinate crew members from questioning the captain or speaking up with concerns. Tom Cordell wryly explains it this way, "There were two rules in the cockpit: rule number one, the captain is always right. Rule number two, if the captain is wrong, see rule number one."

By the mid 1970s, Diehl says detailed accident investigations made "the magnitude of judgment, crew management and situational awareness problems" crystal clear. Although more thorough checklists and better technology could—and would—reduce procedural and perceptual-motor errors, the decisional mistakes presented a bigger challenge because of the human psychology involved. Human factors like personality traits, stress, attitude, motivation, risk tolerance, relationship to others, cultural background, all play a role in individual decision-making. Training people to make decisions a certain way is a complicated operation, but the need for change in this area was becoming undeniable.

Back in the cockpit of Little Ami, Gary Estes remembers the cowboy days well. "Things are different now—better," he says as we jockey out of the seats to finish our tour of the big jet. "And that's because of United Flight 173."

Gary Estes and "Little Ami," one of the last of the DC-8s, at the Naval Air Museum Barbers Point, Hawaii, 2014.

Chapter 5

Mayday!

United Flight 173—December 28, 1978

"The bottle caps are up, Buddy," Mendenhall said, swiveling back into his engineer's chair. "Looks like the gear is down and locked."

But McBroom wasn't so sure. Even if the gear was down, he couldn't shake the idea that something was badly wrong with it.

"Why don't you try resetting the circuit breaker again, Frostie."

Same result. The right main landing gear lights were still flickering on and off. McBroom took a drag of his cigarette, and left it in his lips, squinting through the smoke as he flipped to the "Landing With Unsafe Gear Indication" section of the emergency manual. There wasn't much. All it said was that the crew should determine if the gear was: "retracted, partially extended or down but not locked." If it was partially extended, the recommendation was to jerk the aircraft to the side whipsaw-like to help throw the gear down the rest of the way. If the lights still showed unsafe gear but the wing tabs were up, then it said the captain "could land the plane at his discretion"—as if there was a choice.

McBroom didn't think they needed another shaking so decided against swinging the airplane around. And anyway, what if it made whatever was broken even worse? He kept thinking of the double jolt they'd felt. If the wheels were locked, why did it jolt twice? Wouldn't the gear just slam into position once and be done? Or was there a good reason to think that despite the extended wing tabs, the right main landing gear was damaged in a way that would make landing on it unsafe?

It was also standard procedure to recycle the gear—retract and then re-extend it. But nobody in the cockpit wanted to do that. What if they got the gear up and then whatever was broken made it impossible to get it back down again? That would leave them in an even worse situation.

There was also the suggestion to make a low pass by the control tower and let the guys there get a visual on the gear. McBroom knew this was a standard procedure, but it was dark, and there was air traffic. By the time PDX got the area cleared for a flyby, they'd be lower on fuel. Plus, he didn't like the idea of buzzing the airport with a DC-8 full of passengers, and then have to climb out to altitude again, burning yet more fuel. Besides, even if the gear was down, and the guys in the control tower could see it, they still wouldn't be able to tell if it was actually safe to land on.

Don't think so, McBroom thought. Not worth it. "What's our fuel?"

"Showing 10,000," Mendenhall replied.

They still had some time to get things figured out, but not a lot. McBroom, Beebe and Mendenhall ran the what-ifs, focusing on the possibility of gear collapse on landing. McBroom visualized the Portland airport in his mind. The main terminal sat between two runways: Two-eight left, which was the longer runway on the south side of the terminal, and Two-eight right, which sat to the north of the terminal, very close and parallel to the Columbia River. If they landed on Two-eight left and the right main gear collapsed, McBroom imagined the momentum of the big jet throwing it to the right toward the terminal complex. If they landed on Two-eight right, they could end up in the river.

He didn't like either option, and wondered again—what the hell was wrong with the landing gear? No matter how many ways he looked at it, and despite the wing tabs being up, the huge double 'kerwham' they'd experienced convinced him that something mechanical had broken, and would give way on landing.

And there was something else bothering him. Something he remembered from years before when he served on the accident investigation teams for two United Airlines crashes. The first in Denver in 1961 involved another United DC-8. The second in 1965 in Salt Lake was the crash of a Boeing 727. He was still haunted by the memory of the people burned to death in the fire that had engulfed both aircrafts after the fuel tanks ruptured on hard landings that tore the gear off dropping wing to pavement. There was no question that in an emergency you had to land with sufficient fuel on board to get the plane safely on the ground. But the flip side of carrying a load of fuel in a crash landing was all too clear to him, and he'd said to himself, and to colleagues soon afterward, that he never wanted to be caught in that situation.

At 5:30 pm McBroom felt they'd exhausted United's "crew concept" trouble shooting protocols and were no closer to the answers he needed. He wanted help from dispatch and the maintenance and engineering guys at United's west coast base.

"Let's get San Francisco on the horn. Maybe they've got some info on the landing gear."

As if on cue, Joan was back at the cockpit door looking for an update. Now almost fifteen minutes into the problem, McBroom had to make a decision, knowing that what he was about to say was both the only prudent thing to do, and also would change the tenor of their situation. It would frighten the passengers.

"We're still abnormal on the gear," he said to her. "Go ahead and get the cabin prepared for a possible emergency landing. I'll make an announcement."

This was it for Joan. It was like a switch flipped to automatic, it was what she'd been trained for. It was a relief to have something to do, something else to think about after the rotten month she'd had—sick for most of it, late for this trip, everything had been a struggle, a mess really since her divorce. But this, she knew it by heart. It was a checklist to follow, just like the one she'd been using to get her life back together lately: will updated, affairs in order. Her training centered her. She was focused.

As 'A-Stew' she was in charge of the first class section, and supervising the other flight attendants' emergency preparation procedures in the rest of the cabin. She had a good team on board. All the girls were level headed and very experienced except maybe Dianne who was the most junior crew member.

As expected, she found Sandy and Nancy going through their manuals and told them what McBroom had said.

"It's really more of a precaution," she said, setting a reassuring tone so they in turn would convey it that way to their passengers. "Nothing at all may happen, but we need to be ready."

A moment later, Captain McBroom echoed that in his announcement, saying that the flight attendants would explain how to do everything, and then adding for levity that there was a "real old" off-duty captain on board who would be able to help, as well.

Despite the humor, the tension among the passengers skyrocketed. Some wept or began praying and counting their rosaries as the flight attendants handed out extra pillows, blankets and envelopes for eyeglasses, pencils, pens and dentures. Unprotected infants traveling on parents' laps were to be wrapped in blankets and placed on the floor at their feet or against the nearest bulkhead according to now very controversial procedures still in use today. But one mother simply refused to let go of her child, a decision she would say years later probably saved his life.

Sandy, Joan and the other flight attendants demonstrated the brace position, instructing the passengers to be ready to brace against the seat in front of them or tuck their heads down and grab their ankles when the signal was given. Over the PA system, Joan asked for any police officers, firemen or other able-bodied men on board to volunteer to change seats and assist near the emergency exits to help with possible evacuation. In the forward section of the coach cabin, a vacationing sheriff's deputy, Bill Griffith, answered the call and moved to an exit row, leaving his thirteen-year old daughter, Gwen where she was.

In the smoking section at the rear of the aircraft, Oregon corrections officer Captain Roger Seed thought it best to stay put beside his prisoner, twenty-seven-year-old Kim Edward Campbell, but unlocked Campbell's handcuffs. He was serving a sentence for robbery and had only just been recaptured a few days earlier in Colorado after he'd walked away from a work camp detail in the Oregon woods. Both were put in charge of helping at the rear exits doors.

Joan made her way forward, poked her head in the cockpit door and waited a moment. Frostie was on the floor peering with a flashlight into a small hatch, trying to get a look at the nose gear.

"How you doing?" McBroom asked her. He'd been flying this route with her for a couple of months, and once again, he appreciated her quiet calm, and the feeling she gave that things were well in hand.

"We're ready for your announcement," she said, ignoring the opportunity to give a more personal answer. "Do you have the signal for protective position? That's the only thing I need from you right now."

He paused, his mind still full of doubts and questions. Cabin procedures were her domain, and without thinking he gave into a moment of uncertainty.

"Ah, what would you do? Have any suggestions on when to brace? Want to do it on the PA?"

Joan was caught off guard at his sudden vulnerability. Or was it meant as an acknowledgment of her experience? She knew him to be a by-the-book captain who wasn't given to hesitation.

"I, I'll be honest with you," she blurted. "I've never had one of these before. My first you know...."

McBroom recollected himself, a little embarrassed at the lapse. "All right, what we'll do is we'll have Frostie, oh, about a couple of minutes before touchdown, signal for brace position."

"Ok, he'll come on the PA..." she filled in the gaps.

"And then, ah..," he paused again, distracted by his crewman maneuvering back into his seat.

Joan continued, nudging him along. "And if you don't want us to evacuate, what're you gonna say?"

"We'll either use the PA or we'll stand in the door and holler," he finished with a smile.

"OK, one or the other," she said, returning the smile. "We're reseating passengers right now and the cabin lights are full up. We're ready for your announcement anytime," she added as she left.

Off-duty pilot T. D. "Duke" Garrett, who'd been sitting in the first class section, told Joan as she passed to reseat him wherever he could do the most good, and then went to the cockpit to get the flashlight he always carried in his flight bag. It was customary for dead-heading crew members to leave their gear in the cockpit with the flight officers.

The cockpit was a familiar sight for him, dark except for the glow of the instruments, and a little hazy from cigarette smoke. The crackle of radio traffic filled the space. McBroom, Beebe and Mendenhall were in their shirtsleeves, manuals open around them.

"Less than three weeks, three weeks to retirement," Garrett said trying to keep his voice light as he reached into his bag. "You better get me outta here," he added only half joking.

McBroom glanced over his shoulder at his 'real old' sixty-one-year-old colleague—the one he'd poked fun at in his announcement over the PA. "Thing to remember is don't worry."

"Uh, yeah." Garrett paused, not wanting to interfere, but he'd been doing this a long time. "If I might make a suggestion—you should put your coats on, both for your protection and so you'll be noticed, so they'll know who you are."

"Oh, that's okay," McBroom replied absently.

Garrett grabbed his own officer's hat and pressed his point before turning back into the cabin.

"But if it gets hot, it sure is nice not to have bare arms."

"Yeah. If anything goes wrong, you just charge back there and get your ass off, okay?"

McBroom had other things on his mind at the moment but could see the wisdom of the suggestion, even though "getting hot" was the last thing he intended happening.

They had ARINC—San Francisco dispatch and maintenance—on the line now, and had briefed them on the problem. What were the probable causes? McBroom wondered. Had there been similar incidents with landing gear? And if so, had planes landed safely on gear that had fallen free on extension? McBroom and his crew were mystified. With more than 27,000 hours of flight experience he knew that normally, after you thought about a problem and analyzed it, you could usually figure out what was wrong and arrive at a solution. But this had him and his fellow crew members stumped.

McBroom knew that the maintenance specialist, on the other hand, would have access to a variety of information that the cockpit manuals didn't supply. He could punch in a computer code and call up the mechanical history of a particular aircraft, or a mechanical aspect connected to the whole fleet of airplanes. They had all the service bulletins and maintenance records at their fingertips. McBroom hoped the specialist would tell him something the crew couldn't know about, something that would explain everything, reassure them, or at least give them the information they needed to feel they could land safely.

But the United base in San Francisco wasn't much help. Not that they weren't sympathetic or concerned, but the radio connection kept cutting out, and they volunteered nothing about any previous landing gear issues on the DC-8, nothing about the other eyebolt failures they'd had on their fleet of aircraft. In short, they said nothing that would tell McBroom that he was dealing with a problem they knew about and had experience with.

McBroom calmly reported what had happened and their status: seven thousand pounds of fuel, clear conditions, preparing the cabin for emergency landing and evacuation, didn't want to hurry the girls, and then, with the radio connection faltering added with a little less confidence, "Suspect that we've had some kind of, ah, linkage failure...that type of thing if you people..."

But the voice on the line was focused on the wing tabs and asked if the visual indicators showed okay on both main gears. McBroom said yes, and asked, "Is there anything else for us to do?"

"Negative one seven three, this is maintenance; uh, I think you've done everything you can do."

"Ok," McBroom replied, adding, "I'm reluctant to recycle in the event the machinery is bent, we might get something stuck up there."

Again the voice asked if the 'bottle caps' were up, showing the gear was down and locked.

Yes. And yet. McBroom replayed the massive double impact in his head. They still couldn't get a steady green indicator light to confirm safe equipment.

He knew the aircraft well, and felt certain that something was terribly wrong with right main gear. In the end, Neil Reynolds, the United dispatcher, said they'd have everything ready at the airport, and repeated, "I think you guys have done everything you can do." And that was that. It was 5:49 pm.

What could be taking so long? Joan and the other flight attendants wondered to each other. The captain hadn't specified a time frame for preparing the cabin, but you didn't dilly-dally. She and the others finished reseating and briefing the passengers on the emergency landing procedures within about twenty minutes of the announcement. Of course, maybe the airport wasn't ready yet, or there was too much air traffic. Or maybe everything just seemed to be moving slower. They didn't doubt that the flight crew had things under control, it was just that the waiting was wearing on the passengers. Most on board were taking the situation in stride, but some were having a tougher time of it. Joan and Sandy had assigned some buddies to the latter. As long as there was something to do, or say, you could keep folks' attention on preparations. But at a certain point they were all just waiting now for the announcement to brace for landing.

Joan asked off-duty Captain Garrett to move from first class to the row nearest the middle galley door, and then headed back to check on how her colleagues were doing. She smiled at the passengers as she passed, and paused to reassure those she could see needed more attention; among them was the woman sitting next to Aimee. It was a kindness Aimee would remember in the years to come.

The lights in the cabin were bright, which seemed to help, along with the soothing, low roar of the four engines as Joan passed the wing section. The cream-colored cabin walls gleamed next to the warm gold upholstery of the seats. These big, older jets felt safe. A lot of the newer, plastic-filled aircraft seemed flimsy by comparison to the solid metal DC-8; this was like traveling around in a Cadillac.

"You all set back here?" she asked Sandy and Nancy.

"Yep, briefed and re-briefed," Sandy replied. "Any idea when we're landing?"

"Soon, I think. Buddy says he'll have Frostie give the brace announcement over the PA. Let's wrap things up and be ready to take our seats. I'll go check on Marty and Dianne."

In the cockpit at ten minutes to six first officer Beebe was dealing with the air traffic reports coming in from Portland approach control and following their flight heading instructions.

"Uh, what's the fuel show now, Buddy?" Beebe asked.

"Five."

Mendenhall interrupted, "The lights in the fuel pump....."

"That's about right, the feed pumps are starting to blink," McBroom finished. He knew the fuel pump lights had a tendency to blink during turns or altitude changes when the fuel got a bit low. It was just the way the fuel sloshed around in and out of contact with the sensors in the tanks.

"United one seventy three heavy turn left heading one six zero."

Factoring in the landing delay McBroom needed updated figures. "Hey Frostie, give us a current card on weight; figure another fifteen minutes."

"Fifteen minutes?"

"Yeah, give us three or four thousand pounds on top of zero fuel weight," he said counting on his experience with the fuel gauges.

"Not enough," Mendenhall replied. "Fifteen minutes is gonna really run us low on fuel here." Concern crept into his voice as he began the calculations.

"United one seventy three heavy continue your left turn heading zero five zero."

"Call the ramp," McBroom said. "Give 'em our passenger count including laps. Tell 'em we'll land with about four thousand pounds of fuel, and tell them to give that to the fire department. I want United mechanics to check the airplane after we stop, before we taxi."

Mendenhall was a little rattled now, and it showed in his message to the controller.

"United one seven three will be landing, ah, in ah, little bit and the information I'd like for you to pass on to the fire department for us... we have souls on board: one seven two, one hundred seventy two plus five ba- ah lap, ah children; that would be five infants. That's one seventy-two plus five infants."

"One seven three copied it all and I'll relay that on. Ah, we're showing you at the field about zero five. Does that sound close?"

Mendenhall turned to McBroom. "He wants to know if we'll be landing about five after."

"Yes," McBroom replied. "All done?"

"Yes sir. Ready for the final descent check, final approach, final descent check," Mendenhall repeated hopefully as the voice at approach control interrupted again.

"United one seventy three clear of the first traffic, now there's another one at eleven o'clock, moving twelve o'clock a mile south, southwest bound."

"Okay. Do you want to run through the approach descent yourself?" McBroom asked, letting his co-pilot deal with the radio.

"Yes sir," Mendenhall replied automatically.

"United one seventy three heavy traffic at twelve o'clock, a half a mile."

"Yeah, we got it down below," co-pilot Beebe responded.

"Okay, approach descent check is complete," said Mendenhall.

"How much fuel you got now?" Beebe asked the engineer. It was 5:56 pm.

"Four, four thousand, in each—pounds."

"One seventy three heavy turn left two eight five."

McBroom turned to Mendenhall. "You might just take a walk back through the cabin and kinda' see how things are going, okay? I don't want to hurry 'em, but I'd like do it in another, oh, ten minutes or so."

Mendenhall left his two fellow officers discussing the shut down procedures. Beebe ticked off the list aloud.

"If we do indeed...have to evacuate assuming none of us are incapacitated, you're gonna take care of parking brakes, spoilers and flaps, fuel shut off levels, fire handles, battery switch and all that..?"

McBroom nodded toward the cabin, his mind in two places. "You just haul ass back there and do whatever needs doing."

The faces of the crew flashed through his mind and settled on Joan.

"I think that 'Jones' is a pretty level-headed gal, and..." he said, referring to her by her nickname.

"Pardon?" asked Beebe, having lost track of McBroom's train of thought.

"I think the 'A' stew is a pretty level headed gal," he repeated, as if to reassure himself. "Sounds like she knows what she's doing and been around for a while. I'm sure Duke will help out..."

But Beebe was focused on the more immediate issues that he imagined the landing itself would deal out.

"We're not gonna have any anti-skid protection, either," he observed gloomily.

McBroom recollected himself and countered, "Well, I think the anti-skid is working. It's just the lights ain't working." He paused, and then added. "I won't use much braking; we'll just let it roll out easy."

"You plan to land as slow as you can with the power on?" Beebe asked.

"Ah, I think about ref or thereabouts," McBroom said, referring to the standard DC-8 threshold crossing speed. "Try and hold the nose wheel off. I'm tempted to turn off the automatic spoilers to keep it from pitching down, but let's try and catch it," he added.

In the cabin, Mendenhall took measured steps down the aisle trying to convey an air of calm for the anxious eyes that met his. He couldn't answer everybody's questions, or quell all fears but perhaps his presence would be a signal to the passengers that the crew had things under control. In fact, it likely helped quiet his own nagging doubts to be away from the cockpit for a moment, tasked with checking preparation procedures and spreading reassurance. It wasn't unlike being a dad.

With his own anxiety parked firmly in the back seat of his mind, he stopped beside a family with a small child, and kneeled down next to the mother.

"I know this is frightening," he said gently. "But we'll be at the airport soon. Let me show you how to wrap this blanket around your little boy."

He scanned the other seats in the main cabin. Passengers were putting on their coats as instructed, and had been given blankets and pillows. He could see that the girls had done a good job of preparing the cabin as he made his way back to the cockpit.

In first class, he paused at the Andor family where Joan was helping them pack blankets and extra pillows around the three children, the oldest, three-year old Lisa, belted in her seat and holding a Raggedy Ann doll her baby sister had gotten for Christmas. Joan caught Mendenhall's eye. "I was just on my way to let you all know that we're about ready back here."

"Yep, looks good," he replied. "I'll tell Buddy."

At 6:01, four minutes had passed when Mendenhall returned from his cabin tour and took his seat in front of the panel of glowing instruments.

"You've got another two to three minutes," he reported.

"Okay," McBroom replied. "How are the people?"

"Well, they're pretty calm and cool. Some of 'em are obviously nervous, but for the most part they're taking it in stride. I, ah stopped and reassured a couple of them; they seemed a little bit more anxious than some of the others."

"Okay, well about two minutes before landing—that will be about four miles out—just pick up the mic and say 'assume the brace position.'"

"Okay," Mendenhall said automatically, as he scanned his instruments and the fuel gauges, alarm welling inside him. "We got about three on the fuel—and that's it." At their low altitude, with gear down and flaps extended, he knew they were burning fuel fast. McBroom's response told him the captain's mind was still on the gear problem.

"Okay, on the touch down if the gear folds or something really jumps the track, get those boost pumps off so that—you might even get the valves open."

At 6:02, Portland approach control was back on the radio. *"United one seventy three heavy, did you figure anything out yet about how much longer?"*

Beebe responded. "Yeah, we, ah, have indication our gear is abnormal. It'll be our intention in about five minutes to land on two-eight left. We would like the equipment standing by."

Then he seemed to contradict himself adding, "Our indications are the gear is down and locked. We've got our people prepared for an evacuation if that becomes necessary."

"Seventy three heavy, okay, advise when you'd like to begin your approach."

McBroom took it up from there. "Very well, they've about finished the cabin—I'd guess another three, four, five minutes."

Portland asked again for souls on board and fuel status. McBroom responded with four thousand pounds, then corrected that to three thousand pounds of fuel. The crew spent a few moments calculating the number aboard so it included the crew, reported that and then went back to discussing their impending landing issues: gear warning horn, automatic spoilers, anti-skid.

At 6:06 Joan was back at the cockpit door just as Portland approach control finished instructing them to turn left heading zero five zero—vectoring them once again *away* from the airport. None of the three officers in the cockpit questioned the instructions even though they'd just told approach control that they had only three thousand pounds of fuel and intended to land in less than five minutes. Beebe accepted the heading, repeating the coordinates, while Joan stood waiting to be acknowledged.

"How you doing?" McBroom asked finally.

"Well, I think we're ready. We've reseated, assigned helpers and showed people how to open the exits. They've got able-bodied men by the windows." She paused.

"Okay," McBroom replied. "We're going to go in now, we should be landing in about five minutes…"

But he didn't finish.

The engine noise had changed.

Mendenhall interrupted, "I think you just lost number four, Buddy…"

Joan froze at the words, and then carried on with what she'd started to say as if ignoring what she'd just heard would keep everything normal. "Okay, I'll make the five minute announce…announcement. I'll go—I'm sitting down now…"

"Better get some cross-feeds open there or something," Beebe said urgently.

Joan stood there for a moment, and then backed up uncertainly. "Alrighty," she said with forced perkiness. But it was clear that she and everything else outside the cockpit had suddenly ceased to exist for the officers.

At thirty-six, she'd been a flight attendant long enough to know that cross-feeds were used to share fuel between engines when one wasn't getting enough. That meant their situation had just gone from bad to worse, and she was helpless to do a thing about it. She would take care of her passengers, but the fate of the aircraft was in other hands. She mumbled something else—maybe it was a prayer—

as she turned away from the door to have one more look around to make sure everyone was okay before she took her seat. But there was no mistaking the urgency in the men's voices.

"We're going to lose an engine, Buddy," Beebe reiterated.

"Why?" McBroom replied, mystified.

"We're *losing* an engine," Beebe insisted, with extra articulation.

"Why?"

"Fuel," Beebe snapped.

"Open the cross-feeds, man!" Both Beebe and McBroom said in unison.

"Showing fumes," Mendenhall replied helplessly.

"Showing a thousand or better!" McBroom countered looking at his display.

"I don't think it's in there," Beebe argued, adding the obvious. "It's flamed out."

McBroom activated his radio. "United one seventy-three heavy would like clearance for an approach into two-eight left— *now.*"

"United one seventy-three heavy, okay, roll out heading zero one zero—be a vector to the visual runway two-eight left and you can report when you have the airport in sight suitable for a visual approach."

"We're going to lose number three in a minute, too," Mendenhall announced. "It's showing zero."

"You got a thousand pounds—you got two..." McBroom argued.

"Five thousand in there, Buddy, but we lost it." Mendenhall made some frantic adjustments at his panel. "Are you getting it back?"

"No, number four," Beebe said. "You got that cross-feed open?"

"Open 'em both, damn it," McBroom barked. "Get some fuel in there."

Mendenhall pulled the lollipop-shaped fuel feed toggles on engines three and four and watched the needle on the pressure gauges twitch without much conviction.

"Got some fuel pressure?" McBroom asked hopefully.

"Yes sir," he responded weakly.

McBroom heard the engine whine. "Rotation, now she's coming." But he was frightened. How long would it stay lit? And what about the other two engines? He knew it was a race to the runway now.

"Okay, watch one and two," McBroom said glancing at the instruments. "We're showing down to zero or a thousand on number one," he said, hoping that the fuel gauge readings would keep the promise that there was enough fuel in the tanks to get them to the airport. But then his heart sank as he gazed at the new digital LED gauges, installed just three months earlier. Maybe the tolerance between what these instruments displayed and their actual fuel amount was less forgiving.

Beebe interrupted his thoughts with a confirmation of this fear. "Still not getting it," he said. The engine wasn't responding.

"Well, open all four cross-feeds," McBroom ordered.

"All four?" Mendenhall said, double-checking the hail-Mary move.

"Yeah," McBroom said.

"Alright, now it's coming," Beebe said, grateful to feel the power return, and then added, "It's going to be hell on approach."

"You gotta keep 'em running, Frostie," McBroom urged, though he knew the engineer couldn't do a thing about it.

"Get this fucker on the ground," Beebe said.

"Yeah," Mendenhall echoed softly. "It's showing not very much more fuel."

McBroom could see the airport lights in the distance as the jet headed north through the night sky. They still had the final left turn to make to line up with the runway on the left side of the terminal, but it was too soon. They were still too far out. At 6:08 he activated his radio to request approach instructions. "United one seven three has the field in sight now and we'd like an ASR to two-eight left."

"Okay United one seventy three heavy, maintain five thousand."

Mendenhall gazed at the bad news on his instruments. They'd be lucky if they could maintain anything. "We're down to one on the totalizer," he said grimly. "Number two is empty."

And no wonder. They'd circled for nearly an hour with flaps and gear extended, burning fuel at almost twice the rate of an aircraft flying "clean" at cruising altitude. They'd taken on enough fuel in Denver to arrive in Portland with 13,300 pounds of fuel—including the required forty-five minute reserve. Their time was up.

In the cabin, Joan tensely busied herself with a last pass through, and was heading for her seat when she and everyone else heard it. It was like being just outside a room where four vacuum cleaners are running. At first, the high-pitched whine from the four machines is loud and steady. Then, imagine that one gets unplugged and the whine from that machine fades away, "spools down" so to speak. That's what they call it when a jet engine quits. Without power the turbine spins slower and slower until it's only the wind flowing through that keeps it turning silently like a switched-off window fan.

A few passengers automatically turned to the windows, curious perhaps to see the runway lights below. But it was dark outside. They didn't know what Joan had heard in the cockpit about the fuel. How far away were they from the airport? They had better be very close. She would focus on the three other engines, and hope that the roar would remain steady, that this would all be over soon.

Still at the controls, Beebe felt the jet yaw as the number four engine furthest out on the wing quit, throwing the aircraft off balance momentarily until the yaw damper compensated. McBroom felt it too, and knew it wouldn't be restarting this time. The fuel cross-feeds were wide open, but there wasn't anything left to pump. McBroom grabbed his seat lever and scooted forward. "My aircraft," he said signaling Beebe that he was taking over control of the jet. Beebe resumed his subordinate role as co-pilot but he couldn't keep the hint of fatalism from his voice when he asked McBroom if he wanted the ILS (instrument landing system) turned on, and then without waiting for an answer added, "It's not going to do you any good now."

But it was as if McBroom hadn't heard, or could only think in the most literal of terms. His entire concentration was focused on every detail of the aircraft's descent and touchdown.

"No, we'll get that damn warning thing if we do," he said, referring to the automatic horn the system triggers if the ILS is on and it senses the plane is descending too fast and too far from the runway. This was going to be hands-on, seat-of-the-pants flying all the way in.

Then, once again, the landing gear was in his mind. What would they be landing on? He'd check one last time; maybe, just maybe...

"Reset that circuit breaker momentarily, Frostie. See if we get gear lights."

Mendenhall obeyed and pulled the circuit breaker out and pushed it back in. The nose gear showed steady green, down and locked. But that was it. The right main landing gear lights were dark. Mendenhall just said glumly, "Off."

McBroom activated his radio to PDX approach control.

"How far you show us from the field?"

"Ah, I'd call it eighteen flying miles," said the voice.

"All right," McBroom replied keeping his tone steady.

What the hell had happened? He asked himself. He'd been a pilot for United for twenty-seven years. It was all he'd ever wanted to do, all he'd ever wanted to be. He was good at his job, by the book. Didn't take chances, ran a tight ship. And now of all things... first the landing gear, and then—how could he have misjudged their fuel situation? What the hell had happened?

He searched his memory for a map of Portland around the airport, vaguely aware that Mendenhall was saying something to nobody in particular. "Boy, that fuel sure went to hell all of a sudden," he mused. "I told you we had four...."

But McBroom was thinking of the land and streets they'd be flying over as they approached the airport.

"There's ah, kind of an interstate highway type thing along that bank of the river in case we're short," he said visualizing Marine Drive, the big road he'd followed so many times coming into Portland. But at 6:10 on a weekday evening, it would still be busy. Not a good option. And there was that little municipal airport at Troutdale. They were heading north on a line exactly between both airfields. When the time came, they could turn left to PDX or turn right.

"That's Troutdale over there," McBroom nodded to the right, then shrugged as he thought about it. "About six of one, half dozen of the other." Would they even make it to the turn?

Beebe was in no mood to chat about it. "Let's take the shortest route to the airport."

McBroom radioed Portland approach control again. "What's our distance now?" he asked.

"Twelve flying miles," came the businesslike response.

"Well, shit," Beebe said.

"About three, four minutes." McBroom calculated the eternity before them as the sound of the engines changed again and the plane suddenly felt loose, as if it let out a sigh and relaxed. McBroom sensed one side of the airplane go heavy, and worked to adjust. Everything about the jet felt sluggish now, unwilling to do his bidding. He scanned out of the cockpit windows into a darkness neatly braided with city streetlights, and then at the glowing aircraft instruments before him. They were losing altitude.

"We've lost two engines guys," Mendenhall announced. "We just lost two engines, one and two."

"You got all the pumps on and everything?" Beebe asked urgently, though he knew the answer.

"Yep," Mendenhall replied with simple finality, as he double-checked his gauges and instrument panel. There wasn't a thing left for him to do. Their fuel was gone. Absentmindedly, he pulled his uniform jacket from the back of his seat and slipped it on, then swiveled his chair to face the windows. He was already somewhere else, a sunny beach, squatting beside two little tow-headed children.

At 6:13 pm Portland approach control was calling again to make the routine hand-off of the flight to the controller in the tower, and give the crew the new radio frequency to switch to.

"United one seventy three heavy contact Portland tower— one, one eight point seven; you're about eight or niner flying miles from the airport."

Eight or nine miles. The distance was impossible. Might as well be a hundred. The airport was well beyond their reach. His brain a fog of helplessness and discipline, Beebe responded automatically, reaching for the radio dial and repeating the frequency. "Okay, eighteen seven."

"Have a good one," came the friendly, oblivious reply as the voice signed off to the sound of the last engine wheezing.

"They're all going," McBroom said. "We can't make Troutdale."

"We can't make anything," Beebe corrected grimly.

"Okay, declare a mayday."

Beebe did exactly as he was told, his voice steady and business-like. "Portland tower, United one seventy three heavy, mayday,

59

we're—the engines are flaming out, we're going down, we're not going to be able to make the airport."

In the tower, air traffic controller Ed KingRey received the strangely calm message with disbelief, and raced to the window to see if he could spot the troubled airliner. The blinking navigation lights on the wingtips were just visible in the dark distance—far too close to the horizon.

Through the cockpit windows the lights on the ground were brighter now, much closer. McBroom could see strings of Christmas lights festooning the gutters and gable ends of the houses not far below. He searched for an empty street, or a dark spot that might be a city park or playground, anything but the cheerful rows of holiday-bedecked houses.

Then he saw it, a shadow in the carpet of lights ahead, an ellipsis that said "maybe" on a page covered in "no's". He had no power and almost no control of the aircraft except for the big DC-8's cable drive. Now, with all his might and concentration, McBroom jammed the four engine throttles full forward in case there was anything left in them, and pulled back on the yoke, willing the jet toward his dark target. A flush of fear prickled across his scalp like hundreds of tiny bee stings as he struggled in a mixture of hope and despair to keep the plummeting plane level, its nose up, as the wings greeted the first surprisingly mushy tops of fir trees.

In the cabin it was suddenly dark and utterly silent. Only the battery-powered emergency lights along the ceiling glowed dimly. The sound of the engines was gone. The intercom was silent. There was nothing but the whisper of the wind. It was time, it was up to

Joan to warn everyone, but without power the PA system wouldn't work now.

"BRACE! BRACE! GRAB YOUR ANKLES!" she yelled again and again.

Then from what seemed like very far away, her call echoed back. Her voice had been heard.

Chapter 6

Miracles and Disaster

Southeast Portland—December 28, 1978

Fourteen-year-old Kevin-Michael Moore was off on an adventure. His dad had called before dinner from his job with Western Airlines at the Portland airport to say he'd be home late; United Flight 173 inbound from Denver had reported problems with its landing gear and was delayed—maybe even in danger. Kevin hopped on his metallic-green Schwinn Stingray to see if he could spot the troubled jet. Air traffic regularly flew over his Rockwood neighborhood home out in the east metro area between Portland and Gresham. He'd made it a hobby to track the landing patterns.

Christmas lights glowed on the rows of modest ranch-style homes lining the residential streets as Kevin pedaled south in the subfreezing evening air from his house at 162nd and Everett until, at 6:14 pm, he was a block or so east of 157th and Burnside. That's when he saw it, he recalls in his present-day blog, "Dead Memories." The DC-8 appeared against the night sky like a "three-story building," eerily dark and soundless.

Before he could understand what was happening, the jet's tail snagged a stretch of high tension power lines, sending a shower of sparks and blinding, blue-white electrical arcs into the winter darkness that could be seen six miles away at the airport control tower.

Observers since then credit the power lines for slightly slowing the momentum of the plane, like the braking cable on an aircraft carrier, before the airliner tore through a stand of tall fir trees that ripped off sections of both wings. Then the plane plowed into the ground, flattening a house, before it crossed the four-lane Burnside Street at 157th —momentarily and miraculously empty of rush-hour evening commuters—and kept barreling north, a roaring mass of rending metal that slid, shedding pieces of itself, for more than fifteen hundred feet. What was left of the DC-8 jammed to a halt atop another house amid splintered trees and branches and blackberry brambles in a large, unlighted wooded lot surrounded by homes and apartment complexes.

Kevin-Michael, astride his bike and rooted breathless to a spot two hundred yards away, could only stare. In a house nearby, a woman hearing what she thought was a bomb grabbed her baby and took cover in the back room of her home.

Inside United Flight 173 a few moments earlier, Sandy was standing in the aisle of the coach cabin when everything went dead—no lights, no engines. For a moment it didn't register. Had the pilots shut down the jet engines for the emergency landing? Had she missed the announcement? There wasn't a sound. Something told her to get to her seat. The emergency lights along the ceiling lit her way. Dianne was already belted in as Sandy reached her own jump seat and grabbed the belt. Then she heard someone yell, "Brace! Grab your ankles!" Both flight attendants tucked their heads between their knees and took up the cry.

Out of the corner of her eye, Sandy saw a series of blue flashes before she felt the plane and her body yank forward, then a tremendous shuddering jolt, then another and another again. Thunder filled her ears, replacing the silence of moments before with a deafening roar as she whipsawed back and forth. Papers and pop cans flew past. And then everything just stopped.

Sandy sat stunned for a few heartbeats and then she and Dianne yelled, "Release your seat belts! Get out!" Programmed by their training, the two women dashed to their primary exit doors, Sandy at three/right, Dianne at four/left, but neither would open. There was a moment of confusion as both women redirected passengers to the other's blocked door. Sandy hurried to her second exit station, number four on the right. She released the latch and was relieved to find that this door opened, but then shocked as a tree branch sprang toward her. *Trees don't grow on runways. Where were they?* She didn't have time to think. She heard the hissing sound of the emergency slide, but she felt the exit wasn't safe. It was dark. She couldn't see how far it was to the ground.

Just then, she heard Marty in the rear of the aircraft calling out to the passengers that the aft exits were open. "Come this way!" Without any fuss, the people who had gathered around Sandy and Dianne's faulty exits turned quietly and filed toward the rear.

Sandy paused to scan her section to see that everyone had gotten off as Dianne herded the passengers to the back of the aircraft. Then she heard Nancy yelling from the front area of the coach section, "Is everyone okay back there?"

Sandy couldn't see her because two of the emergency slides at the forward exits on the right had inflated inside the plane, blocking the way.

Sandy made her way toward Nancy and ran into Duke Garrett. They both crawled over and under the slides, and found Nancy alone getting the last of that section's passengers out of her left-side exit door. Where was Joan?

That's when Sandy saw it—the whole front end of the aircraft was gone, demolished and open to the night air. The jetliner she knew so well was unrecognizable. The smooth, porcelain-white walls of what little remained of the first-class cabin were ripped open, exposing wires, conduit and twisted metal. Great wads of shredded insulation hung like strips of whale blubber from the open gash where the plane just ended in a gaping hole, as if bitten off by a monster. Everything that had been neat and comfortable and stylishly color-coordinated just moments earlier was now a riot of destruction. In the surrounding darkness it struck her as a shocking, even immodest sight—like she'd come upon the scene of a crime, an assault.

And where were the people?

Nothing was left of the first class cabin that anyone could navigate from "inside" so both Sandy and Nancy picked their way down to the ground on the left side of the plane to check things from there. Debris was scattered everywhere. A light snow of blasted aircraft insulation was drifting down. They split up when Nancy stopped to help a woman who'd been thrown clear of the plane and hurt her back. Sandy stepped carefully with her flashlight through the rubble until she stopped at the sight before her. A woman in uniform lay flat on the ground in a clearing a little ways from the main wreckage. Sandy swept the motionless figure with her beam, the light catching a pearl earring and then her eyes, unblinking, staring into the night. It was Joan.

A sheriff's deputy was suddenly beside her, kneeling over the stewardess and shaking his head. "She's gone," he said.

Now Sandy's vision had adjusted to the darkness so that she could see more of what was beyond the glow of her light. She could make out bodies on the ground, one still belted and slumped in his seat, which had been launched from the plane. In a daze, she stumbled through the debris, taking in more and more of the disaster around her.

The contrast was stunning. Just moments before in the coach section, dozens of people had walked or limped off the aircraft, shaken and bruised but alive and remarkably calm. But out here, with the front of the jet in piles of destruction, and the cockpit who knew where, she understood the extent of the calamity. With each sweep of her flashlight a new version and vision of death amidst the twisted wreckage strobed into a permanent place in her mind. No! Frostie, too!

Then she heard something—a child? It was muffled, but she could hear the sound close by. She searched with her light and realized that it was coming from beneath a piece of the metal fuselage. Nancy had reappeared and heard it, too. Frantic, they pulled at the parts they could move. Two sheriff's deputies joined in, helping, pulling. Now Sandy and Nancy could see a small hand in the rubble. A moment later the rescuers had the little girl. It was three-year-old Lisa Andor who'd been in the first class cabin with her family. She was badly hurt and having trouble breathing, but alive. Her parents and her two little sisters were not.

Chapter 7

Who Lives, Who Dies

Portland's KGW Channel 8 canceled the evening tele-vision programming in favor of live coverage and got its news crew to the crash scene within minutes, which was fortunate since they had the big spotlights the rescue personnel needed to see what they were dealing with.

The main coach section of the DC-8 was wedged up against an embankment at the end of the dark lot, and was remarkably intact. Passengers in the forward coach area had taken most of the impact and were more badly injured than those in the back. The first class section was gone.

Fir trees ripped off the plane's right wing just fifteen feet from a forty-seven unit apartment complex. The cockpit was folded under the fuselage. The tail section was gripped in power lines, but providentially, breakers had been installed a week earlier preventing mass electrocution.

Two houses were demolished, one flattened as the jet made landfall, and the other, as it came to rest, became a pedestal beneath the rear of the aircraft. Miraculously, both were vacant at the time of the crash. The family in the first, twenty-five-year-old Debra Alloway, her husband Allen and two preschool-aged children, had been evicted just two weeks before, making what she'd thought was the worst Christmas ever into the greatest blessing of her life. A carpet layer working in the house at the time had gone out for a bag of peanuts.

For seventeen-year-old passenger Aimee Conner, the experience still hadn't fully registered.

"My ankle was hurt in the crash, trapped by the seat in front of me. A man helped to get it free," she recalled later.

She made her way to the rear exit where Marty and Dianne were helping passengers off with the aid of Oregon corrections officer, Captain Roger Seed and his twenty-seven-year-old prisoner, Kim Edward Campbell, the latter handing people from the plane to his captor below. The flight attendants and helpers were urging the passengers to hurry. Fire is always a strong possibility in a jet crash, and though there was no sign of it so far, a strong odor of something like fuel was in the air. Trained to evacuate the aircraft within ninety seconds, the flight attendants weren't wasting any time to get people clear of the plane.

It was cold as Aimee stepped out onto what she thought for a moment was a ramp, but then realized was the roof of one of the demolished houses. Her light polyester jacket, which had been perfect in Arizona earlier that day, was woefully inadequate now in the thirty-degree night air, but she didn't feel it much. Even the pain in her injured ankle seemed distant as she took in the scene—people milling about, tree branches and wreckage strewn around her—and understood that they weren't at the airport.

"It was like my mind was expecting one thing but my eyes were seeing something else. Nothing made sense."

She paused for a moment, vaguely aware of a strangely out-of-place garden gate blocking her way. An idea formed that she should call her family in Minnesota to let them know she was all right.

She saw lights in a small house across the street on the corner and limped toward it. A woman answered her knock at the door.

"I was on the airplane," Aimee said to her simply. "Could I use your phone to call my parents?"

Recalling the moment years later, Aimee laughs. "My parents always thought of me as teen drama queen, so when I called and told them I was in an airplane crash, they didn't believe me. I didn't have time to try to convince them because other people like me were coming to the house to make calls, too. When they finally saw the TV news reports start to come in, they were stunned."

For a while, people who hadn't been injured weren't sure what to do. Before the flight attendants were able to organize everyone, some like Aimee wandered off and were taken in to nearby residences, or even found cabs home. Cheryl Lewis and her two children, Cheri (five) and Michael (ten) were taken to a neighbor's front yard and left sitting there for a while until, she recalls, they were bussed to the airport and dumped at baggage claim.

"I don't know why they left us at baggage claim; we didn't have any baggage—it was all on the plane!"

By then fairly miffed, she says she marched to the nearest ticket counter and told the ticket agent, "We just crashed. Now where is it that you'd like us to go?"

After helping evacuate the plane, the prisoner Campbell, too, disappeared into the night when he and his police escort were split up in the confusion.

"Once we got separated, I wasn't sure what to do," he later explained. "I decided to go home."

He wasn't seen again for seven months until he was re-arrested on his way out to dinner and sent back to prison—though thanks to his help during the night of the crash he wasn't prosecuted for the second escape.

A triage center was soon organized at a nearby Baptist church where passengers gathered and were either put on buses to the airport where families awaited, or sent in some twenty ambulances to area hospitals including Gresham, Providence and Adventist. Nevertheless, it was a confusing situation as passengers and their relatives tried to locate each other, and authorities tried to establish a definitive accounting of survivors and casualties.

During the course of the rescue operation, Captain McBroom was discovered alive but injured on the ground near the stub of the right wing and a table-sized section of the cockpit floor with his seat still attached to it. First Officer Beebe was alive, too, though critically injured and unconscious, buried up to his shoulders in wires and wreckage. He would be in a coma for weeks, and then unable to remember anything about the crash later.

In addition to crew-members Joan Wheeler and Forrest Mendenhall, and Lisa Andor's four family members, four others perished in the crash, including Raymond Waetjen, who had been reseated in first class so that he could make a tight connection in Portland. Also killed were Jasna and Anna Pepeonik, the young wife and infant daughter of forty-three-year-old Zlatko Pepeonik, a visiting geography professor traveling with them from Zagreb, Yugoslavia to Portland State University for a nine-month teaching position. Finally, Clark County sheriff's deputy Bill Griffith, who had answered the call to volunteer at an emergency exit, lost his seventh-grade daughter, Gwen who died in her seat in the left-side, forward section of the aircraft where he'd left her.

Two dozen others were badly hurt.

Neighborhood residents remember sirens filling the night as sheriff's deputies, police, and scores of fire and ambulance crews raced to the crash site, arriving within minutes. Newspaper reporters and local television news vans converged on the location, as well, along with an estimated one thousand curious onlookers, some of whom tucked souvenir pieces of the jet into their coats, and have them to this day. Neighbors opened their homes, taking in at least thirty dazed and injured passengers where rescue personnel could tend to them on the sofas and floors of warm living rooms.

The dead were gathered in Grace Clark's yard, an instant cemetery.

"They laid canvas down on our front lawn by the porch, and the bodies were laid on it, ten of them. It made you very aware of what had happened," she recalled later, adding that the plane had missed her bedroom by a mere forty feet.

For a little more than two hours, starting shortly after the moment of impact at 6:15, a "Green Alert" was activated, and Portland's well-practiced regional disaster plan, which had been put in place ten years earlier, played out across the city's hospitals and among three hundred emergency responders. The power company worked to restore electricity to several thousand customers who went dark when the ill-fated jet severed power lines. Pacific Northwest Bell quickly added telephone communications at motels near the airport to aid investigators and to handle the surge of information people needed about loved ones. The Red Cross appealed for blood donations and was swamped by a record response as people almost instantly lined up outside their S.W. Corbett Avenue headquarters and gave two hundred thirty-three pints in just five hours.

At 8:45 pm the Green Alert was called off when the last of the injured had been sent to hospitals, and the crash site was secured. But fearing the worst, Multnomah County Medical Examiners William Brady and Larry Lewman made plans to rent three large refrigerated vehicles to hold the high number of expected fatalities, only to discover later, to their disbelief, that the death toll was limited to ten.

Phil Cogswell, a reporter for The Oregonian described what he saw when he arrived:

"Coming onto the crash scene, the most remarkable impression was the aura of calmness, almost normality, which made the floodlighted scene of the airplane fuselage sticking out of a grove of trees even more grotesque."

In the light of day after the crash, police, airline authorities and medical personnel shared their astonishment that casualties both on the plane and on the ground had been so low. Photos show the wrecked orange-red-and-blue-banded United DC-8 tangled in a taut cat's-cradle of power lines and nested in a snarl of downed fir trees less than a stone's toss from occupied homes and apartments on three sides. A policeman at the scene said, "It's just amazing. If they had to crash, they couldn't have put it down in a better place."

Early Friday morning, December 29, just hours after the plane went down, investigators from the National Transportation Safety Board (NTSB), the Federal Aviation Administration (FAA), and United Airlines were already combing the wreckage for clues to the cause of the accident. Police and a team of Explorer Search and Rescue Boy Scouts were tasked with guarding the site. Only mail and luggage were allowed out. One seventeen-year-old Explorer scout on the scene, Jeff Schroeder, took the opportunity to record what he saw over the next three days in a series of remarkable photographs, many of which can still be seen online. A crane was brought in to help lift trees and large pieces of the aircraft so officials could get at the cockpit voice recorder and other instruments and operating systems that might yield an answer to the big question on everyone's minds: What had brought down the jet?

On New Year's Eve, the temperature plummeted to the coldest of the year at thirteen degrees. Snow snarled city traffic and blanketed the wreckage of United Flight 173 in a layer of white that visually smoothed the raw details of the scene, even while re-emphasizing the surreal, Gulliver-like scale of the DC-8 carcass in the pale winter light. There was a Sunday pause in the flurry of activity that had been underway since the crash. Neighbors brought hot drinks to the chilled guards huddled around a fire barrel and wondered when the streams of curious, camera-wielding citizens would abate.

By Tuesday, investigators had combed the wreckage for evidence and determined that the fuel gauges read zero. Less than ten gallons of fuel remained in the one tank left intact after the crash of the doomed jet, which accounted for the fortunate absence of fire, and also focused a line of questioning.

NTSB officials were waiting at Gresham Community Hospital to interview Captain Malburn McBroom six days after the crash on Wednesday afternoon. Though in stable condition, his broken ribs, leg and shoulder, concussion and back injury rendered him too weak after a seventy-five-minute session to answer, or even remember, all their questions, but it was the start of many interviews to come in the years ahead.

As for the answers contained in the wreckage, the investigators were swift in collecting their evidence and wouldn't get a chance later to go back over the remains of the aircraft. On January 4, just one week after the crash, United sold the remains of DC-8 #N8082U for scrap, and a day later the jet, and any story it had left to tell, was being cut up and hauled away.

Chapter 8

A Little Survivor

December 28, 1978—The night of the crash...

Elizabeth "Lisa" Andor arrived at Portland Adventist Medical Center's emergency room bleeding and unconsciousness. Her parents were not among the others being transported with her from the jet crash site, and the three-year-old had no identification. The medical team didn't know if her family had been taken to another hospital or what had become of them. Lisa couldn't even tell the doctors her name. All they knew was that she was in critical condition and needed medical care for her broken ribs, punctured lung, head injuries and her leg, which was fractured in three places and required a pin.

But the doctors could not proceed without permission from whomever was responsible for her. Efforts to find and contact family members had so far failed, so a judge with the Multnomah County Juvenile Services Division made her a temporary ward of the court for medical purposes so she could be treated.

Meanwhile, across the Columbia River from Portland in Vancouver, friends and neighbors of Lisa's family feared that something bad had happened when TV news reports started coming in about the crash. The Andor family had spent Christmas Eve—their youngest daughter Rosina's first birthday—with neighborhood friends before leaving to visit relatives in Chicago, and they were due back on a flight that night.

75

Gabor Andor's old friend and fellow Hungarian immigrant, Louis Csonaki, lived nearby the family's Vancouver home and, hearing the news reports, felt compelled to check on them. He drove to their house hoping against hope that he'd find the lights on, that perhaps they'd gotten home earlier, or that some of the family had remained behind. But he knew that wouldn't have been like them. They did everything together.

The home was dark.

Another neighbor, Bill Billow, watching the television news, was among the first to realize the worst had happened when he spotted the gut-wrenching image of the Raggedy Ann doll he'd given to baby Rosina for Christmas caught on camera in the twisted wreckage of the plane's demolished front section.

In the hospital, Lisa was treated, and stabilized as the night wore on. Nobody came to claim her and the nurses took turns staying with her in case she woke up and was afraid. By the next day, however, her mother's sister Maria and grandfather were en route from Chicago to deal with the family calamity.

Lisa spent nearly a month in the hospital before she was well enough to go home. She was told a week after the crash that her parents and sisters were dead, but at the age of three, Lisa understood only that they were not there and she missed them.

Shortly before she was discharged, Multnomah County Circuit Court Judge William Riggs granted primary guardianship of Lisa to her aunt and uncle, Maria and Steve Affatigato, and secondary custody to her maternal grandparents after a two-day hearing in which John Stasulat and his wife, the Andors' good friends and Lisa's godparents, also sought custody. The judge said all three families were "nice, well-qualified people." But knowing that accident-related lawsuits were likely, he also made Lisa a ward of the court, saying, "So we can assure everything is being handled properly for her."

Vancouver attorney William "Bill" Klein, who represented the Affatigato family in the guardianship suit, knew what the judge was talking about. Lisa had lost everything. Her family was gone and her injuries were severe. There was a battle ahead for the little girl that her future would depend on, but Klein would need help.

Two weeks after she was released from the hospital, Lisa moved from the west coast for good to her new home in Chicago where, similar to the way it had been in her own family, she would have two sisters—her cousins Rosalia and Joyce. But instead of being the oldest of three girls, she was now the youngest. She was still in a body cast, later to become a leg brace to keep her damaged foot from falling when she walked. Visits to bone specialists would become routine. She had a new future ahead, but it would be a long journey of recovery from her injuries and her loss.

In the meantime, United Airlines' insurance agents had already swooped in to settle as many claims as they could in advance of the lawsuits soon to be filed against the company. On January 4, 1979, just seven days after the accident, crash victims received a letter from United's insurance company. In it, United States Aviation Underwriters assured passengers and their families that "there is nothing to be gained by a precipitous lawsuit," that a settlement offer would be made and that people "should not commit themselves needlessly to inordinate legal expense."

This caught the attention of attorneys and investigators with the Oregon State Bar who said it inappropriately discouraged people from seeking legal counsel and, in effect, was giving legal advice. However, the two-year-old defense strategy had withstood legal challenges in other recent airline mishaps—the airline simply accepted liability and quickly paid out a compensation package to victims in exchange for their pledge to forego lawsuits. The practice had been very successful in limiting cash settlements to predictable amounts by dramatically reducing the number of lawsuits that went to a jury where the risk of massive and unpredictable punitive damages had loomed as a possibility for years—even though many state laws and courts had typically not permitted them in airline injury or death cases.

Just a year and a half before United 173 crashed in Portland, the defense technique got its biggest early test—and many would say victory—in March 1977, when two 747s collided on the runway in Tenerife, Canary Islands, killing 583 people. Under the new strategy, which became known as the "Tenerife Approach," victims were immediately contacted directly with offers. In the end, all but nine cases were settled within a short three years with compensation payments eventually totaling $75 million—an amount considered shamefully low by plaintiffs' attorneys.

Robert Alpert, vice president of United States Aviation Underwriters, and one of the architects of the Tenerife Approach argued in an April 1979 interview with the *American Bar Association Journal* that plaintiffs' attorneys who complained about the letter sent to Portland crash victims "aren't interested in the welfare of these people [victims]." He said that in cases where the airline assumes liability, "victims don't need to share their recovery [settlement money] with lawyers." He added, "Aviation accidents are errors. Punitive damages don't apply."

Actually, Alpert, himself was in error on the last bit. While a few states did prohibit recovery of punitive damages in aviation wrongful death cases at the time, in Oregon punitive damages *could* apply for the reason that they provide a punishment and thus a deterrent when it can be proved that an accident was not just an error, but the result of wanton misconduct. The idea is that where public safety is concerned, knowingly causing or contributing to an accident must be prevented, and more likely will be if the financial stakes are high enough. Unlike general liability damages, which are covered by insurance, and can be written off as a business expense, punitive damages are often *not* covered by insurance because they are, in essence, a fine for wrongdoing. Moreover, the amounts levied can be unpredictable and extremely disciplinary. That's the deterrent.

The Tenerife Approach is no longer legal, but in 1979 it was a novel and effective strategy, and most of the victims of Flight 173, anxious to put the ordeal behind them, bought Alpert's position that the accident was simply the result of an error. They took what they could get in private negotiated settlements ranging from a ticket refund and new luggage to several hundred thousand dollars. According to William Crow, one of the Portland attorneys representing United Airlines, of the 181 claims that were filed after the accident, about forty developed into lawsuits, and by 1983 all but three were settled out of court. But the exceptions were significant, and one would make legal history.

Meanwhile, the financial impact of the accident barely registered for United. It had been a banner year for the conglomerate which owned United Airlines, Westin Hotel Group and an insurance claims adjusting organization called GAB Business Services. In February 1979 just two months after Flight 173 crashed, United (UAL, Inc.) released its annual report featuring on the cover a smiling blond flight attendant gazing out of an aircraft window at a sunny aerial view of New York City and the Plaza Hotel, one of the corporation's crown properties. Inside the report, investors got the good news hinted at in the cheerful cover image: record-breaking airline profits of over $284 million for 1978, nearly triple that of the year before. Operating revenues surged eighteen percent, as well, to $3.4 billion, the highest earnings and revenues ever achieved by any airline the report said, thanks in large part to a scheduling change that kept planes in the air longer each day.

Expenses and liabilities didn't include any mention of accident costs except in a short, vaguely-worded boilerplate paragraph labeled "Contingencies and Other Commitments" that said UAL, Inc had "certain contingencies resulting from litigation and claims incident to the ordinary course of business." It went on to assure investors that there was nothing to worry about saying, "Management believes, after considering a number of factors, including (but not limited to) the views of legal counsel, the nature of the contingencies and the prior experience of the companies, that the ultimate disposition of such contingencies will not materially affect UAL's consolidated financial position."

Chapter 9

The Questions Begin

Two months after the accident, in March, McBroom was convalescing at his home in Loveland near Denver, and up from one to two packs of cigarettes per day, when he presented himself in his wheelchair to seven investigators at the FAA offices in Aurora, Colorado. Crowded into room 103 that morning were four attorneys from United Airlines, the FAA, and the Airline Pilots Association; accident investigators from the NTSB and McDonnell Douglas Aircraft Corporation, maker of the DC-8; and a human factors specialist working with the NTSB on the role of human error in air accidents.

Since the crash, McBroom had received more than three hundred letters of support—and a cake—from people in Washington and Oregon thanking him for his skill in limiting casualties. But he was consumed with grief over those who were lost and injured, and had spent the time since the accident asking himself many of the questions he was about to get during the deposition. He was also drinking more.

For weeks he'd pored through aircraft manuals, fuel gauge specifications, landing gear structure and maintenance records and the cockpit voice recorder transcript searching for his own answers about what had happened to the fuel—and to the landing gear, which had set the disaster in motion.

With his attorney by his side, McBroom looked older than his fifty-two years in a dark, open-necked shirt and gray Glen plaid jacket. His elbows rested on the arms of the wheelchair for support, and his spare, five-foot-seven frame barely filled the seat, but he was as ready as he'd ever be for the three-hour deposition he was about to give.

McBroom's lawyer, Albert Malanca, knew the experience would be tough on him, and spoke first.

"Captain McBroom, I'm happy to report, is progressing on the way to recovery, but he is far from there. We hope that all the questions will be expeditiously put and move the hearing along because I'm not too sure how many hours he could physically take it."

"We want to complete the record today," assured the NTSB senior hearing officer James Kuehl. "If Captain McBroom is feeling a little bit weary, we'll take a fifteen or twenty minute break." And then he added, "It's just a matter of semantics, but it's very important: this is *not* a hearing, this is a deposition. This proceeding is an administrative fact-finding investigation and there are no adverse parties and no adverse interests."

But after a few preliminaries, E. Doug Dreifus, the chief investigator for the NTSB didn't hold back. With the transcript of the cockpit voice recorder in front of him, he confronted McBroom again and again on his thinking during the final minutes of the flight.

"At 1802:49, it says here that you will land in about five minutes on 28 left, but you didn't head directly back to the airport. Do you remember why not?"

"No, sir, I don't."

"You gave approach control a reading of three thousand pounds of fuel. What was your thinking about the fuel remaining? Did you have any thoughts on that?"

McBroom paused, trying to find the answer. "I don't specifically remember. I don't specifically remember my thoughts. I could speculate..."

"Don't speculate," Dreifus interrupted, then pressed on. "At 1807:06 when you lost your number four engine due to lack of fuel, what were your thoughts? What were your thoughts about your fuel situation, if you can recall?"

"It frightened me," McBroom said, remembering with visceral clarity the sudden, stomach-churning disorientation he'd felt that night as the engine quit.

"Sir?" Dreifus asked, skepticism creeping into his voice.

"It scared me; it made me aware that I might not have as much fuel on board as I think I have, because I was surprised when the engine flamed out. I did not suspect it to be the fuel."

Dreifus leaned in. "When the engine *did* flame out and it was apparent to you after a discussion that it *was* the fuel, why didn't you head directly back to the field instead of asking for a vector for approach?"

"As I recall, we were bent in a left turn on a southwesterly heading. A direct course would have been possible," McBroom explained, trying to re-gather the particulars in his mind. "But you present a problem of a considerable heading change at low altitude. I don't know."

Dreifus pulled back and changed tack. "Do you have any fuel figure you'd like to have at the threshold of a runway in a DC-8? Normal or emergency, do you have a fuel figure in your mind at all?"

"Well not to be facetious, but as much fuel as you reasonably can," McBroom began. "We have prescribed limits of all kinds that we contend with routinely in our business and the safety margins are built in for redundancies of every kind, and that pertains to fuel as well. You like to have a little reserve. It's a fudge factor—like money in the bank—that enhances your possibility to deal with something unexpected."

McBroom paused, then continued. "We all approach this business with the unexpected in mind. I likened our situation that evening to that. We didn't have a clear-cut solution as to what was wrong with the gear. We all three felt it was worth the time and effort to prepare the cabin. My feeling is that our survival is directly attributable to that."

McBroom took a breath, remembering, then added, "It was my feeling and belief then, and it still is, that I had enough fuel to descend five thousand feet and traverse fifteen miles and make a turn into a good airport on a good night with no other problems. I can't sit here and say to you that I wanted to be over that threshold with one thousand pounds, no sir, I'm not that good. I wanted to be over that threshold with as much damn fuel as I could salvage, and at the same time accommodate the cabin preparation. Now why we didn't start sooner, I don't know," he said shaking his head. "I don't know."

Dreifus wasn't satisfied and pressed again, "Then, I don't want to put words in your mouth—that evening you *didn't* have the exact fuel figure you wanted to be at threshold—were your thoughts that you wanted to be at threshold...."

Now the hearing officer Keuhl jumped in to McBroom's defense. "I think he just answered that question. I think he answered it quite well."

Dreifus got the message. "Thank you, Mr. Keuhl," he said simply.

As the minutes wore on, Dreifus questioned McBroom on his knowledge of the FAA and United's fuel reserve requirements, and then pivoted again.

"When you were holding, Captain, could you keep the field in sight?"

"I had the field in sight at all times except when I was on the wrong side of the airplane relative to our heading," he replied.

"Were you really aware, consciously aware of your distance from the airport?" Dreifus queried, then added again, "Was that in a *conscious* area, do you recall? It was a clear night and you know yourself the distances involved in clear nights."

Now both Malanca and James Barron, the attorney with the FAA's Chief Counsel's Office objected.

"I think the question doesn't have to lead the witness into what he feels. Mr. Dreifus may have his opinion on what clear visibility may do to distance; why don't we let the witness answer the question instead of having a speech," said Barron.

"The question was, Captain," Dreifus corrected himself. "That night when you were holding, did you have a conscious feeling of how far you were away?"

"Yes, sir, and I....."

But Dreifus didn't let him finish. "Did you dump any fuel, Captain?"

McBroom was caught off guard at the abrupt change in question, but didn't hesitate.

"No, sir."

Dreifus kept going. "Did you intend to burn fuel to a minimum?"

"No sir."

"During that last portion of the flight, say about 1800 on, Captain, 1800, 1805, did you feel that fuel was a critical situation?" asked Dreifus.

"Yes, sir," McBroom replied. Then suddenly unsure of himself, he added, "While I have no recollection of that, I think yes, I would have been aware the fuel situation was critical."

McBroom was shaken now as Dreifus moved on to the pilot's understanding of the fuel gauge system, asking him if he knew the difference between the LED digital display, which had been recently installed on his aircraft, versus the older analogue system, and if he knew how to read them.

The questions were so simple as to be insulting, and they rattled McBroom. With more than 27,000 hours of flight time under his belt, 5,500 of which was as a DC-8 captain, he knew good and well that the old analogue system gave a direct read of fuel amounts—the number you saw was what you presumably had in the tank. But with the new LED display you had to multiply the number on each fuel tank gauge by one hundred to get the correct supply figure. It was the same with the fuel totalizer gauge, which gave total fuel on board—in all eight tanks—except you had to multiply that number by a thousand to arrive at the correct figure. He knew all this but somehow got the answer wrong, and had to be helped along to understand what was being asked.

"Did you get any training on this system, Captain, this new digital system?" Dreifus asked.

"No, sir, not training as such. We got, as I recall, a multi-page bulletin—perhaps four pages, both sides at the onset of this idea, which explained the way this system would work," McBroom replied, adding that the new system was rolled out gradually and he'd had experience with some of the test installations early on.

"Well, prior to the accident," Dreifus continued. "Had you flown both the DC-8s with the digital and the DC-8s with the analogue system—one day one plane, and one day the next?"

"Yes, sir."

"Have you ever misread that system, that you can recall?"

"No, sir," McBroom answered, dispirited and embarrassed.

"Do you know of anyone else in your crews that has ever misread it that you can remember?"

"No, sir."

McBroom shifted in his wheelchair and took a deep breath of relief as Dreifus gathered his papers and said he was done. McBroom's shoulders were hurting. It was hard to find a comfortable position. The nerve damage and badly-mended shoulder fracture he'd suffered in the crash left him in constant pain. He stretched his neck one way then another trying to ease his discomfort as Dr. Alan Diehl, the human factors specialist, launched without a break into his questions.

Studying the role of human errors in flight accidents was still an emerging field of inquiry in 1979, and this was one of the first times the NTSB had made it an integral part of an accident investigation. Although McBroom didn't know it at the time, Diehl's participation and subsequent recommendations would make the airline captain part of a text-book case that would soon change the airline industry— and other industries as well.

But on this cool, late winter morning, Diehl's focus on how McBroom had been feeling and sleeping prior to the accident, and what his relationships were like with his flight crew, seemed a little touchy-feely compared to the no-nonsense line of questions he'd gotten so far.

"Prior to the accident did you ever have a tendency to doze off occasionally? Was there a feeling of not being sharp that night? Any trouble sleeping?" Diehl began.

"No sir. I started running last April and was running every other day including layovers. My health, if anything had improved and I was sleeping better," McBroom replied, acutely aware of how much all that had changed since the accident.

"Were there any disruptions or irritations during the flight, or immediately prior to the flight that you can recall? Any changes in work load?"

"No sir."

"Captain, do you smoke?"

"Yes, sir," McBroom said. "I then was smoking a pack or perhaps a little better than a pack a day. I have about doubled that since then."

"Captain, how would you describe the other two crew members in terms of their performance that night?"

"Both of them I would say were above average in cooperation and friendliness, competency. They both knew the airplane well. I had a very good crew." McBroom fought a wave of guilt as he thought of his first officer still in the hospital, and his engineer's death.

Diehl continued. "I'm thinking of a couple of instances on the CVR—the cockpit voice recorder where they voiced some concern— the one where the second officer says there's not enough fuel. Do you feel that the other two crewmen were assertive enough with you that night—if they had some concern that they didn't speak loudly or pointedly enough?"

McBroom didn't hesitate. "No sir, that's not my feeling at all. There is no doubt in my mind that the copilot would have spoken up. Frostie was perhaps a little more diplomatic, but I think either one of them felt free enough to say anything they had on their mind."

But Diehl wasn't so sure. He'd listened to the CVR tape and read the transcripts over and over. He knew a lot about the top-down cockpit culture among airline pilots. He had studied and written articles about their infamous lack of collaboration and self-awareness when it came to listening to their subordinates. As he gazed at the compact man across the table—weakened though he was—he couldn't help but see an old-school pilot who probably wasn't even consciously aware of the extent to which he fostered the hierarchical atmosphere in the cockpit that squelched open, honest communication among the crew members. Here was the perfect storm he'd seen again and again in his studies of flight accidents where human error was the primary cause—i.e. *most* accidents. Pilots didn't know how to listen and include others in their decision-making, and subordinates were reluctant to question authority, or assert themselves enough in critical situations. It was a problem he was determined to change.

Diehl finished jotting some notes and then looked up at McBroom. "Captain, those are all of the questions I have at this time."

McBroom was tired after a solid hour of questioning, and his lawyer asked how much longer there was to go. Keuhl called a recess saying he, too, was getting concerned about the time being spent, considering that the other four investigators still hadn't had a chance to ask their questions.

Malanca worried that McBroom was running out of steam and urged before the investigators left the room, "Maybe during the recess, everyone can get their heads together and sort of coordinate so we will not have to repeat any questions."

They reconvened after fifteen minutes, and despite Malanca's concerns about repetition, the deposition continued for the next two hours with question after question about McBroom's awareness about the fuel, fueling procedures, his knowledge of fuel measurement tolerances and quantity indicators, as well as whose responsibility it was to monitor the fuel. Apart from a few focused on whether the landing gear indicators showed down and locked, the bulk of the questions concerning the fuel hinted at the conclusions about probable cause the investigators would come to a few months later in their accident report.

But the problem with the landing gear that had triggered the whole disaster barely figured in the interview beyond its place in the sequence of events and the effect it had in distracting the crew. It would be virtually ignored in FAA and NTSB safety recommendations. And yet, the significant role it—and United Airlines, itself, played in contributing to the accident *would* come out, revealing a broader package of responsibility than the NTSB was soon to confer.

At 12:45, McBroom was drained and depressed as the deposition came to a close, despite some kind words at the end from Charles Goldstein, the representative of the Airline Pilots Association (ALPA), who wanted it in the record that the captain had done a masterful job of getting the crippled airliner on the ground with so little loss of life.

"Anyone who saw the airplane, the way it remained intact, that was a skillful job and we are proud of that landing," Goldstein said. "I say that on behalf of the members. Thank you very much Captain McBroom."

Tears sprang to McBroom's eyes at the gesture of support, but he knew in his guts that the stage was set for a "pilot error" determination in the NTSB's accident report. And frankly, part of him agreed. Once again, he felt the surge of remorse and confusion that had kept him awake nights since the crash, one question echoing in his head: how could he have made such a mistake?

But there was something else, another voice that said it wasn't as simple as that. There was more to what had happened that night, and just pinning the blame on him without understanding more fully what contributed to the accident would do nothing to prevent such a situation from arising again. He had to know for his own peace of mind—if he would ever have any again—why the landing gear failed and why he'd misjudged his fuel situation. It just didn't make sense.

Chapter 10

A Pilot Disgraced

June 7, 1979. It was a typically hot, muggy day in Washington, D.C., the air like wet flannel, when McBroom got the news he was both dreading and expecting. Six months after he had crash-landed in Portland, the NTSB finished its investigations, and released its accident report. He sat in the NTSB hearing room and listened, and wasn't allowed to speak, as the safety board laid the blame squarely on the captain's shoulders citing his "failure to monitor properly the aircraft's fuel state and to properly respond to the low fuel state and the crew-members' advisories regarding fuel state. This resulted in fuel exhaustion to all engines."

In short, incompetence, pilot error. It didn't soften the blow that the report went on to say "his inattention resulted from preoccupation with a landing gear malfunction and preparations for a possible landing emergency." As if those didn't matter!

But they also went further, adding, "Contributing to the accident was the failure of the other two flight crew members either to fully comprehend the criticality of the fuel state or to successfully communicate their concern to the captain."

McBroom had urged the NTSB to delay their final determination in the hopes that his co-pilot Rod Beebe might recover from his trauma-induced amnesia enough to provide valuable insight into the actions of the crew that night, which might somehow support his own actions and perceptions. But Beebe was still in no shape to help. He couldn't remember anything about the crash, or even going to work that day. The NTSB refused McBroom's request for a continuance, and at least in his mind seemed bound and determined to rush to judgment.

But the worst part of the report to him was the safety recommendations arising from the investigation. This is the "lessons learned" section directed to the FAA so that it can set new rules aimed at preventing a repeat of a given type of accident. To McBroom's astonishment, not a word was said about addressing fuel gauge inaccuracies or eyebolt failures—the very problems he felt were largely responsible for everything that went wrong that fateful December night.

Though these issues were acknowledged in the report, the gauges were deemed satisfactory based on a fuel control test that United Airlines, itself, performed on the salvaged instruments at its own maintenance facility shortly after the crash. The NTSB used the results of these tests along with United's fuel quantity system error analysis rather than performing its own.

As for the landing gear problem, the report said the NTSB made its own metallurgical examination of the piston rod and the mating end from the right main landing gear retract cylinder assembly at its laboratory in Washington, D.C. The results of this examination "showed that the primary cause of the separation of the rod end from the piston rod was severe corrosion caused by moisture on the mating threads of both components. As a result of the corrosion, the joint was weakened to such an extent that only a comparatively low tensile load was required to pull the rod end out of the piston rod." In short, the eyebolt rusted out, and then it broke.

The NTSB recognized that this corrosion caused the right landing gear to free fall when it was deployed, which damaged the down-lock indicating system so it wouldn't work, and began the chain of events that led to the crash. It acknowledged that McDonnell Douglas had sent service bulletins to its DC-8 customers urging the bolt be changed. The report even noted that United had never made the repair on the doomed aircraft, though it knew of the service bulletins *and* corrosion on the eyebolt of McBroom's own jetliner. Yet the NTSB suggested *nothing* by way of preventative action on other DC-8s in its safety recommendations.

Instead, the recommendations were all about crew training to make sure that flight officers understood how to read and analyze different fuel gauge systems, and that they learned how to communicate with each other more effectively.

Reflecting the work and influence of the human factors expert at McBroom's deposition in March, the NTSB noted that although the captain is in command and responsible for the performance of his crew, the actions or inactions of the other two flight crew members must be analyzed: "Admittedly, the stature of a captain and his management style may exert subtle pressure on his crew to conform to his way of thinking. It may hinder interaction and adequate monitoring, and force another crew member to yield his right to express an opinion."

The new age of Crew Resource Management (CRM) was born when at the end of its report, the safety board urged the FAA to "Issue an operations bulletin to all air carrier operations inspectors directing them and their assigned operators to ensure that their flight crews are indoctrinated in principles of flight deck resource management, with particular emphasis on the merits of participative management for captains and assertiveness training for other cockpit crew members."

Apart from the personal disaster the findings meant for Mc-Broom, he suspected the NTSB of at least partly using the pilot error determination and crew-training recommendations to forward a human-factors agenda that made pilots like him a scapegoat for accidents with more complicated causes. If bolts were allowed to rust out, and gauges were inaccurate, all the cockpit communication in the world wouldn't make an aircraft airworthy or its instruments reliable.

Still haunted by the crash, McBroom had made his own investigation, in the intervening months since his NTSB deposition, into fuel gauge and landing gear problems on the DC-8. He soon discovered that he wasn't alone in his concerns about the fuel gauges. In a television show aired in San Francisco shortly after his accident, station KPIX interviewed five United pilots who said they had experienced instrument-read errors large enough to explain why McBroom thought he had enough fuel to make the airport when he actually didn't. Pilots had been complaining for years about these discrepancies in low fuel situations, partly the result of wiring problems between fuel tank probes and the cockpit instrument displays. It didn't matter whether the displays were the old analogue or new LED style read-outs, the issue was in the tank probe wiring—and it could mean the difference of 3,900 pounds, or about nine minutes of flight time.

Captain T. D. Garrett, the off-duty pilot aboard McBroom's flight, summed up many pilots' views in a later deposition when he said, "I don't trust gauges that much. I don't trust any gauge." Mc-Broom's co-pilot echoed the sentiment about the new gauges in an *Oregon Journal* interview when he later observed, "They were no better than the old."

During the TV program, United Airline's vice president for safety, Captain J. D. Smith, said the company was aware of the complaints and had recently installed new wiring on the tank probes. That was cold comfort for McBroom; lots of airlines besides United were operating DC-8s, and absent the authority of the NTSB and enforcement powers of the FAA, the likelihood that the gauge problem would get attention was low. But it gave him something to work on, and a basis on which to support his petition for reconsideration with the NTSB, which he filed two months later in August.

In the meantime, with the NTSB accident report in hand holding him responsible for the crash, the FAA had the documentation it needed to deliver the next blow to McBroom: it pulled his pilot license at the end of the year citing "careless and reckless operation."

McBroom prepared an appeal on that, too, and began gathering the evidence he would need to make the FAA and NTSB do something about the gauges and the landing gear problems. "All in all the DC-8 is a fine, fine airplane," he said in a *Rocky Mountain News* interview. "But if I can get those problems fixed then maybe those ten people didn't die in vain."

The airline industry was about to be on a completely different wavelength, though. Crew Resource Management was the big new idea, and it had United, in particular, focused on making operational changes based on the NTSB recommendations. Thanks to studies that showed crew error was responsible for a major share of air crashes, and in the wake of the Tenerife catastrophe in 1977, and the Portland accident in 1978— both blamed on pilot error—United rolled out a program, developed by NASA, aimed at reducing human error by emphasizing participatory decision-making and assertiveness training for its cockpit crews.

Former United Airlines pilot Tom Cordell remembers it well. "After the Portland crash, the company brought us all to Denver for retraining. And it was a big thing because they took most of us off the line for it."

Word was already out among the hard-bitten, mostly ex-military flight crews that the new training had something to do with learning how to communicate, listen and be assertive, and some of them joked that it reminded them of the women's lib stuff they were getting from their wives. One long-time pilot quipped, "They drag me in here just to tell me I'm an asshole? I already know I'm an asshole!"

First they made the flight crews listen to the cockpit voice recording of the Portland accident, while watching the transcript on a screen.

"Listening to that tape, you just had this terrible feeling in your chest about what was happening," Cordell recalls. "Then when they [McBroom and his crew] turned away from the airport that last time, some of the guys in the room couldn't stand it and started throwing crumpled up paper at the screen."

Then the airline did something unusual and innovative in order to get the point across. "They made us watch a movie: *Twelve Angry Men*," Cordell says with a laugh.

In the 1957 film directed by Sidney Lumet, one lone juror in a seemingly open and shut murder trial keeps raising questions about the evidence with the other eleven jurors despite the overbearing personalities of two particularly authoritarian men in the group. Thanks to the juror's persistent questions, it becomes clear that the suspect is probably innocent. The process saves the suspect's life.

Cordell says the lesson was, "Keep talking if something is bo thering you; be proactive." He adds, "The crash of Flight 173 was watershed event in the industry. After 1978 it wasn't just a good ide to speak up if you were worried about something, it became your job.

United Airlines is credited as being the first commercial air line to adopt and require CRM training following the Portland acci dent. The other airlines quickly followed suit, and it wasn't long befo re the training techniques even spread into other high-stakes setting like firefighting and surgical theaters.

The healthcare field got the wake-up call in 1999 when th Institute of Medicine published *To Err is Human*, a scathing accoun ting of the number of medical mistakes committed each year in hospi tals where surgeons—like pilots—were prone to be authoritarian an go unchallenged. Today, consulting firms like Safer Healthcare trai medical staffs throughout the U.S. and abroad in Crew Resource Ma nagement techniques like active listening, situational awareness, an team-based problem solving.

Using the story of United Flight 173 as a launching point, an the communication model developed because of it, medical personne are now trained to confront potential problems directly by following three-part alarm script. A first level of intervention is expressed with "I'm concerned about..." If that fails to yield results, the next level is "I'm uncomfortable..." Finally, if someone says, "This is unsafe" o "I'm scared..." the entire team must come to a halt to address the is sue.

In 2004 firefighting agencies jumped on board, as well, afte the book, *Crew Resource Management for the Fire Service* came ou urging municipal and wild land firefighters to recognize CRM as the "force multiplier" needed for error management and successful decision-making in emergency situations.

It hasn't been a fix-all. Human errors and disasters still happen, but most observers agree that the use of CRM practices, adapted from the airline industry and originating with United Flight 173, have improved teamwork and safety in many high-risk professions.

As innovative and effective as Crew Resource Management was after the United crash in 1978 in addressing the issue of human error in flight accidents, for a long time the training and focus was aimed exclusively at cockpit crews—in fact the program was initially called *Cockpit* Resource Management.

Ten years passed before another aviation accident in 1988 finally took CRM beyond the cockpit into the maintenance base. In that near catastrophe, an Aloha Airlines Boeing 737 on an inter-island flight in Hawaii lost eighteen feet of its fuselage skin along a large section of its roof at an altitude of 24,000 feet, but managed to make a successful emergency landing with one casualty; a flight attendant was sucked out and lost at sea. After the accident, an analysis showed more than 240 cracks in the skin of the aircraft. Two experienced Aloha Airlines maintenance inspectors had each examined the plane prior to the flight, somehow missed the cracks, "pencil-whipped" the paperwork—and judged the plane airworthy.

The NTSB accident report slammed both the airline's "fragmented and ineffective" maintenance program, and the FAA for allowing it to go unchecked. This got the attention of the FAA, which issued an Airworthiness Directive (AD) requiring *all* air transport companies to make comprehensive improvements to their maintenance programs, particularly in the areas of corrosion control and structural inspection of aging fleets.

The writing was finally on the wall where airline maintenance and inspection was concerned. One 1992 study found that eighty percent of aviation accidents involved human error, and of the top twelve types of mistakes made, maintenance and inspection failures came in fourth after pilot, crew and design faults.

But lessons from the Hawaii accident and the growing body of work that pointed to maintenance and inspection problems in the aviation industry didn't come soon enough to prevent the devastating Sioux City crash that killed 112 people a year later in 1989. In a convergence of design and manufacture errors, and maintenance and inspection failures, the blade on a United Airlines DC-10 engine fan disk broke off in flight sending metal shards through the aircraft's hydraulic control system. The pilots, credited with practicing excellent crew resource management techniques, spent a heroic forty minutes battling to control the airplane and get it on the ground. In the end 184 people miraculously survived the crash in an Iowa cornfield.

In its analysis of probable cause, the NTSB went straight to "human factors limitations in the inspection and quality control procedures used by United Airlines' engine overhaul facility." They'd failed to detect a fatigue crack in a defectively-designed fan disk manufactured by General Electric. There were plenty of errors and failures to go around among United, McDonnell Douglas and General Electric, but ultimately much of the evidence developed in the subsequent lawsuits would remain secret under protective orders and never released to the public, according to David Rapoport, one of the attorneys involved in the cases.

Still, attention to human factor failures beyond the cockpit was finally growing. In 1991, Continental Airlines was the first to develop a training program based on crew resource management for its maintenance operation. At its heart was the understanding that anywhere humans are involved in a system, errors can and will occur leading to delays, in-flight emergencies, accidents, and loss of life. This new program, soon to be called Maintenance Resource Management, recognized that many people along an organizational chain may contribute in active and passive ways to errors. Likened to a stack of Swiss cheese slices, the idea is that if the holes—"windows of opportunity"—line up because of action or inaction, and an error is allowed to pass uninterrupted all the way through, accidents happen. MRM aimed at reducing those errors by taking a more system-wide approach to the problem. That meant going beyond the cockpit crew to include aviation maintenance technicians, support personnel, inspectors, engineers, and managers.

Given the evolution of Maintenance Resource Management more than a decade after the crash of United 173, it might well be argued in hindsight that McBroom was right, and that the NTSB caught one boat, but missed another in its analysis of the Portland accident. Using the Swiss cheese example above, the investigators ignored several hole-filled slices, so to speak, when it failed to include the maintenance issues responsible for the landing gear failure in their findings of probable cause, and in their subsequent safety recommendations.

Nowadays, those dots would likely be connected along the chain of events leading to the crash. But it apparently didn't compute in 1979, and try as he might, McBroom couldn't get the NTSB to think more broadly about the real and unresolved factors contributing to the accident.

In his letter addressed to the NTSB in August 1979 appealing their findings, McBroom laid out the results of his own investigations into the faulty eyebolt and fuel gauges, and urged the NTSB Chairman to fill in the gaps in the accident report: "Until the record is complete," he wrote, "[and] all the facts are in and the proper conclusions are drawn from those facts, the probable cause of an aircraft accident, to say nothing about actual cause, is impossible to ascertain."

McBroom couldn't understand why the NTSB was in such a hurry to close the investigation and skip over the serious safety issues that not only played a role in his crash, but also remained unsolved. He noted that the fuel quantity indicating system was presented to flight crews as reliable and accurate, when in fact it has "tolerances that allow up to forty percent of the required 45-minute reserve fuel to not be there," McBroom wrote in his appeal, "These tolerances were not known to me and are still not known to flight crews of DC-8s."

He also wondered why the NTSB was ready to let United off the hook by ignoring in its safety recommendations the airline's history of eyebolt failures on its DC-8 fleet—five of which the NTSB, itself, noted in its own report.

McBroom cited the service bulletins the company had received from the plane's manufacturer McDonnell Douglas urging its customers to change the defective bolt, and asked why the FAA hadn't made the fix mandatory by issuing an Airworthiness Directive.

"While it's not my function to investigate this accident," he wrote. "It is somewhat my responsibility that an unsafe condition which has existed for thirteen years, finally see the light of day."

It wasn't due to ignorance of the problem that the FAA had done nothing, according to John Galipault, president of the Aviation Safety Institute during that time. By 1980, the FAA had compiled its own multi-year Service Difficulty Record of twenty-one DC-8 landing gear failures because of corrosion reported by operators including United, Delta and Flying Tiger. Some had failed while the aircraft was parked, or while being loaded, some while taxiing, and some while airborne—with eerie similarities to McBroom's flight. Indeed just two weeks after McBroom's landing gear broke, another United DC-8 landing gear failed while taxiing in Chicago. Nobody was hurt that time. Despite more than a decade's worth of records of such problems, the NTSB still wasn't willing to acknowledge the obvious trend, and told a reporter for *The Oregonian* after the Chicago incident, "At this time, we have no indication of a pattern of landing gear failures on DC-8s."

Referring to that data and echoing McBroom's concerns, Galipault warned in a Newhouse News Service article, "What do you suppose would happen if that gear gave way as a DC-8 was roaring down the runway for takeoff, or if it collapsed on landing?" He, too, urged the FAA to require improvements to the gear in his own report documenting the issue, but didn't get a reply.

The eyebolt repair remained optional, which from the beginning had allowed United, and every other airline flying DC-8s to address the issue—or not. Attorneys for the airline would later argue correctly, if somewhat cynically, that United had always operated within FAA guidelines.

None of the DC-8 landing gear history was shared with McBroom when he could have used the information. But the icing on the cake for him was what United's DC-8 Maintenance Controller Leland Buhr said in his post-accident NTSB interview: "The eyebolt usually fails on retraction." *Usually?* The word was damning proof to McBroom that the airline—and more importantly *Buhr*—knew all about the problem. In fact, it was Buhr, himself, on the radio the night of the crash when the crew called the maintenance base for help to determine what their landing gear problem might be. That Buhr had said absolutely nothing about the bolt failures stunned him. Why had he left them in the dark?

"Had my crew and I been advised of the history of the gear, perhaps we would have chosen a different path," he wrote. "In any event, since UAL maintenance had nothing to offer, we had to go on what we felt our situation was."

McBroom, though grounded and on sick leave, was still an employee of United at the time of his NTSB appeal, which may explain why he stopped short of condemning the airline's maintenance decisions that allowed the eyebolt to rust out, or the failure of the FAA to insist the problem be solved. He ended his letter saying, "If the 'probable cause' is truly mine, then so be it; but we do not enhance air safety if an airplane with known safety related problems is allowed to go free."

A few months after his appeal went to the NTSB, McBroom challenged the FAA's suspension of his pilot's license. But both messages fell on deaf ears. Disgraced, and now known unkindly in the industry as 'Fumes McBroom', he had very little leverage or influence outside of the news items that appeared in the press now and then many of which tended to support and echo his oft-repeated safety concerns.

In June 1980, exactly a year after the NTSB found him at fault, McBroom resigned from United. They'd given him a desk job in marketing, but nothing to do.

"It was like being in jail after all those years in the cockpit," he said in an interview with *The Columbian.*

Instead, he devoted himself to pressing the FAA to issue two new rules: making the landing gear bolt replacement mandatory, and increasing the reserve fuel requirements for air transport. Again, he got no traction with the agency.

In January 1981, McBroom still hadn't heard back from the FAA and was discouraged. "This is an extremely serious air safety issue worthy of being looked into," he said in *The Columbian* article. "I have just about concluded they do not intend to do anything."

Bill Brockdorff, the FAA's chief of the Los Angeles airframe branch assured in the same article that they would respond but didn't know when, explaining that the agency was swamped, and other safety problems were more pressing. "If the bolt fails, airworthiness can continue on airplanes of this type. We believe the landing gear will still come down and lock," he said, adding, "We have a limited number of people and have to prioritize our work."

To McBroom, that was ludicrous. Sure, the plane might continue to function aloft with a broken eyebolt, as his did under that definition of "airworthiness," but only if you never intended to land. By that reasoning why even have landing gear designed with an eyebolt? Was an eyebolt the same as tonsils? Non-essential?

Having replayed the chain of events countless times in his head, and having examined every piece of evidence he could find, he was now convinced that the failure of the eyebolt had caused the right main landing gear—the weight of a Ford Mustang—to crash down (first jolt), and then smash through the outer stops on the aircraft— hence the double jolt. To him, that meant the gear was down all right, but likely in a splayed position.

McBroom felt that it was unconscionable for the FAA to call a DC-8 with such eyebolts "airworthy." Even worse, he believed this very attitude had gone hand in hand with United's safety sidestepping on his aircraft, which allowed the bolt to rust out in the first place.

He soon discovered he wasn't the only one who felt this way. But this likeminded thinker came in the form of an adversary. In December 1981 McBroom was called to Portland for another deposition—the first since his disastrous NTSB encounter. A little girl was suing him and United Airlines citing negligence and wanton misconduct.

As one of the defendants named in the case, McBroom wasn't on Lisa Andor's side, but the answers he gave during the deposition as an 'adverse witness', and the documents he had assembled in his own quest to shed more light on the accident, supported her claims and would help her.

And in a way it would help him, too. At the center of the complaint was the issue of the eyebolt, and the evidence Lisa's attorneys were gathering would both mirror and bolster McBroom's own findings. The NTSB and FAA had ignored his concerns about fuel tolerances and maintenance, but here was a new chance to be heard.

Everything he had learned would come out in a court of law, and if this little girl won her case, it would show that real problems existed and remained unresolved. True, he was again on the receiving end of accusations about his negligence in the crash, but this time United was, too. Maybe it would finally prove that he wasn't the only one to blame.

Chapter 11

Dancing With Elephants

Three years after United Flight 173 went down, most of the claims and lawsuits filed after the crash had been settled, but Lisa Andor's was just getting up a head of steam. William "Bill" Klein, the Vancouver, Washington attorney who handled Lisa's guardianship after the accident, recognized that her case against the airline had the potential to be far-reaching and complicated, and so in the weeks following the crash he had reached out to his old friend Stewart Whipple, and his colleague Alan Johansen, both Portland trial attorneys experienced in complex litigation.

After visiting Lisa in the hospital, and learning more about what had happened, Whipple agreed to lead the trial work to come. A father of five, himself, he remembers being struck by the little girl encased in a plaster cast. Even years later, the memory brings a catch to his voice. "She was a sweet girl, and seeing her in the hospital—it was sad."

And the case intrigued him. "You don't crash as a result of fuel starvation without some horrendous mistakes involved. Something is wrong when an experienced pilot runs out of gas."

But he could also see that the case would be a challenge. They'd be up against a corporation with virtually unlimited resources. It would require years of preparation before it even got to the courtroom. However, as he delved further into the circumstances surrounding the accident, he began to view it as a landmark case "because of

108

the nature of the crash, the safety issues involved and extent of the injuries and damages."

On June 8, 1981 Whipple, Johansen and Klein filed a complaint against United Airlines in the Multnomah County Circuit Court asking for $4.5 million, of which $3 million were punitive damages, reflecting the preliminary discoveries they had made about United's maintenance practices. The legal team felt that punitive damages were appropriate in this case, first because Lisa was entitled to them given the circumstances and extent of her loss, and second, because they would make United—and all scheduled airlines—pay better attention to the vital issue of aircraft maintenance.

"Passenger carriers such as airlines are held to the highest duty of care because your life is in their control when you're on board," Whipple later explained. "They have a duty to do everything in their power to protect your safety."

When injury or death happen because safety has been intentionally disregarded, punitive damages serve as a deterrent to the wrongdoer, and an example to others, signaling that such behavior is unacceptable no matter who you are in society. Plaintiffs' attorneys see punitive damages as the slingshot in David's hand when you're up against a Goliath.

The challenge in Lisa's case, however, was that nobody had ever successfully wielded such a slingshot against an airline. The "Tenerife Approach" —accept-liability-and-pay-direct settlements legal strategy that air carriers and their insurance companies had pursued since the Canary Islands crash in 1977—was a formidable and by now well-tested advantage.

In addition was the fact that punitive damages in injury and wrongful death cases were still the wild west of legal territory in the early 1980s. Some states allowed them, others didn't, and some decided case by case. Legal scholars and defense attorneys complained that there was no consistency or clarity in the application of punitive damages, and that the amounts claimed and/or awarded made little sense.

"It's almost a lawless area," said Matthew Spitzer, a University of Southern California law professor in a 1984 interview with the *L.A. Times-Washington Post Service*. "It's hard to discern any rules or principles to guide juries and judges."

And yet other observers pointed out that punitive damages serve as leverage for often less-powerful victims in settlement negotiations, and improve access to the courts for people who would otherwise be unable to afford legal representation. They also offer a sort of supplementary, private-citizen law enforcement by shoring up inadequate regulatory oversight by government agencies like the FAA. "Punitive damages force carriers to upgrade their procedures," said William Shernoff, one of the nation's top plaintiff's attorneys in 1984.

Still, Lisa's lawyers knew it would be an uphill battle. No court had ever awarded and upheld punitive damages against an airline, so there was no direct precedent that would support their claim. Indeed, just the opposite was true, as had been fulsomely demonstrated in the wrongful death suits that arose after a devastating 1979 crash in Chicago. American Airlines Flight 191 went down, killing 273 people—all on board and two on the ground. A three-judge federal appeals court panel favored airlines by affirming the Illinois law *against* punitive damages even though the NTSB cited systematic cost-saving and improper maintenance procedures during the DC-10's engine overhaul in its finding of probable cause—a worthy foundation for punitive damages if they had been allowed.

So the stakes were high in Lisa's case. If her attorneys prevailed, the verdict would not only take care of Lisa for the rest of her life, it would also have a far-reaching impact on the airline industry, itself. It would send a message that passenger safety can't be sacrificed to save money. It would also open the door to similar actions in air crashes.

To be sure, the legal team was entering unpredictable waters in a very small boat compared to the one United was in. They knew it's often an all or nothing voyage that victims and their attorneys set off on together.

Like most of the other lawsuits filed by victims of the United crash, the complaint Lisa's attorneys crafted accused Captain Mc-Broom of negligence, echoing the NTSB conclusions that blamed the pilot for failing to properly monitor fuel supply and continuing to fly the airplane until it ran out of fuel.

But unlike most other lawsuits, the complaint focused the lion's share of its accusations on the airline, itself, saying the crash and deaths were "caused by defendant's [United] flagrant misconduct, deliberate disregard of the rights and safety of others, and negligence." It went on to clarify that United "knew that integral parts of the right main landing gear mechanism were severely corroded and structurally unsafe to human life," and that it continued to operate the aircraft with this knowledge, along with the awareness that there had been five previous failures of same landing gear mechanism on its own fleet of DC-8s.

Finally, the complaint also charged, *along* with McBroom, that the fuel gauges were inaccurate, that United knew about that too, and that United had failed to let McBroom or his crew know of the inaccuracies in the fuel indicating system.

Calling the suit "a classical case for deterrence" of reckless conduct where public safety is at stake, Lisa's lawyers said punitive damages would send a message to the airlines that safety must come before profits.

In 1981, United's legal team, led in Portland by William Crow and Steven Rosen of Miller Nash—to this day one of the city's biggest firms—already had three years' worth of experience in the Flight 173 cases, and had dispatched most of the 181 claims and lawsuits in pre-trial settlements. United also assembled the services of a Washington, D.C. firm with expertise in NTSB and FAA issues to assist as needed, and a Chicago team of insurance litigation specialists.

By then, virtually all the cases except Lisa's had been consolidated and transferred to federal court as is often the practice when there is a common group of victims and claims from diverse origins. For United, whose ultimate goal was to reach out-of-court settlements, this was both an efficiency measure and a good thing because federal judges were known at the time for "hammering away at both sides to get a resolution short of trial," as Whipple later noted.

For plaintiffs, though, the consolidation meant that their cases became part of a legal cattle call run by a harried, court-appointed plaintiff's supervisor put in charge of herding the claimants and their attorneys through a tightly constrained judicial chute designed to get the lawsuits concluded.

Nevertheless, there was still good reason for United's defense team to worry. In May 1982, with just six lawsuits left unsettled, U.S. Magistrate George Juba set the ground rules for the remaining cases scheduled for trial in federal court. He made news by ruling, over the objections of United's attorneys, that an Oregon law permitting punitive damages in wrongful death cases *would* apply in the remaining federal cases, and could be allowed if a jury saw fit to award them. United's legal team argued that since the victims of the crash had connections to five other states which prohibit such damages, *those* laws should apply. But Juba disagreed saying that because the crash happened here, "Oregon has the strongest interest in applying *its* law of punitive damages."

That was bad news for United. With punitive damages officially on the table, plaintiffs got a bigger slingshot to wield in settlement negotiations with United's lawyers. Even more troubling, it entitled plaintiffs to demand and discover a broad range of company documents, witness depositions and financial records for evidence not normally permitted in simple compensation claims. Finally, it reconfirmed the possibility of jury awards designed to punish the airline for wrongdoing. This all made it even more important for United to keep the last six lawsuits out of the courtroom if at all possible.

They were almost successful. In January 1983, they got their initial test in court when the first lawsuit from the accident went to trial, and a jury awarded $125,000 to a couple who had been injured in the crash. The majority of the award, $80,000, was designated as general—but not punitive—damages for pain, suffering and emotional distress resulting from the experience. That was a relief for United, but also a close call.

After that, with the rest of the federal court trials on the docket for February and March—only one of which involved a wrongful death claim—they settled the remaining cases out of court in a two-month flurry of activity for amounts ranging from $135,000 to $400,000—all covered and approved by United's insurance carrier United States Aviation Underwriters, and its 'Tenerife Approach' vice president Robert Alpert, who had earned a reputation as being a very hands-on and successful settlement negotiator following the crashes of both United 173 and American Airlines 191.

But Lisa's case was still pending in the state circuit court where it had been filed, and where her lawyers had battled United to keep it. Hers was the last left standing, and while Juba's federal court ruling on punitive damages was not binding in the state court where Lisa's case would be heard, it did set a tone and a foundation that in a broad sense supported her claims for punitive damages. United would face her in a Multnomah County courtroom exactly a year later in March 1984.

Chapter 12

The Great and Powerful

On a cold, early spring day in Chicago, Lisa's guardian aunt, Maria Affatigato arrived at One IBM Plaza for her first deposition with one of United's legal defense teams, Wildman, Harrold, Allen and Dixon. She was the acting plaintiff on behalf of Lisa Andor in the lawsuit against United and Captain McBroom. She had signed the complaint against them just a few months earlier, and United wasted no time calling her in for this initial examination.

The offices of the hard-charging firm of insurance litigators known simply as "Wildman" in Chicago—also United's home town —had offices on the third floor of one of the city's newest and already iconic skyscrapers, a dark monolith of black anodized aluminum and gray-tinted glass designed by the great modernist architect, Ludwig Mies van der Rohe, and completed in 1972, a few years after his death.

Headquarters of its namesake, IBM, the ebony tower rose fifty-two stories against the day's pewter sky, and was topped by the company's multi-story initials—a giant beacon both by day and at night, viewed by many as an unabashed symbol of corporate power. Fittingly, perhaps, the law firm, which also represented gun manufacturers and the tobacco industry, would later adopt the slogan: "When it's your business on the line, you need a Wildman."

Maria's attorneys, Stewart Whipple and Bill Klein, had flown in from Oregon to accompany the forty-year-old housewife for her

115

deposition with Wildman's Robert Haley, who was conducting it o behalf of United's lawyers, Bill Crow and Steve Rosen who wer leading the case in Portland. The three visitors were ushered into conference room where a court reporter was already set up with he beige stenotype machine at one end of a large table. Haley took hi place across from Maria, a stack of files and a yellow legal pad a hand.

Maria had never had her deposition taken before, and thoug her lawyers had done their best to prepare her, it was still unnervin when she had to raise her right hand and solemnly swear to tell th truth. Her Catholic faith was strong, and she didn't take such thing lightly.

Then without further preliminaries, Haley began an exhaus tive, often painful, three-hour investigation of her life, and that of he dead sister Rosina and brother-in-law Gabor Andor. And Lisa, toc who had been in Maria's care at her suburban home near Chicago fo almost a year and a half since the loss of her family in the air crash.

Having been born and grown up in Italy until she was in he late teens, Maria spoke English as a second language with an accent She had married fellow Italian, Steve Affatigato, a tool and die maker and was now the mother of two girls, Rosalia, age eight and Joyce age five. She'd worked as a seamstress for a piecework company fo thirteen years until just days before the accident when her sister anc family had come out to visit for Christmas. She hadn't been employec since.

Maria and her younger sister had been very close—indeed the whole family was extremely tight-knit. And though Rosina and Gabol had moved to Vancouver, Washington, they traveled with the childrer to Chicago several times each year to visit her parents and Maria's family thanks to Gabor's United employee flight privileges.

Haley, United's attorney, wanted to know everything about the entire family, and Maria remained self-possessed for the first hour as she answered his detailed questions about all her relations: birthdates, siblings, religious affiliation, citizenship, the schools they attended, the jobs they'd held, property they owned, debts owed, health history, bank accounts, income, and so on.

But the loss of Rosina, Gabor, and their two youngest girls had been devastating, a wound that was still very fresh, so when Haley asked about Gabor's personality, what kind of father he was, what kind of marriage he'd had with her sister, and then wanted Maria to recall the day of the accident, she began to have trouble following his line of questions.

"When was the last time you saw Mr. Andor?" Haley queried.

"December 28th, in the morning." She would never forget that date.

"What time of day was that?" Haley pressed for precision.

"Six o'clock in the morning," Maria replied, then wasn't so sure. "Six or eight o'clock."

"Where was it that you saw him?"

"My mother's house," she said, wondering why he was only concerned with Gabor. She added to clarify, "We were *together* at my mother's house."

"What were you doing the last time you saw them?"

Again, she paused, confused by what seemed an obtuse question. "What were we doing there?"

"Yes."

117

Maria went with the obvious: "Well, we were trying to dress the children to leave," she said, recalling the flurry of the morning departure with Rosina's three little ones.

Haley continued with specifics. "What time of day was their plane leaving?"

"I don't know. They were on standby." What did that matter? She wondered.

"Who took them to the airport?"

"Steve, my husband. He always did—pick them up, and bring them back."

"Did anyone else go, other than your husband?"

"My father. My father would stay there until the plane left," she said.

"Did you last see your sister at the same time?" Haley asked, finally including Rosina in his questions.

"Yes," she said quietly, remembering.

Haley changed tack. "Had your sister ever been hospitalized?"

Again, Maria was caught off guard by the question. "No," she answered without thinking.

Whipple, her attorney interrupted to help her be absolutely factual. "For child birth…"

She corrected herself. "Just for child birth."

Haley focused in. "Had she ever had any sicknesses or illnesses?"

"No." Where was he going with this? Her sister was dead.

"Had she ever had any injuries that you know of?"

"No, no injuries."

"She did live with you for a period of time in Chicago, am I correct?"

"Yes. We always stay together until she get married. So we stayed thirty-one years together," she said, trying to drive home for this lawyer how close they were and what they had meant to each other.

But Haley wasn't listening for that. He pressed on and asked if Rosina had ever seen any doctors. He was trying to get a bead on her overall health, and thus what her likely life expectancy would have been barring the crash that killed her. His job was to establish whether Rosina had any history of illness or injury that might have reduced her life span had she gone on living. That's part of the metric used to determine the amount of compensation a victim's family might get. The probability of a long, healthy, productive life, which has been cut short by an accident, means a larger dollar figure must be calculated to make up for what's awkwardly termed the loss of 'companionship, services and potential income.'

Haley switched to the two little girls and then Gabor, asking similar questions about their health prior to the crash, but came up with the same thing. They had all been healthy; both Rosina and Gabor had job skills, employment and worked hard—they'd had excellent prospects before their deaths.

Very little of this detailed family history would ultimately come out or be used during the trial later—indeed United's lawyers wouldn't want the jury to hear much of anything about Lisa's family since it would only provoke sympathy for her loss, which might translate into a higher compensation award. The defense team would make sure that the evidence presented was narrowly restricted when the time came. But in the meanwhile, United hoped that the case would resolve short of the courtroom, so Haley needed to get this information in order to help craft a settlement offer.

The deposition had begun at two o'clock, and now as it was nearing three thirty, Haley launched without a break into the meat of the case: Lisa, and the injuries she had suffered in the crash. He had to understand what it might cost in the future for her care. This was something Maria was all too familiar with having been her primary caregiver since the accident.

The crash had changed Maria's life, too, along with that of her family. She had almost lost count of the doctors she had taken Lisa to see since returning with her from Portland after her weeks-long stay in the hospital there.

Lisa had been unconscious for six hours, and in critical condition for three days after the accident. Maria still vividly remembered her horror when she first saw the transformed little girl lying in the ICU with tubes in her chest, blood coming from her ear and the wounds on her leg and foot before they operated and put her in a full leg and body cast.

She'd been through the list of injuries so many times since then with the specialists she'd sought out in Chicago, it was easy to tick them off now for Haley: right leg broken in three places, along with nerve and muscle damage; collapsed lung, broken ribs, punctured ear drum, fractured disc in her neck, concussion, face lacerations.

That first month back in Chicago had been especially tough. Lisa was still encased in plaster, and couldn't move or use the toilet, so she'd had to go back to wearing diapers, a regression that would plague her for years. They'd rigged up a bed for her in a little Radio

Flyer red wagon—as they'd done in the hospital in Portland—and carted her around the house in it so she could be with the rest of the family.

Then, after the cast was removed at a hospital in Chicago, the doctor discovered a terribly infected three-inch-long gash on her broken right leg above her knee, which Maria was told had developed because the cast had been put on too tightly in Portland. Lisa had to spend another two weeks in the hospital.

Things had improved since then. After a year and a half, Lisa's wounds had healed to scars, but because of nerve and muscle damage she had to wear a special shoe bolted to two metal braces strapped to her right leg to hold her foot up when she walked. With or without the one-pound device, she tended to trip and fall, and could only walk for short distances before she tired, complaining that her foot was "too heavy."

The right leg had not continued to grow at the same rate as the other one. It was shorter now and thinner, so Maria explained that a doctor instructed her how to give Lisa therapy at home by pulling her leg firmly by the ankle while turning her foot one hundred times each day—a procedure Lisa did not enjoy.

Haley was meticulous in his questions about the length and placement of each and every scar and injury. He listened to Maria carefully, documenting the problems from an adversary's point of view, and then moved on to the psychological impact of the accident.

Maria told him that Lisa had nightmares every other night, often screaming and searching the bed with her hands in her sleep. She had to sleep in a bed between her two cousins' beds with the light on. She talked about seeing her father with blood on his face. She also had a habit of sitting alone crying on the steps of their basement

121

stairwell holding a photograph of her two little sisters. Understand
ably, she was now afraid of airplanes, and would turn off the TV if
program about them were on.

Life was so different now. Maria wanted to tell Haley abou
what it had all been like: to lose her sister, her two nieces, her brother
in-law, her job. She said she was proud of how her own two daughter
had accepted their little cousin and coped with the fact that they nov
had less of their mother's attentions. Maria knew it had been hard o
them. Yes, Lisa's injuries were improving, but she needed a lot o
care. She had bad days, and was hurt in ways that often seemed be
yond Maria's power to help or understand. Lately, Maria had resolve
to take Lisa to the famous Mayo Clinic for a complete examination
Maybe they could connect the dots and give Maria a course of treat
ment that would restore her, heal her leg injuries, her chronic earache
and respiratory ailments, and offer a clearer picture of what the futur
might hold for the little girl.

But Haley wasn't there to hear about her feelings or fears, an
kept the questions matter-of-fact, interrupting Maria when she strayed
off point, and when she said she was scared about possible hearing
loss in Lisa's ears.

"Let me say something here," Haley stopped her. "Let me
move to strike the portion about your being scared from the answer."

Maria recollected herself, remembering where she was, wha
these questions were for, whose side this lawyer was on. She wa
tired, and anxious to be done with all this talking and remembering
She had a family to feed at home.

The deposition finally came to a close shortly after five. Haley
gathered his files and the legal pad he'd been jotting notes on, while
the court reporter packed up her equipment. Maria was relieved, and

vaguely aware that her attorneys were telling her she had done just fine.

But the ordeal of the case was only beginning. There would be another deposition to face, more doctors, school assessments, and then later, her testimony in the courtroom before a judge and jury.

Chapter 13

The Trial at Last

The hip destination city of Portland today is a far cry from the mostly-ignored, mid-size metropolis it was in 1984. If a Portlander traveled abroad—or even to New York or Chicago—and someone asked where she was from, the sensible answer went something like this: "You know where San Francisco is? And Seattle? Portland is in between those two in Oregon." There would be a puzzled pause as an unexpected state—Oregon—appeared on the map in the questioner's mind's eye; and then it wasn't uncommon to get the sudden ah-ha, "Oh, yeah; I heard it rains a lot there."

The crash of United Flight 173 put Portland briefly in national public view in 1978 and early 1979, as disasters do, but six years later, the city was known chiefly as the home of the Trail Blazers basketball team, a fast-growing company called Nike, and a bearded, bicycle-riding, ex-beatnik named Bud Clark who'd been a well-loved neighborhood pub owner before he emerged from behind his Goose Hollow bar one day and beat the pants off the city's political insiders to become mayor. But that's the kind of town it was: laid back, athletic, sometimes unpredictable, and ok, it did rain a lot.

So sure enough, it *was* raining on the cold Monday morning in March 1984 when Maria Affatigato, Bill Klein and her two trial attorneys, Stewart Whipple and Alan Johansen, paused in the granite-clad entry of the historic Multnomah County Courthouse to doff rain coats and stow umbrellas before climbing the wide marble staircase to the courtroom awaiting them.

In the five years since the crash that took so much of her family, Maria had both dreaded and awaited this day, and now she leaned on the company of these men. Bill Klein, a stocky, tennis-loving people person had been her attorney and support through so much already—all the day to day legal details that had gone with trying to recover from the disaster. Stewart Whipple and Al Johansen, on the other hand, would be her and Lisa's champions of a different sort, the ones about to engage United publicly in court. Johansen, a portly, well-liked descendant of Finnish immigrants, was a meticulous scholar known for his razor sharp ability in complicated legal matters, and for a wry sense of humor he expressed at Christmastime by wearing a button that said "Bah Humbug!" Stewart Whipple was a fit sixty-two when the trial began. He had been a trial lawyer for three decades and had earned a reputation as a tested and successful litigator in a wide variety of defense and plaintiffs' cases. Tall, self-possessed, hair silvering, he approached his trial work with the discipline and commitment of an athlete.

In the time leading up to the trial, Maria's attorneys had tried to shield her from as much of the ongoing legal wrangling as possible as they and United's lawyers filed motions, took witness depositions, filled files and then boxes with documents and exhibits they would need, but there had always been something case-related Maria had to attend to.

Lately, the administrators at Lisa's school were sending her worried reports about Lisa's reluctance to engage in activities in or out of the classroom. They said she hung back at the sidelines during recess, and tired quickly of academic tasks. And no wonder; since the accident, Lisa was still plagued with nightmares so she almost never got a good night's sleep. Now eight years old, her nighttime problems were terribly embarrassing for her. She couldn't have sleepovers with friends or go to overnight camps, and there didn't seem to be anything the doctors or psychologists could do for her except advise patience.

This was important information in the lawsuit, so Maria had to carefully document everything, all Lisa's physical and psychological troubles. She had filled a suitcase with her notes, school records and medical reports, ready to travel whenever she had to fly to Portland. At the same time, she had to find ways as a surrogate mother to cope with her youngest child's issues—an experience that was often exhausting and frustrating for both her and Lisa, especially because the problems were so intertwined with a still-present grief rippling for them both just below the surface.

Although it wasn't well understood as Lisa's trial got underway, modern experts in early childhood trauma and grief would instantly recognize these classic symptoms of psychological injury, and appreciate the long-term impacts. But in the early 1980s, the common thinking was that children under the age of six who experience traumatic injury and the sudden death of family members don't remember and don't understand it and are therefore less affected by it. Resources available today through the National Child Traumatic Stress Network amply demonstrate how uninformed this thinking was.

As her attorneys led Maria through the doorway into a fluorescent-lit courtroom, her stomach was fluttering. She recognized United's lawyers at one of the tables. The older one, Bill Crow, had taken her second deposition seven months earlier focusing on an update of Lisa's progress since the Wildman deposition in Chicago.

He'd also taken a recorded statement from young Lisa, asking her what scars she had, if she remembered the accident she was in, and what she liked to do during recess—if she "liked to run and play."

Maria felt her tension mount. She knew she would have to relive the terrible night of the crash as her attorneys made their case. She didn't know how she would handle that, but finally, here was the chance for a jury of regular people like herself to hear about what happened, to understand, and decide how justice might be served.

However, the twelve people who had been chosen for the jury three days earlier would *not* hear everything. United's lawyers had filed motions to exclude details of Lisa's dead family and how their loss had affected her. They wanted the jury to hear only about how the experience of the crash had injured Lisa physically and psychologically. That's how it works in complex legal actions—each matter is dealt with individually. In the intervening years, with mounting family and medical expenses, Maria, had made a pick-your-battle decision and settled with United in the wrongful death cases of her sister, brother-in-law and the two children. Those four claims had been compensated and closed, leaving only Lisa's to be tried, and only Lisa's injuries to be considered—if you could somehow keep them all distinct from the loss of her family in the jurors' minds.

For Maria, it was an awkward situation in Judge Phillip Roth's chambers just prior to the trial that morning as he and the lawyers for both sides discussed ways to present Lisa's trauma from the accident during the opening moments of the trial, and at the same time avoid mentioning anything about her parents and two sisters. To be sure, anyone who followed the news would already know about them. It was unrealistic to think that they could just be ignored, and nobody wanted to make the jury think something was being intention ally concealed from them.

In the end, Judge Roth said the jury would be instructed tha Lisa's case was "strictly an exclusive claim for the child's injuries and had nothing to do with any possible claims in respect to the los of her parents or family."

Maria sat and listened to all of this, along with a subsequen discussion about whether the graphic details of a news videotape o the crash scene to be shown in court would be prejudicial to United' defense. She heard the judge disagree.

"I think every day we see on TV scenes that are far wors than that—bodies strewn all over," he said coolly. "Here it is quit mild; mild in the Court's opinion. We didn't see any limbs throw around, any parts of bodies splattered."

Maria couldn't listen to any more. Four of those bodies wer *her* family. The room felt hot and stuffy. She wanted to leave; sh couldn't catch her breath. Suddenly she was aware that Bill Crow wa saying something to the judge about her.

"Your Honor, before we bring the jury in, there is one othe matter I would like to bring to the Court's attention, and that is th behavior of Mrs. Affatigato."

The sixty-four-year-old Judge Roth was a bit hard of hearing "What's that?"

"The behavior of Mrs. Affatigato," Crow repeated a littl louder. "As you can see, she is crying. I want the Court and Counse to caution her about that."

Phillip J. Roth, a short, rotund man, was a seasoned, no-non sense judge who'd served on the Multnomah County Circuit Cour bench for nearly twenty years since 1965. He was often in the news paper for presiding at high-profile criminal cases where he was used to dealing with some of Oregon's worst felons, and known for running a tight courtroom.

But he was also known for a recent criminal lapse of his own that perhaps presaged judgment calls to come. Just three years earlier in 1981, he was arrested and arraigned for attacking his estranged second wife with a fish bat one night as she was returning home from the theater with a friend, whose car window he'd also smashed. The assault was ultimately never prosecuted—the wife, the friend and the judge settled the case out of court for an undisclosed amount of money and the charges were dropped—but Judge Roth was formally censured for his conduct a year and a half later in June 1982 by the Oregon Supreme Court, and the stain on his record and reputation was still fresh. A local attorney recalls that the judge immunized himself against his shame with a dark sense of humor. Alongside the legal credentials framed on the wall of his chambers were the alarming mug shots taken of him on the night of his arrest.

Judge Roth now turned his attention to Maria who was indeed weeping, and overcome with embarrassment.

"Mrs. Affatigato, it is very important that you cannot let yourself go with any emotional tizzy or this," he admonished. "You have to calm yourself, because it can affect..." he paused and decided to skip the explanation. "I will have to ask you to leave the courtroom. We cannot allow this in front of the jury, to have you go into tears or depression or anything like that. Do you understand?"

Maria struggled to regain her composure. It helped that the judge was speaking to her as if to a child, and without any note of compassion. In her blossoming irritation at the scolding, she felt her tears abate.

129

"Yes," she replied.

But the judge went on. "If you feel you are really getting upset, I want you to take a walk outside of the courtroom." He turned to the attorneys for back up. "And gentlemen, advise the Court, and I will keep an eye on her, too. But we cannot allow that."

Talking about the trial more than thirty years later, Maria recalls having to leave the courtroom frequently as the experience and the photos were so painful.

So it didn't help that one of the first witnesses called to the stand was Multnomah County Deputy Sheriff Robert Smith. Maria and Lisa's lawyers wanted the jury to have a fresh picture in their minds about what happened on the night of the crash now five years earlier. Smith had arrived at the scene just moments after the jet went down. Whipple asked him what he was doing prior to the accident, and Smith explained that he'd been issuing a traffic citation a few blocks away at 160th and Stark when he said he heard a low rumble.

Then his memories tumbled out.

"I thought I seen something pass overhead, I wasn't sure, it happened so fast. I heard another sharp crackling noise, and the whole sky and everything lit up in a blue-white flash, like a flash on a camera. Then I heard another loud noise and all the power to my back, facing south, all the houses went dark."

He said he thought someone had hit a utility pole, so he jumped in his car and headed northwest toward Burnside in the direction of the commotion.

"I observed telephone poles flying through the air with lines attached to them dragging along the ground."

That's when he knew something major had happened. He pulled over, radioed dispatch, grabbed his walkie-talkie and flashlight, and started running down the blacked-out street.

"As I approached, I observed people coming out of a tree line, a kind of wooded area. I ran into several people and they asked me the direction to the terminal."

Terminal? It took him a moment to register.

"I was extremely shocked at what was going on. Then I looked up and I seen this large tail of a United Airlines plane sticking up, with power lines caught around it."

He was still the only officer on the scene. With his flashlight he noticed "a residue like dew, but not wet," covering the ground and roadway behind the aircraft—the insulation from the aircraft, he would later learn—and then he smelled what he thought was jet fuel.

"Having been in Vietnam and been shot down in three different helicopters, I recognized the smell of this type of fuel."

Given the downed power lines he'd seen, and his suspicion that there might be live electrical systems on the plane, he believed fire and an explosion were imminent.

"So I started screaming at these people to run west on Burnside. Then I went from the rear of the airliner forward, and they had the balloon-type ramps on the left side and people were sliding down. I grabbed ahold of things and climbed up into the aircraft."

Once inside, he said he met a stewardess who was holding her injured arm, but trying to help people out, and a man who identified himself as a doctor who was also aiding in the evacuation at that exit. He recalled seeing ten to fifteen people still in the cabin gathering their things.

"I started pulling the people away, and demanding that they get out of the plane. I thought the plane was just going to burst into flames."

At this point, Smith hadn't encountered any serious injuries, but as he looked forward in the aircraft toward the galley he saw that another one of the escape ramps had inflated inside the compartment, blocking the way from the floor to the ceiling.

"I climbed up and pushed down on the inflatable thing, and as I looked forward—from then on there was no front of the fuselage of the airplane, the whole front had been demolished. I shined my flashlight forward. I observed several people still strapped in their seats."

At that point he radioed dispatch again and said there were serious injuries and possible deaths.

By then, he said, another deputy sheriff, Ard Pratt had arrived on the scene. Together, they checked the vital signs of the people who'd been in the forward section, and then pulled them out, laying them about thirty feet from wreckage. Then they turned their attention to the piles of wreckage to see if they could find any survivors.

"As we went through the rubble and debris of the front of the airliner, I made notations as to where people were found, and removed them off to one side with the other bodies. All the debris was stacked so deep that we had to remove it to dig down further. Then one of the stewardesses came and told me she thought she heard a baby or someone moaning under a large section of the airliner."

From what he could see, it was perhaps an emergency exit door or window section of the fuselage. He, Pratt and a neighbor who had come to help, lifted the wreckage and found three seats fastened together.

"There was a small child stuck between the cushions of one of the seats, and she was actually folded down and sandwiched in between them. I pulled her out; she was bleeding from the mouth and gasping like she couldn't get a breath. I carried her off to one side and administered mouth to mouth for what seemed like a long time, but I acknowledge it was maybe five minutes."

The first ambulances began to arrive, and when they did, Smith carried the little girl to the road and handed her over to the medical personnel. He learned later that the child's name was Lisa Andor, and that she had survived. He went to see her in the hospital a couple of days later.

Smith ended his account of that night to a dead silent courtroom. Then after a few moments, Maria's lawyers had the lights dimmed so the KGW news video could be shown, but with the sound turned off as United's attorneys had insisted to avoid "the hearsay of the news announcer," who was in the studio and not an actual on-scene eyewitness. The jury would only be allowed to see the crash footage in silence.

But the images that flashed across the screen captured the chaos and destruction of the accident site, and they were too much for Maria. As quietly as she could, she followed the judge's earlier advice and stepped out.

Chapter 14

Safety and Punishment

In legal cases like Lisa's involving punitive damages—or punishment for wrongdoing—the burden of proof weigh heavily on plaintiffs. They must prove that the harm they've suffere(is the result of more than mere carelessness or mistakes, that it i rather the result, according to one legal definition, of a "willful o wanton disregard of risk of harm to others of a magnitude evincing ; high degree of social irresponsibility."

It's not that the accused *intentionally* set out to hurt some one—that's a worse level of misconduct veering into crime—but if i can be proved that they committed an action or inaction *knowing* ('foreseeing' is the legal term) that the results might well lead t(harm, then it is considered conduct amounting to a deliberate disregard of the rights and safety of others. In recent decades, the tobacc(industry has provided high-profile examples of this kind of misconduct, and some blockbuster punitive damage awards in both individ ual and class-action cases involving a large group of victims.

But this is rare. Despite the widespread misperception tha punitive damage lawsuits and awards are lavish and out of control such lawsuits are statistically infrequent—making up only about fivt percent of civil cases in 2005 according to the Bureau of Justice Statistics—and the amounts awarded are modest, averaging $64,000 That's because punitive damage cases are often seen as controversial they're not easy to prove, and the standards for applying punitivt damages in the U.S. vary from state to state—if they're permitted at all.

However, laws going back to Biblical times, and more recently to our own legal roots in England, have for good reasons provided for civil punishments that extend beyond simply compensating a victim for injuries or material loss. Such punishments address the enormity of a wrongdoer's offense and are designed to inflict a penalty severe enough to deter repetition or imitation, improve behavior and express society's condemnation of the misdeed.

Emily Gottlieb, Deputy Director for Law and Policy at the Center for Justice and Democracy explains in a 2011 white paper on punitive damages that, "Throughout U.S. history, a critical function of our civil justice system has been deterrence of unsafe practices through imposition of financial liability upon wrongdoers."

When it comes to corporate misdeeds, a financial penalty is often the only way to force a change since, as she notes, it is well recognized that some companies engage in a pragmatic if callous calculation that weighs the cost of removing a bad product from the market, or changing unsafe practices, against the cost of paying liability claims later if or when they occur.

The aviation industry is no stranger to this criticism, as Capt. David Simmon, Jr. lamented nearly thirty years ago in his 1988 article for the Flight Safety Foundation: "The corporate accountant is a safety inhibitor. Their influence on the airline industry has increased dramatically since the arrival of deregulation [1978]. Some accountants look at the safety department as another expense which must be reduced to the lowest possible cost."

Gottlieb adds that government regulatory agencies rarely prosecute companies for deaths or injuries from unsafe practices or defective products. That often leaves it up to the individual to take companies to task through the courts for corporate wrongdoing.

In two examples she gives—the dangerous intrauterine device called the Dalkon Shield in the early 1970s and the exploding gas tank on the 1970s Ford Pinto—it was revealed in court that the companies had decided not to make design changes or recall the product, judging that the benefits of doing so didn't justify the costs. But that changed when juries levied massive punitive damages against them in addition to compensatory damages. The supplemental penalty had a real impact on the companies, changing conduct that might well have continued as an insurable cost of doing business.

Over the last thirty years, the threat or imposition of punitive damages has undeniably improved consumer safety. Other infamous products and practices that were changed or removed after the responsible companies were hit with such penalties include: tampons that caused toxic shock syndrome, pizza delivery time guarantees that encouraged reckless driving and caused accidents, high-dose contraceptive pills that led to kidney failure, jeep roll bars that collapsed in accidents, and potentially lethal hospital ventilators. There's even a museum now in Connecticut—The American Museum of Tort Law—founded by consumer advocate and attorney Ralph Nader, and dedicated to the tort (wrongful injury) lawsuits that have removed many dangerous products and practices from the public.

Gottlieb argues that the positive impact of punitive damages on safety extends even further: "The amount of money society saves as a direct result of the deterrence function of punitive damages—injuries prevented, healthcare costs not expended, wages not lost, etc.— is incalculable but significant. Some have estimated this savings to be perhaps a trillion dollars a year."

It's hard to say what consumer safety would be like without the remedies offered by punitive damages, but Gottlieb's view on this is unequivocal: "The imposition or threat of punitive damages is so critical to the fight against reckless corporate behavior that any effort to restrict them undermines the safety of us all."

Yet we are in the process of doing just that. Moves in the last thirty years by legislatures and the Supreme Court have already eroded the powers of punitive damages to help victims of corporate wrongdoing under pressure from corporations and defense attorney lobbies pushing "tort reform"—Nader pointedly calls it tort *de*form.

In a September 2016 speech at the Center for the Study of Responsive Law, Richard Newman, trial attorney and executive director of the American Museum of Tort Law, said this assault on the laws and remedies that protect individuals after wrongful injury can be traced in part to the success of public relations campaigns by insurance companies and corporate lobbies in recent years aimed at capturing "the hearts and minds of the American people [in a] battle to make them think that the system really was broken." As proof of how "persuasive and powerful this assault on tort law has been," he noted that virtually everyone is familiar with the catch phrases "frivolous lawsuits, greedy trial lawyers and runaway verdicts," and many have been convinced that the laws should be changed. Even though statistics show nothing could be further from the truth, these catch phrases are so well-known and ingrained now in the public psyche that the facts have little power to change people's minds.

As of 2016, five states, Louisiana, New Hampshire, Massachusetts, Nebraska and Washington, had passed tort law legislation banning punitive damages outright. Absent a ban, many states have instituted flat-rate caps, or relative caps limiting punitive damages to no more than one, two or three times the amount of compensatory damages. This reflects the U.S. Supreme Court decision in 2008 that slashed the amount Exxon had to pay in punitive damages for the 1989 *Valdez* disaster from $5 billion to $507 million using a 1:1 ratio.

Such caps not only make punitive damages a predictable and budget-able expense item, they may actually offer companies an incentive to compute the costs and benefits of safety by providing a figure from which to do the calculation.

Caps and ratios also have a harmful impact in individual cases where the injured party's compensation—and any correlating punitive damage award—is largely calculated on their lost earnings. For children, low-wage or unemployed victims who have little to no income, the implication is clear and patently unfair to the weak and underprivileged since compensatory and therefore punitive damage awards would be negligible.

Other recent restrictions and barriers include requiring unanimous jury votes in punitive damage cases, or raising the burden of proof of the "reprehensibility" of the wrong.

Perhaps more disturbing is the now common strategy by corporations to prevent lawsuits and avoid the judicial system altogether by forcing people purchasing their goods and services to sign binding arbitration agreements that bar them from suing the company in the event of injury, or joining a class action lawsuit. Terms of Service agreements for everything including credit cards, bank accounts, computer applications and games, telephone equipment, ride share programs, and nursing homes to name just a few often include this arbitration requirement leaving limited options for remedy even if someone is harmed because the product or service was faulty or dangerous, or if corporate misconduct was involved. The typical language in such agreements—which most people sign without reading—requires the user to give up their constitutional right to a trial by jury, and offers a broad, warm blanket for businesses: "You agree that *any* dispute or claim relating *in any way* to your use of the services will be resolved by binding arbitration [emphasis added]."

There is no public hearing or disclosure in such arbitrations, and they are run by private arbitration companies that many legal observers say favor the corporations that hire them. So far, consumers can still opt out of these clauses—and they should, but rarely do.

In an article Ralph Nader wrote in April 2016 for Harper's Magazine entitled *Suing for Justice: Your Lawsuits are Good for America,* he warns of this erosion of tort law protecting citizens. Some states, he notes, have passed legislation shortening the statute of limitations on misconduct, thus shortening the time a victim has to file a lawsuit. He laments the "assault by a thousand cuts" on tort law that now includes a federal law which "prohibits almost all suits by victims and their next of kin against an aviation company if the offending aircraft is more than eighteen years old." A win for the aviation industry to be sure.

Finally, and perhaps most surprising, federal and state tax agencies currently allow companies to deduct punitive damages on their taxes as a business expense, while at the same time deeming them taxable income for the plaintiff. Critics charge that if companies can simply write off such expenses on their tax returns, punitive damages are no longer punitive at all. In fact, it's been said that in effect, it makes the U.S. taxpayer an underwriter of corporate misconduct.

Vermont Senator Patrick Leahy says this is just plain wrong. He introduced a bill in 2012 and again in January 2015 to eliminate the practice, saying in a February 3, 2015 *New York Times* article,

"This loophole allows corporations to wreak havoc and then write it off as a cost of doing business."

As of 2016, the deduction was still allowed.

Most of these modern restrictions aimed at access to the courts and remedies for injury including punitive damage awards were not fully in place as Lisa Andor's trial began in 1984. Since then the aviation industry and other business interests and their insurers have been successful in lobbying state and federal legislatures to pass the time limits, punitive damage bans, caps, ratios, and tax deductions outlined above.

But even without these now-present hurdles, it still wasn't easy to prove that punitive damages were warranted in the Andor case. Her attorneys would have to convince the jury that United had done more than just make a mistake, as its lawyers insisted. The evidence would have to convince them that the company had weighed the costs and benefits of its landing gear maintenance and *decided* to take a gamble that led to injury and death. The jury would have to find further that United deserved to be financially punished not only to make up for Lisa's injuries, but also to force the company to improve its safety practices. It would be an uphill battle, but not as steep a hill as it is today thanks to the success since then of the "Tort Reform" initiatives and limits now in place. Still, the Andor case would teach important lessons for both plaintiffs and defendants, and also act as a civil justice signpost for the road ahead.

Chapter 15

McBroom Remembers

Six women and six men were chosen to serve on the jury of the *Andor v United Airlines* trial. They ranged widely in age, with about half in their late thirties and forties; and in keeping with the common wisdom about state court (versus federal court) juries, they were a conservative group of modest economic means, composed primarily of working and retired citizens ready to do their civic duty for the next two and a half weeks. Among them was a secretary, a former tugboat operator, a dentist's widow, a florist, a semi-retired seventy-nine-year old house painter, a school district maintenance worker, a twenty-eight-year-old getting started in the ear testing and equipment field, and a woman who'd worked in her husband's electrical contracting business.

Even though five years had passed since the accident, Portlanders remembered the night vividly and could say where they were and what they were doing when the jet crashed. Virtually everyone who followed the news knew about Lisa, the little girl who survived but lost her family. The newspapers had run many articles about her long hospital recovery and subsequent move to Chicago.

Now as the trial got underway, she was back in the news, not just because of people's interest in her, but also because only one other lawsuit from the crash—out of some forty filed but settled—had gone all the way to trial. Lisa's case was the only one seeking $3 million in punitive damages—a penalty that, if awarded, would certainly get United's attention. It made her trial stand out as an unprecedented, high-stakes action against a commercial airline, which could have far-reaching legal implications for the entire aviation industry.

Amid the renewed publicity, finding a jury of people who could approach the case dispassionately was not easy. But following extensive pre-trial questioning called "voir dire"—an inquiry into the jurors' personal backgrounds, and attitudes toward money and big business—the attorneys for Lisa and United now faced the dozen citizens who sat before them, note pads in hand. After five years of preparation, the show was about to begin.

Looking back now on what it took to get ready for the trial, Whipple shakes his head a little. "It was a monster case," he says, recalling the endless hours he devoted to it—and all his other cases—at the expense of so many family activities. Then he adds smiling, "That's why I never encouraged you kids to go into the law."

In their opening statements, the attorneys for both sides had presented an overview of the case they said the evidence would prove. As is the practice, Lisa's side, the plaintiff, got to go first. The early testimony of the sheriff's deputy, followed by the silent news video of the crash scene, set a dramatic tone on the first days of the trial. Then, by way of an introduction to the testimony of the pilot, the jury heard the tape recording of the conversation between the crew and the control tower during the last twelve minutes of the flight before they declared a mayday and the plane crashed.

Given the publicity surrounding the case, it was with some anticipation and curiosity that the jurors awaited the arrival of the now infamous Captain Malburn McBroom, the pilot who had run his plane out of gas, and who was not only an important witness in the case, he was also one of the defendants. However, when Whipple called him to the stand, it was only as a formality since nobody stood up. United's attorneys had informed him and the court earlier that McBroom "wasn't available"—though word in the hallways was that he *was* in town at a hotel, and would appear during the defense phase of the trial. Lisa's attorneys chose not to compel his appearance since they knew they'd have a chance to cross examine him later, and they already had what they needed from him in deposition form.

But the jury was disappointed at his absence. A deposition is legal testimony, but it's not the same as seeing and hearing a witness in person. Without that, the jurors were treated to a reading of the deposition transcript, with Stewart Whipple playing himself and Bill Klein delivering McBroom's responses to the questions.

It was an exhaustive four-hour Q&A beginning with McBroom's life and training as a pilot, his knowledge of different aircraft systems and experience with regulations, operations, in-flight problems including hydraulic failures, instrument malfunctions and emergency procedures. His answers were fluid, knowledgeable and detailed thanks to his many years of experience. He'd flown just about every transport aircraft of the time: Convair 340, DC-3, DC-4, DC-6, DC-7, DC-8, DC-10, Boeing 727 & 737. He'd also been active on safety committees through his union, the Airline Pilots Association (ALPA), and served on three accident investigations with the NTSB.

By the end of the first two hours of the deposition, it was clear to the jury that McBroom knew his stuff—indeed, as his daughter would later recall in his obituary, flying was a dream come true for him, his life's work and goal from the moment a barnstormer buzzed the farm his family worked on as sharecroppers in Texas when he was a child. Being a pilot was quite simply who he was and what he was.

So when the questions in the transcript finally veered toward the night of the accident, everyone was paying close attention hoping to get an answer to the burning question: how could such a pilot crash due to fuel exhaustion?

McBroom described his and the crew's surprise and concern when at 5:15 pm, as they were in their approach to land, the right main landing gear came smashing down with two enormous jolts, yanking the giant aircraft sideways and short-circuiting the gear indicator lights. They thought they'd hit something. Realizing that they hadn't, they tried to figure out what was wrong with the gear.

"I asked Frostie to go back in the cabin and check the two mechanical indicator buttons on the wing, and I turned on the wing flood light to help him see them. Frostie came back and said they were up indicating the gear is down and locked."

But McBroom said he wasn't convinced given the massive double impact of the gear falling. Neither he nor his crew mates had ever experienced anything like it. "I was concerned about the gear. I wasn't persuaded the gear was down and locked. I'm still not persuaded."

And he added the others were worried, too.

"This flight crew had many thousands of hours of flight experience. The sound and the feel that shook the airplane were so out of the ordinary we were all concerned."

But try as they might, he said, "We couldn't get a handle on this one; we couldn't satisfy ourselves as to what was the problem."

Twenty-five minutes into the situation at 5:40 pm, he said they called Neil Reynolds at United dispatch and DC-8 maintenance specialist Leland Buhr, both in San Francisco.

"Mechanically, airplanes are fairly technical, and that's when you bring in the maintenance base. The person designated on that watch is there to provide answers to the crew on anything that would assist them in handling whatever problem they have. I told them we had a gear problem and what the sensations and indications were."

He described to them the troubleshooting they'd done and standard procedures they'd followed but said he didn't want to recycle the gear for fear that if it did go back up they might not get it back down. Buhr and Reynolds had agreed on that, he recalled, but didn't have anything else to say about the problem or any history of similar occurrences. Only that the crew had done everything they could.

"Did he [Buhr] at any time tell you that United had had problems with the retract piston rod cylinder eyebolts failing and the gear falling free?" Whipple asked.

"Not that I recall."

"Would that information have been helpful if it had been given to you?"

"My sense is that yes, it would have been nice to have known anything that would have helped to resolve in our minds the question of what we had," he replied, adding, "Whether or not it would have made a difference, I'd just be speculating."

"If you had been assured by the maintenance personnel at central dispatch in San Francisco that the gear was down and locked and that you could make a safe landing, you could have landed ten minutes earlier, couldn't you have?" Whipple asked.

"I don't think anybody could have assured us that the gear was down and locked given the severity of the jolts when the gear came down. I don't think my own chief pilot, the president of the airline, anybody could have persuaded me that the gear was down and locked," he said. "I expected, and I believe my first officer also did that there was a high probability the right main landing gear would collapse upon landing."

During the course of his conversation with dispatch, Mc Broom recalled that he reported the fuel he had on board by that time was 7,000 pounds. He said he was aware he was into his forty-five minute reserve fuel required by the FAA.

"Once we are below 8,400 pounds on board we are in fact using reserve. Yes, sir I knew that."

But again, dispatch had nothing to say about that, offered no comment about how long it might last according to their calculations or that they were making any calculations of their own.

But that wasn't unusual, McBroom explained. Even though under federal air regulations and United's own policies the dispatcher has joint responsibility with the captain for the safe operation of a trip, the only times McBroom recalled that dispatch would get involved in monitoring fuel consumption while an aircraft is in flight is in the event of a hijack, or if the plane is diverted to an alternate airport. A flight in a holding pattern due to a gear problem didn't provoke Neil Reynolds to concern himself with the plane's fuel situation. But neither did McBroom ask for any assistance in the matter.

"Were you at any time concerned about your fuel supply in terms of your time for landing?" McBroom was asked.

"Yes sir. The pilot is always concerned about fuel. Those things don't stay up there without fuel, not to be facetious. I knew I had so much fuel on board and that translates into so much time. I fully expected to accomplish the objectives and land at the airport."

"And just what was the fuel burnout rate that night based on the plane's altitude of 5,000 feet, speed at 180 knots and flaps at fifteen degrees?"

"What I remember is 12,000 pounds per hour," McBroom said.

"Were you intentionally trying to burn off fuel?"

"No sir."

Given his near certainty that the gear would collapse, McBroom asked the cabin crew to prepare the passengers for an emergency landing and evacuation. He'd fully visualized the possibilities they faced at the airport:

"Our touch-down speed would have been about 135 knots. We weigh in excess of 200,000 pounds. You have two choices of runway [in Portland]. If you land on the right runway and the [right] gear collapses, the airplane drops on number three or four engine wing tip. You can control it directly down to eighty knots or so. Beyond that the crew becomes a passenger. The airplane, based on my experience with accident investigation, will go 2,500 to 2,800 feet and veer to the right, and going too far right in Portland you go into the river. The concern of landing on the left runway is a similar situation. Only if we go right we could very well end up getting involved in the terminal complex which sits between the two runways."

That was why he wanted to prepare everyone as well as possible for a difficult landing. He said he didn't recall that he gave the flight attendants a specific time frame to complete the preparations, but thought he might have indicated ten or fifteen minutes. The flight attendants, themselves, would later recall that they'd had more than enough time—enough to go through the procedures twice.

McBroom remembered that when Joan, the lead flight attendant came back to the cockpit at 6:06 pm to say they were ready in the cabin, any thought of being on top of the situation evaporated when one of the engines quit. He was surprised, he said. He hadn't realized that their fuel status was so dangerously low. Indeed he believed he had fuel until twenty-three minutes past the hour, though he said his plan was to land earlier.

"There was some discussion back and forth between the three of us, and suggestions to open the cross feeds, and how much fuel the gauges were showing. It took a little while to get the engine relit," he said. "The fact that the engine flamed out frightened me. That tells me I don't really know how much fuel I have on board. It occurred to me at the time that when the gear broke, we had perhaps damaged a cross feed line—either that or some of the plumbing, and we had somehow lost the fuel overboard."

There was also the possibility, he offered, that he had made a miscalculation or that the gauges were showing more fuel than they actually had. McBroom was asked which it was.

"Well it has been a concern of mine since the accident. I think you can read the comment of Frostie my engineer that 'the fuel sure went to hell in a hurry.' The rate of burnout appeared to increase in the latter minutes of the flight. Whether we were actually losing fuel overboard due to line damage from the impact of the gear, or whether it was the gauges, or whether it was this captain, I can't tell you."

"And were you ever informed by United prior to December 28, 1978 that fuel gauges had certain tolerances in terms of accuracy?" Whipple asked.

"Not that I recall."

148

"Did you learn subsequently that there was a discrepancy between the gauge and the actual fuel in the tank?"

"Some three or four months subsequent to the accident I was told that there is an acceptable tolerance in an otherwise normally functioning indicating system. It's not an inaccuracy."

"And what is that tolerance?"

"It's plus or minus 426 pounds. On eight tanks, it's 3400-3500 pounds. In addition to that there is an allowable tolerance within the totalizer system of an additional 1,000 pounds."

"Would you have done anything differently if you had been aware of those fuel gauge tolerances?"

"All I can tell you is that as I respect other limits in aviation, I would have respected those," McBroom answered.

"But because you were not aware of those limits, you did not take them into consideration?"

"No sir."

His fuel situation now perilous, McBroom said he asked for clearance to land and his distance to the airport. "I began to consider the possibility that I couldn't make the airport and looked for some alternative place to set the thing down."

Then engines one and two quit.

"I picked out a spot I thought was probably a neighborhood park. There were no lights in it and I assumed no houses. I don't remember the other engines quitting, though I know they did. I remember going into the upper portion of the first grove of trees and how surprised I was. I could feel it. I expected it to be more abrupt. It was quite soft. We were doing 200 feet per second or so. I remember I wanted to get the nose at twelve degrees, and I don't remember anything beyond that."

It was 6:15 pm, exactly an hour and 12,000 pounds of fuel since their arrival in Portland airspace.

McBroom said he regained consciousness some time later. A section of the floor with his seat, throttle and radio still attached to it had been ejected from the plane, and he found himself sitting on the ground near what was left of the right wing.

"A person I remember took me by the arm and kind of from behind and asked who I was. I said, 'I'm the captain.' I remember saying, 'I won't go until everybody else is gone.' And he said, 'Everybody else *is* gone.' And the next thing I remember is being in the hospital."

Going back to the gear problem, McBroom was asked to further explain what he meant when he said that he was still not satisfied that the gear was down and locked after it fell free.

"I suppose it's a sense comprised of a good number of years and hours in the cockpit, putting the gear up and down lots of times in different airplanes, the sound of it, the feeling of it," he began. "The fact that it violently shook this pretty massive airplane *twice*—I couldn't reconcile that with the gear going down and into the locked position. Also the landing gear indicating system was damaged in that process. There was no doubt in my mind that mechanical damage had occurred. Right or wrong, there was no doubt in my mind based on what I perceived and what the crew members perceived that it was mechanically broken." He paused and then added, "Now the button on the top of the wing is a part of the mechanism. Was the indication valid? That's the question in my mind."

Based on the investigation after the accident, he said there *was* evidence to believe that the gear was not down and locked in place.

"The width of the landing gear at touchdown as recorded by the NTSB was a good deal wider than usual. The dimension from center of the truck [wheel assembly] to center of the truck on my airplane was twenty feet, ten inches. When the gear touched the ground where we landed, it made an impression in the dirt that was documented by the NTSB as being thirty-three feet in width. I construe from that the gear was outboard from where it should have been," McBroom said, adding, "I was aware that within a few days after the accident the landing gear parts were sold for salvage and I assume melted down. To my knowledge, nothing was saved."

Whether the gear was in fact down and locked, or bent outward as McBroom testified that he believed it was, opinions would vary. But there was good reason to think that he was right. In addition to the touch-down measurements in the NTSB report, Harold Bayer, a former vice president in charge of product support at McDonnell Douglas, testified later during the trial that DC-8 landing gear is designed to be able to "free fall" into landing position if there is a problem with the hydraulics. But the term 'free fall' is misleading, he explained, since resistance is still in place: "You still have the back pressure in the hydraulic cylinder," he said. In other words, it's a controlled descent. He agreed that this controlled descent would *not* have been the case in McBroom's aircraft when the eyebolt suddenly disconnected.

One passenger's recollection of what *that* kind of free fall had been like supported McBroom's perception that the gear was badly damaged and possibly displaced. Fay Saxton was seated over the wing above the right landing gear and wrote in a letter that when the gear came down, "It sounded like it was tearing metal off the bottom of the plane."

Maybe it was. But nobody would ever know for certain—or what might have happened had the jet crash landed at the airport. Both the right and left landing gear were ripped from the aircraft in the crash and found lying on either side of the main cabin some yards away. They were indeed scrapped within the week. United engineer William Witt, who was on the accident investigation team, was the one who measured the touch-down width of the landing gear. That was the number used in the official NTSB accident report. But later in his deposition he changed his story saying he'd "made a mistake," and then testified that the right landing gear *was* down and locked *even though no physical evidence or photographs existed or were ever presented to support the claim.*

The down-and-locked question—and whether that was really beside the point—would be up to the jury to decide.

Still, a few pieces of the landing gear assembly and some of the instrument gauges *were* saved as part of the NTSB accident investigation. After the NTSB was done with them, they wound up in the Portland offices of United's defense attorneys where they remained for years before the trial. Those landing gear parts wouldn't answer the down-and-locked question, but the piston rod retract cylinder with a broken eyebolt from the right main landing gear would tell an important tale in the coming days.

As for the fuel gauges, United flight crews and dispatchers later got a telling, but tardy technical bulletin from Ed Carroll at the company's Denver Flight Standards and Training Center; it would be provided to Lisa's attorneys as a trial exhibit.

In it Carroll explained what the FAR 45-minute reserve fuel rule meant and how it was to be calculated for domestic flights. The memo also set some helpful new guidelines for the "absolute minimum" quantity of fuel each aircraft type should have when it reaches the outer marker of an airfield on final approach. The number of pounds for a DC-8 was listed at 3,000, and was to be considered the *same as zero* fuel at touch down. Carroll wrote, "SFOEG [San Francisco Engineering Group] has advised us that the gauges which are operating normally should be accurate to within 3 percent plus or minus. In addition, when fuel is critical don't rely on the totalizer, but add up the individual gauges."

Carroll concluded by acknowledging the tolerance issue McBroom had raised: "Certainly no one wants to land with so little fuel that the engines flame out at touch down, so some cushion is in order. In addition, an allowance should be made for fuel gauge tolerances."

The memo came too late for McBroom, but apparently another pilot missed it, too. Two months after it went out, the airline earned the headline: *United Does it Again,* when a flight en-route from San Francisco landed in Portland out of fuel on touch down and had to be towed to the terminal.

It had been a long day of trial when the court adjourned at 5:15. The jury had gotten a crash course in every sense of the term. They were exhausted as they left the courtroom with notepads full of information to process and a pretty good idea that a lot more lay ahead.

For Maria, too, the day was thankfully over. McBroom's testimony had both answered and raised a lot of questions about what had happened that fateful night. But the worst part was the vivid detail of his account. Those images made it hard to stop herself from imagining what it had been like for her younger sister during that last hour on the airplane as she and Gabor, no doubt filled with fear, did what they were told to prepare themselves and the children for the coming emergency landing.

Chapter 16

Crevice Corrosion

It was with increasing confidence and a sense of ownership that the jury members gathered now in the gray mornings in the jury room before trial began and chatted briefly about the news over last-minute coffee (they weren't supposed to discuss the case, but it was hard not to, one woman recalls). A kind of bond was growing between these disparate strangers, the sort of connection that develops when people are thrown suddenly into a shared responsibility they haven't chosen but must navigate as best they can. They relied on small talk about news headlines, the weather and the movies to pass the time outside the courtroom. One woman brought in a pan of her "No-Fail Fudge"—a recipe another jury member said was so good, she uses it to this day.

Though still cold and showery, spring flowers were blossoming on the trees, and the presidential campaign was well underway with Ronald Reagan seeking a second term. It still wasn't clear yet whether Walter Mondale, or Gary Hart in his first presidential bid, would capture the Democratic nomination. On the big screen, the movie *Silkwood* had just come out to strong reviews—a damning story of corporate cover-up and misdoings. In the busy, marble-floored hallway outside the courtroom, Michael Jackson's smash hit *Thriller* might've been heard leaking from the headphones of someone's Walkman.

For United Airlines, Inc. 1984 was shaping up to be good year in terms of financial performance after some not so great ones during the recession of the early eighties.

"Hard work begins to pay off," the forty-eight-year-old chairman, president and CEO Richard "Dick" Ferris would later write in the annual report as he summarized the company's "dramatically improved profitability." The airline's net earnings surged to $258.9 million, more than twice the previous year's profits. Operating revenues of $6.2 billion were up sixteen percent. "It was a great year," he wrote near a picture of his determined and smiling face.

Ferris wasn't kidding about the hard work. In the ultra-competitive world of the airline industry he did what it took to deliver results with what one writer called "caveman aggression." The company had shed almost a quarter of its work force from 1979 to 1982 and at the same time—taking advantage of deregulation ("The greatest thing to happen to the airline industry since the jet engine," Ferris said)—United expanded flight schedules, added new service to twenty-four airports in 1983, and increased daily aircraft hours-in-the-air by almost ten percent. They were also now contracting maintenance services to other airlines as "a source of revenue and a means of improving utilization of employees and equipment." Everyone was working harder, and despite frequent labor disputes with the airline's mechanics, pilots and flight attendants' unions, employee productivity kept driving up and up according to company records.

With similar resolve, the company dealt with its various and sundry legal issues, most of which didn't rate a note in the company annual report. But one did, and it was an instructive playbook to legal observers of the time. Specific mention of a potentially very costly class-action lawsuit appeared uncharacteristically in the 'Contingencies and Other Commitments' section of United's 1979-1983 Annual Reports, preparing shareholders for bad news.

Since 1966, the company had been embroiled in a sex discrimination battle with a group of former flight attendants who were fired or resigned between 1965 and 1968 because of the airline's no-marriage rule of the time for female but not male cabin attendants. A flagrant violation of the Civil Rights Act, the court found the rule illegal, and this ultimately spawned a class-action lawsuit.

Unfazed, the company spent the next fifteen years and untold amounts of money fighting through appeals all the way to the U.S. Supreme Court, which ruled against United in 1984 to the tune of $38 million in damages and back pay.

Ferris, whose narrow gaze, even when smiling, hinted at the clenched-fist approach he took to dealing with whatever came, charged the penalty to non-operating expenses, assured stockholders the loss wouldn't hurt the company's consolidated financial position, and then got back to business.

"It's a wonder those women were able to endure as long as they did," Whipple later observed in the knowing way of a fellow combatant. "And to think of all the upfront time, work and costs their lawyers had to bear—who likely handled it on a contingency-fee basis, not knowing how it would end up."

This siege-like approach to litigation was a smoke-on-the-horizon signal to other plaintiff's attorneys, indicating what they might expect in a lawsuit with the corporate giant. Time, money, legal resources, United was known as a merciless, formidable foe; it could and would go to extraordinary lengths to defend its position, right or wrong.

The Andor case was playing out in Portland a few months be
fore United would get the September 1984 U.S. Supreme Court dis
crimination ruling against it, and even though Lisa's trial didn't figur
in the corporate financial statement, the case was not being ignorec
United's attorneys had assembled an extensive array of witnesses—
costly defense strategy, a former defense attorney explained, sinc
they must all be interviewed, transported, fed and housed. The hop
is that, notwithstanding precise relevance to the issues of the case, th
sheer number of witnesses and amount of testimony will produce ₄
favorable impression on the jury—or at least enough doubt to swa·
the verdict for the defense.

Whether the strategy would work with this jury was yet to b·
determined, but one thing was immediately evident: these jurors wer·
an attentive group—so attentive, in fact, that not only did they tak·
extensive notes on the testimony during the first days of the trial, they
started sending notes to the judge, asking questions of their own, es
pecially when a metallurgical engineer took the stand testifying abou·
the severe corrosion that he—along with the NTSB—had found o·
the broken eyebolt from the right main landing gear.

Noting their keen interest in the plaintiff's testimony wit·
some misgivings, United's lawyers finally asked the judge to mak·
the jury stop asking questions, and Judge Roth had to explain to then
that as a matter of procedure it was up to the attorneys to do the ques
tioning and try the case.

But they were clearly interested in understanding what th·
metallurgist Roger Olleman had to say. Using boards mounted wit·
pictures of the eyebolt magnified so the jury could see the ring, th·
shank and the threads, he walked them through his findings.

He noted that while the metal itself in the bolt appeared appropriate to its job, he was not so sure about the threading on it. He had seen the bulletins from the plane manufacturer recommending a change from cut-thread to rolled-thread eyebolts, but this was a cut-thread bolt, he explained. "The bolt that failed was one of the old bolts, not one of the newer ones."

The difference, Olleman explained, came down to a question of strength and durability due to the manufacturing process. Threads are either cut into the metal cylinder of a bolt by a sharp machine-grinding tool, or forced in by means of a narrow, high-pressure roller. The latter rolled-thread bolt is stronger at the molecular level so less likely to crack, and the smoother surface is less susceptible to corrosion.

"Rolled threads generally have more resistance to fatigue failures," he said.

Olleman pointed to one of the close-up photos of the broken eyebolt. "We have threads here, but there has been a lot of corrosion. There are big pits and a lot of material has been lost off the top of the threads."

He noted that the worst corrosion in the bolt was found in what would have been the deepest interior and least exposed part of the piston rod. His investigation revealed several openings along the bolt where the sealant was missing and would have provided pathways for corrosion-causing moisture. He set up another series of photos and pointed to the gaps and the places that still did have sealant, some of which he said appeared to be original to the plane's manufacture date ten years before the crash.

"One of the more interesting features of this set of figures is that, actually, the sealant was not applied so as to keep water out.

There is a substantial hole through which water had direct access to the threads. And these four channels were wide open for moisture."

He said he could find no sealant on the threads of the eyebolt, or in the interior of the cylinder, both areas where sealant is required.

"If an attempt was made to seal off the threads, it was only partially successful," Olleman added, as he lifted another picture onto the easel showing the extent of the resulting damage.

"Some of the most severe examples of corrosion with which metallurgists are familiar are labeled as 'crevice corrosion'—the kind of corrosion that occurs when there is a narrow opening into which liquid can seep."

He pointed at an enlargement of the bolt showing its unevenly rippled edge. "Some of the threads have actually corroded far below their original depth, and there is practically nothing of what used to be the root of the thread."

The corrosion, he explained, affected the entire mechanism and was extreme, destroying both the mating threads inside the retract cylinder *and* along the bolt.

"The majority of the threads in the interior of the piston rod had no real opportunity any longer to form an engagement with the threads on the eyebolt."

Olleman returned to the witness stand and was approached by Lisa's attorney.

"Doctor, based on your investigations, do you have an opinion as to what caused the retract cylinder eyebolt to separate from the piston rod?

"Yes. The primary problem was crevice corrosion."

Later, United's attorneys put their own metallurgist on the stand but his nearly incomprehensible testimony did more to confuse than enlighten the jury. However a couple of points stuck: first, even though he disputed the amount of sealant present, he agreed that corrosion caused the eyebolt to fail, which meant that whatever sealant was there did, too.

"There's no getting around it, the threads were corroded," he acknowledged.

Second, he identified *two* kinds of corrosion in his examination: red and black. Red is common rust, resulting from heavy exposure to air and moisture, while black corrosion occurs when metal is exposed to water in an enclosed, low-oxygen environment over a long period of time. It forms gradually. That piece of information made a successful landing in the mind of at least one juror who says she can still quote the distinction—and that it bothered her. Both types of corrosion were present, but one was the result of a long-term destructive situation, which indicated that something was very wrong with what United was doing—or not doing—to detect and prevent such corrosion.

Olleman summed it up when he was asked how he would characterize United's landing gear inspections and maintenance program based on his investigation of the gear parts:

"I'd have to say it's inadequate."

But "inadequate" doesn't equal deliberate negligence. You can miss something for a lot of reasons, though to go on missing it for a period of years despite a history of similar failures might point to a level of inept or callous disregard. To be called deliberately or wantonly negligent it has to be shown that you actually knew about a specific and existing dangerous situation and *chose* to ignore it. United's gamma ray inspection records and maintenance deferrals would do just that.

Later in the afternoon, Sanford "Pinky" Pinkiert took the oath and said he worked for United Airlines in the engineering department responsible for maintenance problems in the hydraulic system and landing gear on the DC-8 fleet. He acknowledged they'd had some thread corrosion and rod failures in the piston and eyebolt assembly that holds the landing gear, so in 1973, he helped to design and implement a "non-destructive testing" program using gamma ray or isotope imaging—like X-rays for machines—to detect crack and corrosion problems in areas of the landing gear that United didn't want to actually take apart but couldn't otherwise see from the outside.

It's called "non-destructive" because the test doesn't require any disassembling of the parts being inspected. Apart from the obvious time and cost savings such testing offers, Pinkiert argued that the act of inspecting a component by taking it apart, handling it and putting it back again can cause damage of its own.

But critics say that's a poor excuse for not doing a thorough job of inspection—or as Olleman put it, "inadequate." It also short-circuits the collateral benefits of the 'might-as-well' instinct most people share: when you encounter a problem which is revealed after you've already gone to the trouble of taking something apart, you usually decide you might as well fix it. That instinct didn't get much of a chance to kick in with United's gamma ray program. The inspection findings, it would turn out, rarely even got to the actual fixers.

Gamma ray technology and image quality were fairly crude in the mid-seventies. The pictures were difficult to see unless you had an industrial-strength, high-intensity spotlight shining through the film, and interpreting the images varied according to who was looking at them. Nevertheless, Pinkiert said you could tell if corrosion was there in the cylinder and bolt because the threads weren't tight against each other.

"You can see irregularities in the thread contact area."

And indeed the images did show the corrosion—lots of it, in varying degrees. Despite faded handwriting on much-photocopied pages, the records his department kept were informative. They list 292 gamma ray inspections on the right and left landing gear retract cylinders and piston rods of United's DC-8 fleet between June 1973 and May 1977. Of these, only eighty-two were marked "OK", while the other 210 test results found corrosion in "Light, Moderate, or Heavy" amounts. And although "moderate" and "heavy" amounts of corrosion were found on fifty-three of the landing gears—and at least five piston rod assemblies did fail in the meantime—only thirteen eyebolts were listed as changed during that five-year period.

It was in this context that Pinkiert was now asked to look at the records, which Lisa's lawyers had subpoenaed, and find the test results for the aircraft she was on: United Flight 173, tail number N8082U. The date of the first inspection was August 1, 1973, a year after the aircraft had its first and only landing gear overhaul.

"Now there in the 'Results' column, does that say 'minor corrosion?'" Whipple queried.

"I assume that 'minor corrosion' is what they are saying," Pinkiert replied mildly, squinting at the familiar chart before him, and apparently ignoring his own nickname, "Pinky" scrawled in the upper left corner.

Whipple handed him another page—this one handwritten and missing the neat grid of the previous record. The date May 30, 197⁴ was entered next to the same aircraft designation, and he asked Pinkiert what the "results" column read.

"It says 'moderate.'"

"Does that mean there was moderate corrosion found in the right eyebolt?"

"That would be—" Pinkiert paused, studying. "Yes."

"And then on the left landing gear…"

"That also says 'moderate.'"

Whipple leaned forward with another sheet of paper marked June 4, 1975 next to the aircraft ID and asked what it said about the right landing gear.

"That says 'moderate.'"

"Now the left piston rod, what does that note say?"

"Note says 'long thread'. That means it now has a repaired rod-end as modified by United Airlines. The unit has been removed and replaced."

"So it was deemed corroded to the extent that it needed repair or replacement?"

"Yes. We cut a second set of threads in the piston and used an extended rod end."

Whipple pointed again to the document. "According to this the *right* piston rod was not repaired or replaced at the same time."

"Apparently not," Pinkiert replied, though he couldn't say why.

On April 4, 1977, two years after only the left landing gear on Lisa's airplane got a new long-thread eye-bolt, both sides were inspected by gamma ray one more time and labeled "lightly" corroded. No repairs had been made to the right side, so it was counter to reason, if not counter to fact, that the corrosion levels there had somehow improved over time even though the components had been listed as *moderately* corroded in two previous inspections.

At that point, however, corrosion detection and control on the cylinders and eyebolts ceased to be a concern for United, because as Pinkiert explained, they had installed an improved bungee spring mechanism in another part of the landing gear which they felt would guarantee that even if the eyebolt broke, the landing gear would still come down and lock properly. So they decided to scrap the gamma ray inspection program.

"Did the bungee system solve the corrosion problem of the piston rods?" Whipple asked, trying to understand the connection.

"No. It didn't involve the piston rod."

"So you still had the same corrosion problem with rod ends?"

"The potential was still there," Pinkiert said, nodding.

"Yet as I understand it you discontinued the gamma ray inspection program in 1977?

"Yes."

"Was there any particular reason why you discontinued the gamma ray program?"

"We felt that the improvement on the bungee system removed the safety hazard."

"But the bungee system did not control the corrosion of the eyebolts?" Whipple checked again, hoping the jury was following.

"No, it did not."

"So the bungee system was not intended as a solution to the corrosion problem?"

"Not directly. Indirectly it eliminated the safety hazard."

United apparently developed this reasoning on its own since McDonnell Douglas, the aircraft manufacturer never suggested in its service bulletins that an improved bungee spring system would or could take the place of changing the faulty eyebolts, or adequately inspecting and sealing the retract cylinder assemblies, or that airlines could just skip one if they did another. These were separate matters and the subject of separate safety bulletins to United, all of which were deemed important enough to require attention. McDonnell Douglas VP Harold Bayer confirmed this later at trial saying the bungee "has nothing to do with extending [the gear], or seeing that the gear locks down or is down."

Moreover, the news that the bungee system "eliminated the safety hazard" of corroded eyebolts—or that such corrosion was a known problem—never got communicated to United's pilots, either before or during the crash of Flight 173. So a flight crew would have no idea what kind of emergency they were dealing with when a rusted eyebolt failed and a two-ton landing gear suddenly came crashing down. As one pilot later joked, "They wouldn't say to themselves, '"Must be one of those old corroded eyebolts giving way—so no problem."'

As for the notion that the bungee eliminated the safety hazard, the pilot added, "You wouldn't install a bungee instead of the bolt as a 'back-up.' That's not logical. It doesn't make sense. You wouldn't replace a part with something different. The bungee is not an alternative to the bolt."

Could it really be true that United wasn't even inspecting the piston rod assemblies anymore, knowing as they obviously did from their own inspection records that corrosion was a problem there? Had corrosion simply disappeared? Whipple wanted to know.

Pinkiert said, "No, they'd still seen corrosion on eyebolts, even on the newer rolled-thread types."

"Since December 28, 1978, have you adopted a new program or changed any previous inspection program of the eyebolt for corrosion?"

"No, we have not changed our procedures."

"The only thing you have done, basically is discontinue the gamma ray program?"

"That's right, on a routine basis—or on any basis I should say," Pinkiert confirmed. Even when it was underway, he added, it was "a non-routine type of inspection."

"In other words, there was no regular schedule?"

"No, there wasn't."

"Has anyone at United complained to you about the inadequacy of the inspection program of the eyebolts?"

"No," he shook his head.

"Mr. Pinkiert, with respect to the safety of passengers and the proper operation of DC-8 aircraft, do you consider the proper functioning of the landing gear of critical importance?"

"Yes."

Whipple asked him again if another kind of inspection program was substituted for gamma ray imaging to make sure that the landing gear *was* functioning properly.

"We basically have no other method other than we put a time control on the retract cylinder; and improved sealing of the rod ends."

In fact, putting it on a "time control" meant that it wasn't Pinkiert's problem anymore. Dealing with corrosion in the cylinder components was no longer part of his department's now terminated, non-routine-detection-and-maybe-respond protocol. It was simply shifted over and bundled "as a matter of convenience," he said, with the whole landing gear overhaul schedule. With landing gear change they also change the retract assembly, Pinkiert explained.

But what *that* schedule was, he couldn't say.

"That's on a flight hours schedule. It's quite a number of years apart. I believe it's, well, I'm not sure of the time on it at the moment."

Someone else would have that information, he said, but he didn't have a name. It wasn't his department.

"I guess it's Engineering Planning, or maybe it's—no. I guess it's under Quality Control."

According to United aircraft engineer William Witt, who *did* have that information for the jury, and now testified on behalf of United, the schedule set for landing gear overhaul on United DC-8s in the late seventies was 20,000 flight hours—about seven years. It was a schedule that had been extended three times over the course of the aircraft model's twenty-seven year history, he explained during cross-examination.

When the DC-8 model was new, the manufacturer, its airline customers and the FAA got together and set the landing gear safe-life limit at 12,000 hours. At that point a gear overhaul was due—it was "time controlled." That's when the gear was removed and parts re-placed, including the retract cylinder assembly, and sometimes—but oddly not always—the $124-eyebolt, as was the case with the right side gear of United Flight 173.

But as the years passed and experience with the aircraft was gained, Witt said the safety threshold was pushed out to 15,000 hours by United's people in the Maintenance Planning department who didn't want to bring the planes in as much. This was approved by the FAA, he added.

"Why didn't they want to bring them in as much?" Whipple asked.

"To boil it down, economics. Money economics."

"So you save money by not overhauling it as much?"

"Oh, yes, sir," Witt affirmed.

"Do you know who extended that overhaul time to 20,000 hours?"

"It would have been the same maintenance planning people."

"And did they confer with you?"

"Oh yes, sir, very much. I am very much involved," he said.

Witt explained that he was tasked with giving the maintenance planners comments about whether overhaul on the components could be extended based on a variety of factors.

"We investigated the component history, all the maintenance that has been done on the airplane prior, the manufacturer's service bulletins, the AD notes [Airworthiness Directives], anything combined with that particular component to make sure it was safe."

"Did you know at that time that these retract eyebolts had failed as a result of corrosion?" Whipple queried.

"Not in particular," Witt said vaguely. "No, I can't recall any detail at all of these entities failing from corrosion."

Whipple stepped forward with some pages. "Mr. Witt, do you recognize these service bulletins from McDonnell Douglas?"

"Yes."

"I take it that you are familiar with the documents, that the got to your department?"

"Yes, sir."

"What do they refer to?"

Witt took a moment to read the text. "It refers to nineteen failures of the main landing gear retract cylinder."

"Due to what?"

"They were corrosion failures," he said.

"Did you participate in any way in the solution to the corrosion problem of the eyebolts?"

"Not that I recall." Then he added, leaning back, "It wasn't my responsibility."

"Were you aware of your own gamma ray program?" Whipple asked.

"No sir. I wasn't involved in the gamma ray program. That was another person."

"Well, wasn't that conducted by the engineering department of United?"

"Yes, but I wasn't responsible for that program. I believe you saw Mr. Pinkiert."

"Did you *look* at the gamma ray reports?" Whipple pressed.

"No, sir."

"Even so, you were responsible for the DC-8 landing gear— you didn't have the information with regard to the gamma ray program?" Incredulity crept into Whipple's voice.

"That's correct. I did not."

"Were you involved in the extension of the overhaul time from 15,000 to 20,000 hours?"

"I probably was; yes, sir. I am responsible for that time period."

"Mr. Witt, in your opinion, was Flight 173 equipped with safe landing gear?"

"Yes sir. No question."

"Even though the eyebolt corroded, pulled apart and failed?"

"Wouldn't be anything to affect the safety of the airplane because that pulled apart," he said evenly.

"Why do you have them in there at all, then?"

"In order to retract the landing gear for flight. There's no way to pull the gear up without having that eyebolt in place. If it failed, the gear would just fall into the down-and-locked position."

"So you consider that eyebolt—corroded and rusted to the point that it pulled apart—a safe component?" Whipple pressed.

"It's a component that would have to be replaced before the next flight, because he wouldn't be able to fly it when that..." Witt stopped. "I don't consider that safe."

"*Did* you replace it before the next flight?" Whipple asked, the answer obvious.

"No sir," Witt said. "We scrapped the airplane."

According to the NTSB factual report, at the time it crashed, the airplane used in United Flight 173 had logged a total of 33,114 flight hours. It had flown 21,245 hours since overhaul, but was listed as still having another 3,754 hours to go before its second scheduled overhaul was due—and any landing gear change. The safe-life threshold had been extended again from 20,000 to 25,000 hours.

But with the Andor lawsuit underway and perhaps not wanting to push their luck any further liability-wise, United quietly "did a project," Pinkiert later admitted, to finally inspect and change the eyebolts on its DC-8 fleet.

Chapter 17

An Airman Calls Foul

"The rule of law requires that all parties who contribute to an accident share in the responsibility for whatever harm has been caused." - F. Lee Bailey

During the early days of the trial, Frank Harrell sat in the observer section of the courtroom taking notes and sometimes shaking his head, next to Maria's family attorney, Bill Klein, who was doing the same. Harrell, a trim, sixty-two-year old former naval lieutenant commander, air transport pilot and retired FAA inspector, had been listening to witness testimony, and waiting to be called for his turn on the stand. Lisa's trial team, Whipple and Johansen, had asked for his help six months earlier to review case documents and serve as an expert during the trial.

But Harrell had been studying the accident for longer than six months. He was particularly keen to understand what had happened because earlier in his career, he'd been the FAA inspector and a flight crew certifier assigned to United in Denver. There, he also helped to design and evaluate training programs, and test some 250 pilots when United first purchased its DC-8 fleet. He later did the same with other major airlines. His twenty-one year FAA career with commercial transport aviation covered everything from flight training and procedures, aircraft systems and dispatch to accident investigations. But this one especially intrigued him. It was almost personal given his history with the DC-8 and with United. And what he'd been hearing from the witnesses was frankly astonishing to him.

By the time he was called to the stand, he was more than ready for the questions he would get from Whipple's partner, Alan Johansen. He had a lot he wanted to say about what he had learned from his own investigation, and what he had heard during trial. He'd organized his thoughts and began with this:

"In aviation crashes, an old saying is, 'That accident didn't happen in flight, it was already happening before they took off.'"

What was "already happening," Harrell explained, were the contributing factors: the choices, mistakes, missed dangers, carelessness and related close calls that always pave the way for mishaps.

"In my years with the FAA, I can conservatively say that for each *accident*, there are a hundred *incidents* which need investigating," he said. However, the practice of doing so, of really understanding all the causes and circumstances that create a crash didn't see the light of day often enough.

United Flight 173 was a case in point. It was his opinion from his investigations that the accident was the result of a series of deliberate decisions that disregarded the safety of the passengers—and contrary to the now common refrain that McBroom had made all of those decisions, Harrell said that many of them took place *outside* of the cockpit before and during the accident.

Harrell looked at the jury. "The designated pilot-in-command is the focal point and is responsible for so many things, it is easy and convenient to blame him for everything. But that logic is not only unfair, it never gets to the root of the problem."

Not that he excused the "unforgivably unprofessional behavior" of the captain, but he did have some sympathy for the guy, and a broader perspective on how things really work.

"Support personnel, dispatchers, air traffic controllers, managers, maintenance, and office workers perform their duties on the ground with unlimited resources at hand, and with the ground to rest on when things get rough," Harrell observed.

"A captain doesn't have that luxury. He has to operate the equipment in an emergency under what we call the heat of battle. He cannot park and rest. He is not a superman. He needs all the inputs and assistance he can get from the ground. The more professional he is the more he relies on them."

Harrell paused to let what he was saying sink in. He had a no-nonsense delivery style backed by decades of authority and experience, and yet his tone was pleasant, down-to-earth. He had the jury's full attention when Johansen asked him if he had formed an opinion about the cause or causes of the crash.

Harrell nodded and started with the basics. "The reason the airplane fell out of the sky was fuel, it had no fuel to fly. For that to happen there had to be a history of events leading up to it."

Part of the problem was certainly the crew, he acknowledged. First of all they did not follow the procedures outlined in their flight manual about doing a fly-by or believing that a safe landing could be made if the wing buttons were up showing the gear was down and locked.

Secondly, he said, "It was impossible for me to believe that anyone in the cockpit really had a plan of fuel."

Yes, there was evidence in the voice recorder transcript that fuel was being discussed in terms of quantity on board, but nothing that tied this to burn rate, time left to dry tanks and distance from the airport.

"This simple computation gives a specific time on the clock t
head for the airport. *This was not done,*" Harrell stated flatly. "It i
evident that none of the three crew members nor the dispatcher pei
formed this calculation."

He shook his head and added, "That last turn the aircraft mad
at 6:06 *away* from the airport before commencing the approach int
Portland was just not understandable. At a bare minimum, twent
minutes before running out fuel at 6:14 that airplane *must* be headee
toward the airport. At the very latest that should have been at 5:55."

Harrell leaned forward. "To make the point more graphic an
unbelievable, there was *another* positive indicator that should have
been a screaming red flag to the crew. At 5:49 the feed pump light
were blinking, shouting a message: 'Leave now and get on th
ground.'"

Harrell didn't bother to conceal the disbelief in his voice. A
many times as he'd gone over the crash in his mind, he just couldn'
comprehend what the crew was thinking.

"At 6:13 Flight 173 was eight or nine miles from the runwa
or thirty seconds to dry tanks."

He took a breath and summed it up, "From the time the gea
was lowered and the irregularity was recognized, and with an hour o
fuel in the tanks, this crew failed in the most rudimentary test in th
management of a jet cockpit in not planning for the one area tha
could have saved lives—fuel."

The courtroom was silent as Harrell made this last pro
nouncement. Many of the jurors had paused writing on their notepad
so they could focus on his words. But they knew he had more to say
and Johansen now encouraged him to continue with his thoughts oi
the other causes of the crash.

United's contributions were obvious and several, Harrell began.

"First, United Airlines had records of four previous main gear retract cylinder rod end failures of its own, and three dozen or so on other airlines. Obviously, this was an industry problem of long standing which UAL never brought to the attention of those who need to know it the most: the pilots who operate the equipment," he paused, collecting his thoughts.

"As bad as this turned out to be for this crew, I believe that had the captain been told of the previous failures and that a safe landing might still be made, it is reasonably probable that he would have downgraded his concern and devoted more time to cockpit management and getting the plane on the ground with some fuel."

But that didn't happen, he said. Instead the crew got *no* support.

"In my view, the cockpit was in need of information, and some reassurance that everything was not as bad as they thought. Yet when the captain called SFO Maintenance for advice and a mechanical briefing, all he got was, 'I think you guys have done everything you can do.'"

Harrell was mystified as to why more information wasn't shared, especially when Leland Buhr, the maintenance controller McBroom spoke to, clearly had some to give judging from his later NTSB testimony.

"He *knew* of the prior cases where the cylinder had failed, and called it a 'routine mishap' that usually happened on retraction. He told the NTSB investigators afterward that the 'gear was still safe.'"

Why didn't he tell McBroom that? The lack of teamwork, support, and shared responsibility for safety went against everything

177

he'd ever taught and tested for in the FAA, every industry standard he knew of.

"If Captain McBroom had known the history of the rod failure, and maintenance had reassured him that the gear was safely locked down, and if dispatch had questioned his fuel state, the combined help just might have moved him out of the mental block he was so obviously in."

Although at the time, Harrell didn't have the human factors research available today about the consequences of such "mental blocks" in emergency situations, he understood that the problem arose from the captain's distraction. Nowadays distraction is widely recognized as one of the "dirty dozen" causes of errors and accidents.

McBroom was caught squarely in the distraction trap. He was unable to focus on anything but the distraction of his gear problem and as a result lost track of his fuel situation. Unfortunately, the rest of the crew was apparently also caught in the same trap, and nothing was done to help get them out of it.

"The captain's preoccupation with an irregularity of the landing gear consumed so much of McBroom's thinking, he lost control of the cockpit," Harrell said.

He needed guidance and help to change that thinking, and despite United's own stated policies listing *safety* as the number one priority for *all* employees, nobody came to their aid.

In Harrell's opinion the maintenance controller did more than just "pass up a golden opportunity to brief the crew on the gear problem." Buhr's silence, he said, amounted to a "deliberate choice" at the time.

Similarly, prior to the accident United had other opportunities during numerous recurrent ground training sessions and line checks to share this important information. Harrell explained that such sessions act as the "airlines' conduit to pass on tricks of the trade, and are the ideal time to discuss the latest in airplane problems and systems with crews." But again United Airlines opted for silence.

"Captain McBroom had been a DC-8 captain since September 1971. UAL had experienced the rod end failures since January 1972. There seems to have been a lack of communication for McBroom to have successfully completed *fourteen* training sessions (two per year for seven years) and not have been told of this problem area."

Records showed that McBroom's co-pilot, Beebe, had also completed a recurrent training session just five months before, Harrell added. "Evidently Beebe had no knowledge of the problem, either."

But United's contribution to the crash went beyond deliberate failures to communicate. It also had a lot to do with actually precipitating the accident by producing the conditions that led to it. The testimony Harrell heard from United's engineers earlier in the week had stunned him. Its maintenance program neglected corrosion control and faulty eyebolts in the retract assembly despite safety bulletins; it allowed corrosion to continue despite knowing it was there from its own gamma ray inspections; and then instead of fixing the problem, they just stopped looking for it, choosing to defer any attention and repairs until overhaul.

"This airplane had gone some *33,000 hours* on that rod end," Harrell emphasized to the jury. "The fact that the inspections were stopped, and the replacement of the rod ends and the cylinder would be done on the same time cycle as the whole landing gear means they left a void hoping that it wouldn't fail in the meantime. That's something they gambled on and lost, because it *did* fail."

And for that to happen was the result of another choice, Harrell added.

"Some responsible official had to make a deliberate decision to terminate the inspections."

The same went for changing the eyebolt on the left landing gear but not the right side of the airplane.

"Somebody had to decide not to. I'm sure there was lots of deliberation, but they *made a decision*."

For Harrell, the record was crystal clear regarding "the roots and causes" of the accident, and though to him it *all* added up to a blatant "disregard for the safety of the passengers," he hoped the people in the courtroom could see that there was a distinction to be made between McBroom and his crew's failures under pressure, and United's far more calculated and long-standing misconduct.

Chapter 18

Maria and Lisa Take the Stand

Maria and Lisa had been in Portland for more than a week staying at the Holiday Inn while Maria shuttled back and forth to the courthouse each long day, and Lisa waited with Maria's youngest sister. Her attorneys were nearly finished presenting their side of the case, which now included Maria's own dreaded stretch on the stand. But it was familiar territory, she told herself, the same story she'd been telling for five years now, though updated of course in terms of Lisa's condition and progress—and minus any mention of her lost family as previously agreed.

Maria was aware of the jury's acute interest in her as she took her place in the witness box to answer questions about Lisa's ongoing problems. She worried that her English, which tended to worsen under pressure, would make her seem less articulate and therefore less credible to them, but at the same time she wanted to share her experiences.

As the questions began, she tried to focus on just sticking to what she knew and taking it one step at a time. Lisa's injuries had certainly improved over time, but she still suffered from frequent ear complaints and respiratory illnesses. Her nightmares continued, though the doctors had been saying for years she would grow out of it. She was receiving ongoing therapy for the leg and foot problems, which still caused her to fall often and tire easily in any sustained physical activities. But the little girl tried; Maria had to give her that.

She always wanted to do what her two cousins were doing: bicycling, swimming, yes, even roller skating, though her negligible skills were nerve-wracking at best, and she had to have two pairs of skate shoes, a size for each of her unevenly-grown feet.

She explained all this as her attorney questioned her. The jury had already heard about Lisa from other witnesses: doctors, psychologists, school staff—and more was coming when United put their own child experts on the stand—but nobody knew her niece the way she did.

The cross examination by United's defense attorney was the worst part. Though mercifully short, it was stressful and naturally aimed at contradicting her characterization of Lisa as a little girl with ongoing physical and psychological issues.

Bill Crow did his job and focused on trying to highlight discrepancies in her testimony in order to raise doubts in the jurors' minds. The most intimidating interrogation came at the end when he asked whether she recalled the testimony of Lisa's school counselor and two teachers earlier in the week, and Maria said she did.

"They described Lisa as a happy, cooperative child; I gather you disagree with that?" he asked.

"When she feels good, yes, when she feels well," Maria responded.

"You did hear them describe her as a happy cooperative child, didn't you?" Crow repeated.

"Sometimes," Maria replied, still thinking of Lisa on her good days.

"No," Crow interrupted. "Did you *hear* them say that about her?" he re-emphasized slowly.

"Yes," Maria said, suddenly understanding the answer he wanted from her.

"Now do you recall, Mrs. Affatigato when I took your deposition in August 1983?"

"Yes, I do," she said, reminding herself: *just say yes or no.*

"I'm going to ask if you remember these questions and your answers."

"'Question: Then did she wear a brace for a while?

Answer: Yes.

Question: How long?

Answer: Eight months.'"

"Do you remember those questions and answers?"

"The first brace," Maria said, succumbing again to clarification. "Then the leg got a little taller and we had to change the whole frame, we had to make it longer," she said awkwardly, trying to explain how Lisa had worn two braces, one for eight months until she grew out of it, and another for an additional stretch of almost a year.

"Mrs. Affatigato, can we just stop right there—" Crow interrupted again giving in to exasperation. "If you could just answer my questions, we can get this going a lot faster. Do you remember my questions and your answers?"

"Yes."

"*Do* you remember that?" he repeated.

"Yes."

That's where he left it. Maria was excused from the stand and stepped down feeling bullied again. She was worried for the next witness. She hoped that Lisa would not be frightened. She had wanted to keep her from the ordeal of the courtroom, but there was really no way around it. The jury would naturally want to see the little girl, already the subject of so much publicity, so much testimony, and whose economic fate they held in their hands. Maria's attorneys had promised to keep it brief.

Whipple asked for a few moments while he went out to the hallway and then brought Lisa in, holding her hand. She was eight and a half now, a little plump as she'd always been. The light brown hair she had as a small child had darkened to mahogany curls that framed her round face. She shared her dimpled chin and hooded eyes with her father, but the warm hazel shade was a blend of her parents' blue and brown. She walked to the stand with a slight limp, though otherwise appeared robust and healthy.

Whipple helped her to the witness chair and then stepped back explaining gently that he was going to stand over here and ask her a few questions. But first the judge wanted to have a word with her.

Judge Roth craned over from his elevated position and peered down at the child.

"All right. Elizabeth, I am the judge," he intoned. "My name is Judge Roth. Would you say your name into that microphone there?"

"Well..." Lisa paused uncertainly. "I usually call myself Lisa."

"Lisa, alright. And your last name?"

"Andor."

"Okay Lisa, Mr. Whipple is going to ask you some questions, and do you know what telling the truth is?"

Lisa nodded. "Uh huh."

"And if you don't tell the truth what happens?"

Lisa's eyes widened at the black-robed figure seated above her.

"I don't know," she said softly, a little baffled.

"Well, do you get punished? Do you get spanked if you don't tell the truth?"

Alarmed at the prospect, Lisa thought the right answer must be yes, so she nodded stiffly with her whole body.

"Are you going to tell the truth here?" Roth pressed his point.

"Yes," Lisa replied, her voice small in the microphone.

"Now this lady is going to administer an oath. That means you raise your right hand, Lisa."

Lisa glanced down at her hands and quickly double-checked to make sure she got the *right* hand, then put it up in the air the way she'd seen it done on TV.

The court clerk proceeded. "Do you solemnly swear that the testimony you are giving will be the truth so help you God?"

Lisa wasn't sure what "testimony" was but she knew just what the rest meant.

"Yes," she said, nodding earnestly.

The questions seemed simple for the most part. She was asked how old she was, her birthday, where she lived, what grade and school she was in, her teacher's name, her pets, what the weather in Chicago was when she left. Lisa answered the questions easily. She said that of all the subjects, she liked art best, that she was in the Brownies and that her aunt Maria was teaching her to sew and cook spaghetti. She had a pet cockatiel that would sit on her finger and sometimes nip.

But when she was asked what she did during recess time at school, her voice became quiet.

"Sit," she said.

"I beg your pardon?" Whipple asked, adding that his hearing wasn't as good as hers. "What do you do at recess?" he repeated.

Lisa spoke up and was surprised by the loudness of her voice coming from the courtroom speaker.

"Sit, 'cause I can't volunteer and I can't play because I'm afraid I might fall."

"Okay. What do you do in your Brownie meetings?" Whipple continued on.

"Well, we have treats, and we talk about some things."

"Do you have lots of friends in the Brownies?"

"Yes."

"And I assume they are nice to you and you have a good time with them?"

"Yes. The thing is I can't run very fast," she said. The other kids always wanted to play tag and racing games.

Whipple asked about swimming and ice-skating in the park near her house. Lisa said she couldn't swim very well yet, and that her friend's mother had to take her around the rink holding her while she skated.

United's attorney, Bill Crow was next and led off with the same approach he'd used with Maria by asking Lisa if she remembered talking with him a few months back. Lisa said she couldn't remember *him*, but did recall answering a man's questions.

"Okay. At that time, Lisa, I asked you what you did at recess and you told me—I'm looking at page 4..." he paused over the transcript of the statement he'd taken seven months earlier. "You told me that you played on swings and that was kind of fun. Do you remember that?"

"Yes," she replied, heedless that her earlier testimony about sitting during recess might be seen as any different from sitting on a swing—or that her truth was being tested.

"That is fun, isn't it? Do you have a bicycle?"

"Yes."

"Does it have training wheels?"

"No." She'd recently mastered that.

"Do you like to fly on airplanes?"

"No."

"You don't like landing and taking off, do you?" Crow clarified, glancing at the text before him.

"No." She had told him before that she hated the ear pressure change, and sometimes there was trouble when planes were landing. But he didn't ask her to explain that this time.

"How about when you get up in the air, do you like it then?"

"Yes," she replied, amicably.

"Do you like to look out and see what's outside?"

"No."

"Okay, you say you have a bird as a pet?"

"Yes."

"Are you afraid of it?"

"No." She wasn't afraid of birds anymore, ever since the family got their cockatiel.

"Do you watch much television?"

"Yes," she said, nodding.

"What do you like to watch?"

"The Flintstones."

Crow scanned the list of TV shows in Lisa's interview note from the psychological expert he'd hired, and picked one.

"Do you watch *Dallas*?" he suggested, aware that the soa opera would be seen as unsuitable, and on rather late in the evenin for an eight-year-old.

"Yes," she agreed, affably.

"Thanks Lisa, that's all," he finished.

Maria was glad to have the day behind her as she and Lis returned to their hotel. Their side of the trial was nearly over, but he attorneys had warned her that the next week, as United presented it case, would be difficult, especially in regard to Lisa. The defens lawyers would do what they could to raise doubts in the jurors' mind about the severity or permanence of Lisa's injuries, and try to con vince them that her compensation needs were minimal. They woul have their own doctors and specialists on the stand to testify tha much of what Maria was claiming was temporary or simply untrue She had to be prepared for that.

It was gathering dusk as they pulled up in their taxi. The rai hadn't let up for days. Snow was nicer, Maria thought, missing hom in Chicago. She got out, and as she waited for Lisa to scoot out on th same side of the car, Maria spotted a familiar van parked across th street and felt a wave of alarm.

At first she had thought she was imagining things, that th stress of the trial was making her paranoid. But no, here it was again she was sure of it now, and just like the other times, a man inside th vehicle was pointing a camera at them. She wondered if it was th press.

As she would soon learn, United's legal team had hired the California-based private investigation firm of Krout and Schneider to watch and film Lisa in public in an attempt to show her walking with ease. The agency, specializing in P.I. services to law firms and insurance companies, put three of its Portland-office investigators on the case at the behest of United's attorneys who gave them a photo of Lisa and told them where Maria and Lisa were staying. Two field agents logged some sixty-three hours shadowing the woman and child over the course of four days—in other words almost constantly.

It was a "short-notice" job, the lead investigator, George Ruselli said later. They didn't get much time to complete the assignment, but they did manage to shoot plenty of super-8 footage from the dual stakeouts, which Ruselli then edited and spliced together in time sequence. The resulting five-minute film was screened for the jury on the second to last day of the trial.

To be sure, the footage, which showed the pair out shopping and eating in restaurants, made an impression on the jurors, but not entirely in the way United hoped. For some, the surveillance came across as foul play, and watching the undercover film was awkward, like spying, a sort of peep show. It also highlighted the lengths to which the corporation would go to win against the girl.

Chapter 19

Last Words

These days when Stewart Whipple looks at the eight boxes that hold the *Andor v. United* lawsuit documents, he'll sometimes smile, shake his head and mimic the phrase from a famous 1972 Alka Seltzer commercial: "I can't believe I ate the whole thing!"

That's not too far from what the jury was feeling, as well, on March 28, 1984 when the attorneys for both sides finally made their closing arguments.

"It was just exhausting to have to pay attention to so much information," juror Marlene J. recalls, though she adds, "It was certainly a learning experience."

Indeed, the thirteen-day trial filled 1580 pages of transcripts, bound in twelve volumes, all carefully typed on the lightweight, "onion-skin" paper that people also used for airmail letters back then. Even so, the transcripts fit in just one of those boxes. The seven others held five years' worth of case preparation: trial exhibits, depositions, correspondence, news articles, photos, video tapes and piles of documents and reports known as "discovery" from United, the NTSB, FAA, McDonnell Douglas and more.

Recalling those and other days as a litigator in the courtroom, Whipple observes, "What's important is to be prepared, be disciplined, be honest and be *yourself*." Then he adds, "Putting on a trial is a production, like making a movie but without the benefit of retakes or editing, and mostly without a set script."

And the intended audience—the jury—is right there watching live.

And so they were watching on the last drizzly day of trial, alert in their seats but also tired. Judge Roth had adjourned the court early the previous afternoon with the reminder that today would likely be a long one, adding lightheartedly, "You might bring your toothbrush and nighties, or whatever."

The second week of trial had been devoted to United's defense, and no expense was spared on the parade of nineteen in-person witnesses the attorneys brought before the court to weigh in on medical questions about Lisa on one hand, and United's dedicated adherence to safety practices on the other.

The message strategy elicited from the United witnesses was, and still is, an oft-repeated refrain in aviation crash defense cases. According to one plaintiff's attorney, it goes like this: "The FAA lives with us, we are trained for safety and have a great safety record, we are compliant with regulations, our crew died, too." And in some cases, though not this one, "We built a memorial."

Among those on the stand were officials from the FAA and McDonnell Douglas, United pilots, co-pilots, engineers, mechanics, and even crew survivors: co-pilot Rod Beebe (who was on the stand long enough to give his name, age and profession and say he still couldn't remember a thing about the night), and Martha "Marty" Fralick, one of the flight attendants onboard who helped get everyone off the back of the plane. The point was to show that United's own people were there too, ably doing the jobs they were trained for in the emergency.

In them the jury could surely see that United was not just a faceless corporation. On the contrary, United *was* these good, professional people. So to find United guilty of misconduct, was to find *these people* guilty. This was the syllogism Bill Crow presented to the jurors as he began his summation.

"The judge will tell you that if you should decide that someone needs to be punished, you'll have to determine whether either of the defendants, United Airlines or Captain McBroom, were guilty of wanton misconduct amounting to a deliberate disregard for the rights and safety of others. That's the standard you are going to have to use and that's one reason we are pleased, ladies and gentlemen, to be able to tell you about United Airlines, because United Airlines is made up of *people*—that's what United airlines is, it's people who work for it. It isn't just somebody out here that we can't identify with; we can. And we've brought the people we think are important to let you see who United Airlines is."

Indeed, the faces of United were a polished, professional group—some of them commanding and glamorous in their uniforms.

Crow drove his point by reminding the jury that Fralick, the attractive stewardess they'd seen earlier in the week, had continued to evacuate passengers from the aircraft despite her fear that fire might erupt.

"That's not a disregard for anyone's safety and rights," he said, shaking his head, opting for imagery over relevance.

McBroom, too, had finally made his appearance, and was questioned yet again about the fateful night, about the decisions and mistakes he had made. Although he no longer worked for United, he was a co-defendant and represented the company the night of the crash. The company was happy to admit that *he* had been wrong, and they were ready to pay some compensation for it—but that was the limit of United's liability. McBroom now sat in the courtroom and listened as he was once again thrown under the bus.

"The airplane was safe to land," Crow said. "Captain Mc-Broom knew that. But Captain McBroom believed he had an emergency situation. He made a mistake. And that's why we are here. He didn't mean to hurt anybody. There was *no deliberate, wanton disregard* on anyone's part—on the part of Captain McBroom, or United Airlines."

As for the maintenance problems brought up during the trial, Crow parried. "United is proud of its maintenance facilities. It's proud of its maintenance program. It's one we're happy to tell you about. An eyebolt broke, and we wish it hadn't, but partly because of what United Airlines had done, when the eyebolt broke, the landing gear came to a down-locked safe position."

It was an accident and that's all it was, Crow said, dismissing the crash as an unfortunate mishap that didn't mean United should be punished.

"Mr. Whipple says we had an unnecessary accident, one we would not like to have had; one that does not make United Airlines proud, but it was a mistake. It was *not* anything *deliberate* or *wanton* on the part of anyone." Again, Crow repeated the legal terminology the jury had been hearing and he hoped would soon dismiss.

And, he added, it didn't deserve so much attention during the trial. In fact, United Airlines shouldn't be the focus at all, Crow insisted, steering the discussion away from punitive damages toward the compensation side of things—and Lisa.

"I told you that this case is and should be about Lisa, and the injuries she suffered. And it should *only* be about what happened to Lisa. We acknowledge that Lisa was injured," he offered, making it a little too simple: "She had two broken ribs, a punctured lung, her right leg was broken, and you've seen the X-rays of that broken right leg and it looks like it did hurt. And we believe it did hurt."

And then he went to work. United had hired its own medical professionals to examine Lisa, give her tests, and they testified that she was, "A charming, attractive little girl, and an easy girl to like." She did what she was asked during their exams, responded to questions about the sports she enjoyed, and would grow out of her current remaining physical and psychological issues. Indeed, as anyone could see, Crow said, "Lisa has made a good recovery." And, he added, despite Mr. Whipple's assertions, "Based upon progress from 1978 to the present, we can expect a complete and full recovery in time."

In the meantime—he circled back—if she is tired and disengaged at school, he said, "You heard Lisa testify about her favorite television programs. You know when they come on. I suspect Lisa is tired from *that*."

As for Maria's testimony, Crow hoped the jury could see that she had a problem telling the truth. He pointed out a discrepancy between what she and Lisa had said about having training wheels on the bicycle. He wanted the jurors to take all of this into consideration as they calculated the amount of damages she should receive for her injuries, and ended with, "We appreciate your attention and we are comfortable and confident in your ability to determine what that number should be."

As the attorney for the plaintiff, Whipple was allowed to speak twice in final arguments, the second time being the chance to rebut whatever the defense had said. But as he later noted, recalling his approach, "Less is more. Don't play in the opposing counsel's

194

court." So he kept his second round of comments brief and focused on sticking to his evidence and the fundamentals of his case.

"In our system of justice, the *jurors* are the fact finders. They can draw their own inferences from the testimony."

Whipple reminded the jury of his opening statement at the beginning of the trial, that the case was indeed about "the unnecessary crash of United Flight 173," an accident that didn't need to happen.

"I think, by now you probably know what I meant by that," he said. "I meant that if the eyebolt had not failed, Captain McBroom would have landed at the airport shortly after 5:00 and we wouldn't be here today."

Whipple continued the proposition. "When Captain McBroom called the San Francisco dispatcher, explained the problem, told him he had 7,000 pounds of fuel on board and planned to land at 6:05, and if Mr. Reynolds had said, 'In multiplying your fuel burn by twenty-five minutes, it looks to me like you're going to be almost empty when you land.' Or if he had said, 'Hmm, you are well into your forty-five—minute reserve, so you better watch it, and don't depend on those gauges,' perhaps Captain McBroom would have landed and we wouldn't be here today."

He paused, and then continued. "Likewise, if the maintenance man he called had said, 'You've described a problem we've had before. We've had eyebolts fail, but as far as we're concerned the gear is down and locked, so don't worry about it; go ahead and land,' we might not be here today."

"But we are here," he explained, "because the plane did crash, and it could have been avoided if United hadn't violated every arti-

195

cle—except one—of its own written policy called the Rule of Five: Safety, Service, Profitability, Integrity, Responsibility."

Whipple picked up a document marked with an evidence sticker, showed it to the jury and said, "United's policy says: 'Safety is the most important operating rule of any transportation system. It's the essential ingredient to all measurements of success. It's the responsibility of *everyone* connected with the transportation system.'"

He pointed to the writing on the sheet and read on. "To achieve appropriate safety standards we must control loss. Loss control means prevention of injury or damage to people and property both on the ground and in the air. To achieve safety through loss control, efforts must be directed toward prevention of loss *before* it occurs. Safety therefore requires each of us to exercise the highest degree of care in all operations to minimize the possibility of accidents resulting in injury or damage."

Whipple laid the paper back on the table and explained that the testimony and evidence presented during the trial about United's maintenance practices showed that the only part of the rule-of-five policy United had adhered to was profitability.

"They put profit ahead of safety, at the risk of passengers," he said. "And that's why we are here, and why we believe the punitive damages in this case are appropriate."

He wanted the jury to understand just what that meant, even though he knew they'd shortly hear again from the judge.

"The court will instruct you that if the defendants' conduct constitutes wantonness or a deliberate disregard for the safety of others, it is the law in Oregon that a jury can award punitive damages for the purpose of punishing a defendant and deterring a defendant and others in a similar situation from repeating the same kind of conduct."

196

"I have never suggested that United was sitting down with a sharp pencil trying to cause this accident to happen. They weren't. But they were following practices that made it almost inevitable. And as you heard, they're still following them."

Moreover, he added, they weren't willing to take any responsibility for the crash.

"I thought that before this trial was over, someone would be brought in from United—maybe an officer or a director of the corporation who would come in and say, 'Yes, we knew about the corrosion problem and we shouldn't have let it get away from us. But it did.'"

Whipple paused. "But they didn't do that. All they have done is to come in and say, 'We've got a great program. We've got a great reputation for safety. These eyebolts; no big problem. The bungee will take care of it if it fails.'"

But the bungee won't take care of the eyebolt failure if it damages the aircraft and confuses and distracts the flight crew, he explained.

"So we believe it's our responsibility and yours to help United in improving their standards of maintenance. And the way to do that and call it to the attention of the board of directors in Chicago is to award sufficient punitive damages so they'll say, 'Well here we are back to money again, and it's going to be cheaper to improve our maintenance program and prevent problems like this than to get hit with punitive damages if we don't.'"

Whipple turned back to the evidence table where Lisa's first small leg brace lay among enlarged photos of the plane crash, and her medical reports. He didn't pick anything up, but the jury's eyes followed him as he took a position near them.

"So, then we come to the other reason why we're here today," he began. "And that involves the injuries to Lisa Andor."

He reminded the jury that they had several exhibits in connection with it that showed the scope of the devastation she'd experienced, including the pictures of the demolished first class cabin, the testimony of the sheriff's deputy who found Lisa under the wreckage; detailed hospital records of her injuries and month-long hospital stay; and subsequent examinations by neurologists who found that she suffered some permanent nerve damage to her foot and ankle that would continue to limit her activities, as well as her recreational and vocational choices in later life.

"You also heard the testimony of psychologists," he said, moving to the question of Lisa's emotional damage from the crash.

Again, he encouraged the jury to recall the two psychologists who'd spent significant time examining her. One was employed by Lisa's school, and had been asked to test her as a result of her teachers' concerns about problems she was having with her work. She was now getting special help and doing better because of the intervention.

Another psychologist who examined Lisa at length said her ongoing problems at night were evidence of post-traumatic stress syndrome, a result of unresolved issues connected with the trauma of the accident that would likely continue to manifest themselves well into her future.

Of course in 1984, at the time of the trial, PTSD was not the well-recognized condition it is today outside of military circles, so its appearance in her diagnosis was perhaps unfamiliar to the jury. Even so, Whipple felt that the impact of trauma was something most people could understand based on life experience, and so he kept it simple:

"I ask you to view all of the experts' testimony in light of your own common sense."

The same went for United's culpability. Again, he noted, the jury had the evidence and their common sense, and what's more, a unique opportunity through a punitive damage award to send United—and other airlines, too—a message from society at large: that passengers are entitled to be protected, that proper aircraft maintenance should not be sacrificed for money or profit, that safety is the first and most important obligation of a transport air carrier.

As for Lisa, he said, "We have a little girl who through no fault of her own sustained serious personal injuries, and to the extent that money could help her, she should have some. We've asked for a substantial amount of damages to cover the pain and suffering and mental anguish she has experienced as a result of the accident because she has a long time to live with these problems."

Whipple paused and looked at the jurors before him. They'd listened carefully through complicated testimony for more than two weeks. It was hard work, and he could see they were tired. Everyone was. But he had grown to trust them precisely because they had been so attentive. What happened next was in their hands, so that's how he summed it up.

"This trial has lasted a long time, but *your* verdict is going to have to last Lisa Andor the rest of her life."

And that's what the jury believed as they prepared for their instructions and deliberation.

Chapter 20

Justice Needs a Champion

"It would be enough for me to have the system of a jury of twelve versus the system of one judge as a basis for preferring the U.S. to the Soviet Union." —*Joseph Brodsky*

For companies involved in personal injury or wrong ful death lawsuits, damage control, literally and figuratively, is the main objective. That's why after the crash of Flight 173, United did all it could—mostly successfully—to settle the cases that arose from the mishap short of trial. The last thing it wanted was to face a judge or worse, a jury, because apart from being exposed to immediate fi nancial losses in the form of general or punitive damages, the perils of trial always include the possibility that legal precedents will be estab lished, laying a foundation for similar actions in future accident cases. In fact, that's one of the biggest worries.

And there's another worry. A lot of information comes out in a trial that rips the curtain aside on business practices and records most companies would rather keep from public view. Trade secrets and formulas are traditional examples of information companies under standably wish to limit, along with settlement terms in lawsuits. But since the 1980s, companies engaged in civil litigation have fought to conceal a far broader array of information, beginning with what's produced in the discovery phase of a trial. That's when each side is required to turn over records and documents to each other that will be used in the case. This is often sensitive material—like financial records, correspondence or emails, or in Lisa's case, United's mainte nance reports. Such material may not only reflect badly on the company if available to the public, it might also be re-deployed in other lawsuits as documentation of past negligence, misconduct or foreknowledge of a problem.

Nowadays, much of that information is kept secret, especially in complex, high-dollar cases because litigants automatically file motions for "protective orders" at the very outset of a lawsuit. If granted, protective orders seal records permanently before a single document is exchanged. Unless the litigant is a public agency and therefore subject to Freedom of Information (FOIA) statutes, sealed lawsuit records of private companies are virtually impervious to public scrutiny—forever—unless the case goes all the way to open trial, which happens less and less frequently.

According to one attorney involved in a large-scale environmental pollution case involving multiple insurance companies and their policy-holders, the effect of protective orders is to mask *everything* related to the case "partly because it would be more work to sort out what's covered by the order from what isn't, and partly because it's just more prudent not to try." So in practice, every document produced, whether it's a deposition, a consultant's report or a piece of correspondence, is caught in the secrecy net and comes marked with a protective-order stamp reminding anyone coming in contact with it—lawyers, witnesses, experts, secretaries—that it is cloaked in confidentiality and must be destroyed within a set period after conclusion of the case under penalty of law. In fact, in a bizarre extension of this secrecy, even the protective order is *itself* protected and cannot be shared or viewed beyond the confines of the case.

But for good reasons, there has been a growing push-back on this increasingly routine practice in recent years as Chicago plaintiff's attorney David Rapoport points out. He has been an outspoken opponent of court secrecy, and wrote about it in a scholarly article about protective orders entitled, "The Erosion of Secrecy in Air Disaster Litigation."

"The nature and legal consequences of wrongful conduct should be publicly known. This serves one of the fundamental purposes of our justice system. Nevertheless, air disaster litigation has long been shrouded in secrecy."

Rapoport has been deeply involved in commercial aviation litigation since 1981, and represented a plaintiff in one of the lawsuits that arose after the crash of Comair Flight 5191 in Lexington, Kentucky on August 27, 2006. As he recalls in his article, "The airline designated virtually all of the documents it produced in discovery "confidential" and argued almost all of the deposition transcripts were confidential as well. While this strategy ultimately failed, it succeeded for a long period of time and took a federal court ruling rebuking it to shine public light on important new evidence that was first revealed in pretrial discovery."

Rapoport argues that air disasters often give rise to "high-profile cases usually involving important public safety issues. The new safety information discovered in air crash cases should be available to other members of the industry and the public, yet historically and surprisingly these cases have been shrouded in great secrecy."

As a result, there have been very few open windows into the evidence produced in some of the most devastating air disasters of the last thirty years, including the Sioux City crash. Most cases settle before trial and are thus sealed from view, and protective orders ensure that information developed about the factors involved in the crash, along with all those who may have contributed to it, is limited or destroyed.

But the Andor case happened before the wave of protective orders became standard practice, *and* it didn't settle but went all the way to trial on punitive damages, so the public safety issues Rapoport is talking about were both fully examined and, more importantly, publicly disclosed in the course of the litigation. What's more, those boxes of case materials, never "sealed" and never destroyed, combine to make the *Andor v United* lawsuit a rare skylight into still-relevant safety, corporate and legal details of a commercial air disaster, which has hardly been duplicated since. In fact, under present conditions, *this* story, and whatever transparency or illumination it may provide about the intersection of personal tragedy with corporate power and our court system, would hardly be possible today.

In the last twenty-five years only a few major air disaster cases have ever gone all the way to trial. Rapoport says among those that did go to trial are USAir Flight 1016 in 1997, the United Express Quincy crash in 2003 and the American Airlines 1420 Little Rock crash in 1999. According to him, these all involved operational safety issues like pilot decision-making, air traffic control and airport safety areas. Apart from the Andor case, few, if any, aviation cases involving airline maintenance malpractices have seen the light of day.

"There have been other cases litigated involving maintenance issues, but no trials I'm aware of in recent years," Rapoport notes.

Unaware of their unique position in legal history, the jury in the Andor case now readied their notepads one last time for Judge Roth's instructions to them about how they should deliberate and arrive at their verdict. Although these instructions are mostly boilerplate guidelines for juries in civil trials, each side—the defendant and the plaintiff—typically asks the judge to tailor them to their specific needs and issues of the case.

In Oregon, jury instructions are also far more detailed than in other states, and crucial to the durability of the verdict, especially in punitive damage cases. That's because Oregon's Constitution is unique in the country—and echoes almost word for word the Seventh Amendment of the U.S. Constitution—in preserving the rights and powers of trial by jury by prohibiting the courts from going back and re-examining any fact that has been tried by a jury. Further, courts cannot set aside a jury verdict unless they can *affirmatively* say there is *no* evidence to support it, *or* if they find flaws in the jury instructions. So making sure that the jury understands and follows their instructions as closely as possible is one of the ways the Oregon judicial system tries to prepare juries in the hopes that their verdicts are informed and reasonable and secure.

The judge has the final say on what the jury actually receives as their "marching orders," but either side may go on the record in disagreement by "taking exception" to what's present or absent in the instructions. These are important record-making opportunities, because if legal procedure mistakes are made, or issues are overlooked, or the wording seems prejudicial to one side in the instructions, "excepting to them" is the only way to tag it for a later instruction-based appeal or mistrial motion. Likewise, if the instructions are found to be sound, or all sides have *accepted* them, those are the ground rules that must be followed—and lived with.

Up until the last day of trial, United's attorneys had done everything they could to waylay the case before it reached the jury room. They had moved several times for summary judgments and directed verdicts, asking the judge repeatedly to step in and remove the claim for punitive damages from the case. Those motions were denied but duly placed in the record. Failing that, its lawyers had also tried to close the entire show by moving four times for mistrial—also recorded and denied. Now as the jury prepared to hear their twenty-five instructions, United's lawyers took the strategic blanket approach by "excepting" to virtually all of them so they could keep them in play if needed later on. If United lost this first battle, its lawyers were preparing for the legal siege the company was known for. A successful punitive damages verdict against a scheduled airline had never happened. The money at stake would pale compared to the disastrous legal precedent the case might establish for United and the entire commercial aviation industry. Whatever it would take in time and money, they were determined to prevail in the long term.

It was early afternoon when Judge Roth turned to the jury to explain their final mission. He had spoken versions of these words many times before in other civil trials, and could nearly recite them from memory.

But for these jurors, the words had the vivid impact of a new and important experience. This was the culmination of more than two weeks of listening, and the signal that they were about to transition from absorbing information to arbitrating it. But not just in any old way, as they were about to learn.

"It is now the duty of the Court to instruct you as to the law," Roth began, assuring them that they would also get a written copy of his directives in the jury room.

"Under our legal system, the Court decides all questions of law and procedure arising during trial, and it is the jury's duty to follow the Court's instructions in these matters. On the other hand, the jury is the sole exclusive judge of the facts and of the reliability of the evidence. The jury's power, however, is not arbitrary, and if the Court instructs you as to the law on a particular subject or how to judge the evidence, you must follow those instructions."

Roth paused to let what he was saying sink in. Sitting in judgment was an everyday event for him, but for the people in the jury box this was perhaps the only experience they would ever have to make a life-changing decision for a fellow citizen in a court of law. He could see the jurors were taking this seriously, even though it was likely that they were unaware of the sweep of legal history this moment represented, and why their role in it was important.

Indeed, he knew that most people were happily out of touch with the legal system. Courtrooms, like hospitals, weren't any place you *wanted* to be. And to be sure, jury trials could be a messy business at times, what with the broad range of experience, personality and intellect citizen jurors brought to the courtroom. This wasn't the time to give them a crash course in American jurisprudence and its English Common Law roots, but something Supreme Court Chief Justice Rehnquist wrote in a 1979 opinion would have perhaps offered them a glimpse at why what they were doing mattered.

"The founders of our nation considered the right of trial by jury in civil cases an important bulwark against tyranny and corruption, a safeguard too precious to be left to the whim of the sovereign, or, it might be added, to the judiciary...Trial by a jury of laymen rather than by the sovereign's judges was important to the founders because juries represent the layman's common sense...and thus keep the administration of law in accord with the wishes and feelings of the community...Those who favored juries believed that a jury would reach a result that a judge could not or would not reach."

The last sentence of Rehnquist's observations would prove to be prophetic in the *Andor v United* case. But for now, Judge Roth followed his script and the jury listened.

"Your verdict should be based only upon these instructions and upon the evidence in this case," he told them. "It is your duty to weigh the evidence calmly and dispassionately and to decide the questions upon their merits. You are not to allow bias, sympathy or prejudice any place in your deliberations, for all parties are equal before the law."

Roth explained the meaning of evidence as the testimony, exhibits and legal presumptions presented to them during the trial, but cautioned the jury that the statements and arguments made by the attorneys were *not* evidence.

"They are intended to be helpful to you, and I trust they have been helpful," he continued. "But if your recollection of the evidence differs from the attorneys' then you should rely on your own memory."

As to the testimony of witnesses, he noted, "The testimony of one witness whom you believe, is sufficient to prove any fact in dispute." Then, perhaps referring to United's parade of witnesses, the judge added, "In other words, you are not simply to count the witnesses on each side, but you are to *weigh* the evidence." Likewise, he added, "If you find that any person has intentionally given false testimony, you should distrust the rest of that person's testimony."

In this case, he continued, United has admitted that they are liable to the plaintiff for the personal injuries she sustained in the crash of Flight 173.

"Accordingly, the only issues for you to decide are the *amount* of general damages, the *amount* of special damages, and whether one or both defendants are to also be held liable for punitive damages—and if so, the amount of such punitive damages."

In deciding these issues, Roth wanted the jury to understand that the burden of proof was on the plaintiff to show by a "preponderance of evidence" that her claims were valid. That meant the "greater weight of the evidence" had to fall on Lisa's side.

Moreover, a further hurdle also existed, the judge explained.

"If upon any question in the case the evidence appears to be equally balanced, or if you cannot say upon which side it weighs heavier, you must resolve that question *against* the party upon whom the burden of proof rests."

Roth noted that the law did not furnish any fixed standard by which to measure the exact amount of general damages, but did require that the compensation allowed be reasonable—and it did have an upper limit. The jury could consider the pain, anxiety, discomfort and mental suffering of the plaintiff now and into the future, her impairment and loss of earning capacity or enjoyment of normal activities during her lifetime.

"You must apply your own judgment to determine the amount," although he added, general damages could not exceed the sum of $3.5 million.

The special damages the jury might award would include compensation for the reasonable value of medical care she needed.

This amount, he said, could not exceed $11,275, which was the amount of her actual bills.

Finally, Roth said, "If you have awarded general damages, you may award punitive damages *only* if the defendants' conduct goes beyond mere carelessness to a willful or wanton disregard of risk of harm to others of a magnitude evincing a high degree of social irresponsibility."

He paused to give them a chance to process this important point, then went on.

"In considering punitive damages, you must first determine whether the defendants, or *either* of them, were guilty of wanton misconduct, which was the cause of damage to the plaintiff. Wanton misconduct is conduct amounting to a deliberate disregard of the rights and safety of others. Wanton misconduct is something worse than negligence, but less than intentionally hurting someone."

The defendants in this case were the pilot, Malburn McBroom and United Airlines. The judge noted briefly that the airline is a "common carrier of passengers," a special class of business like train or bus systems. Under the law, Judge Roth said, a common carrier is charged with "an extraordinary duty to inspect and maintain its equipment in a safe condition, and is required to exercise the highest degree of care and skill for the safety of its passengers."

If the jury decided to award punitive damages, Judge Roth said *they could do so against one or both defendants,* but again there were specific guidelines to follow in fixing the amount, which couldn't exceed $10 million. They could consider: "The character of the defendants' conduct, the defendants' motive, the amount of damages which would be required to discourage defendant and others from engaging in such conduct in the future, and the net worth of the defendant."

This last consideration is governed by another rule in Oregon aimed at avoiding prejudice during a trial. The case for punitive damages must be firmly established and on the table before the jury is even allowed to hear the net worth of a defendant. This condition was satisfied in the Andor case, so on the last day of trial the jurors learned that as of December 1983, United's net worth was $1.26 billion.

Judge Roth concluded his instructions by saying that because this was a civil case, nine or more of the twelve jurors had to agree on the verdict, and the same nine or more had to agree on the amount of the verdict.

It's fair to say that getting this action-packed job description after more than two weeks of far more passive employment was a bit of a jolt for the jurors. The scope of the instructions they were to use in arriving at their verdict took many by surprise, and even made some wonder if they were up to the task ahead—not just individually but also collectively, since this diverse group of strangers would have to reach an agreement. This was a level of decision-making few encountered in daily life, and the stakes were high. A little girl's future was in their hands. And the ear of a multinational corporation was within range of their voice.

Judge Roth summoned the bailiff and handed her a sheet of paper printed with the verdict form the jury foreperson was to fill out when they were finished. There was a brief uncertain pause, and then the bailiff led the jurors away shortly after noon.

Chapter 21

Anything Can Happen

"The highest calling of any citizen is to serve on a jury."
—Abraham Lincoln

Nobody had cell phones or lap-top computers in 1984, so unless you had a pager you had to stick close while the jury was deliberating, and be ready to reconvene the moment they finished. Still, Maria's legal team thought it was probably safe to grab a quick lunch nearby, both for sustenance and a much-needed break from the tension everyone was feeling.

But Maria was in no mood to eat. Waiting for a group of perfect strangers to make a life-altering decision for her—a decision that she had zero control over—produces a special kind of helpless stress. For most people, such circumstances are thankfully rare, but for Maria it was déjà vu. She knew that now after hearing all the testimony. People had made *decisions* that took her family from her and from Lisa, and now other people were making decisions that might or might not deliver some justice.

In any case, Maria was worn out. Lisa was waiting back at the hotel where she'd been trying to keep up with the schoolwork assignments her teachers had sent. For now, all Maria wanted to do was go back, lie down for a while and await the verdict with her niece. She was more than relieved when Whipple told her to go ahead, they would call her when it was over.

Still she hesitated, uncertain. She'd come this far, bee
through so much. Bill Klein reached over and put his hand on he
shoulder. He'd been by her side as her attorney from the very begin
ning just after the accident. He'd handled all the family legal matter
for the last five years, and he'd been in the courtroom every day of th
trial supporting her, watching, jotting down thoughts and observation
as his colleagues tried the case. He gave her shoulder a reassurin,
squeeze and nodded. He didn't have to say anything as he helped he
on with her coat.

In fact, nobody had much to say. Everything that could be sai
or done had been. There was no sense in speculating about anything
The three lawyers walked Maria downstairs where she got a cab. I
was nearly over. No matter what the jury decided, she and Lisa coul
soon go home to Chicago and put all this behind them.

Whipple, Johansen and Klein decided to go around the bloc
to Dave's Deli hoping for a plate of their famous short-ribs. It wa
close by and the buffet line would be quicker than sitting down at
restaurant. Anyway, now that the old Congress Hotel was gone, de
molished for a black glass office building five years earlier, nobod
could think of anywhere else they wanted to go. Its destruction ha
created a lunch-time diaspora in the legal community that had neve
been resolved.

Dave's was busy and comforting. Giant, half-carved roasts o
beef and turkey sat spotlighted at the end of a steam-table filled wit
stews, vegetables, gravies, potatoes, and sure enough, the tende
slow-braised short ribs. The heady mix of aromas and the visual feas
on display usually made it impossible not to overeat. But today th
lawyers held back, watching the time, suddenly anxious to finish an

return to the courthouse, even though hours of waiting still stretched out before them.

At least that's what they hoped. The rule of thumb in jury trials is that if you're on defense like United was, the quicker the jury comes back the better because it means the jury has found the plaintiff's case wanting. Likewise, if you're on the plaintiff's side, you hope the jury deliberates longer, enough to really consider the evidence and calculate the damages. But if the jury takes *too* long, it might mean they're hung up on something.

Back at the courtroom, all was quiet; the judge was in his chambers and United's attorneys were at the defense table. Whipple, Johansen and Klein hunkered down to wait, knowing they had to stay put now in case the jury came back or suddenly had a question that needed input from both sides. None of them felt like trying to do anything productive to pass the time, so they sat together in the back of the room and chatted quietly about whatever they could think of to take their minds off the stress of wondering what the results would be.

"It's a lonely vigil," Whipple later recalled. "All you can do is just sweat it out."

The observer section of the courtroom had been especially busy before the jury retired to deliberate. Fred Leeson, a reporter for *The Oregonian*, was one of the journalists following the case, and had been in the courtroom for the closing arguments, as well as off and on during the two-and-a-half-week testimony. A lot of people remembered Lisa since she had been so much in the news after the crash. The public wanted to know what had become of her and what the outcome of her singular trial would be.

Other attorneys had stopped by, as well, to hear the closing remarks in the high-profile case, and were now peeking in periodically to see if the jury was back.

Hours dragged by, passing five o'clock. The hallways began to empty as activity in the courthouse wound down for the evening. It was getting close to dinnertime, but nobody wanted to take the chance to step out now. The jury had been deliberating for five hours, and might be getting close to a verdict.

By seven o'clock, Whipple and company had gone quiet having momentarily run out of things talk about. Each man sat with his own thoughts trying not to replay moments during the trial where questions or testimony might have gone better. Still, one simple conviction remained as a mental bulwark against self-doubt, Whipple recalls: "I believed in the case."

At nine o'clock, the attorneys took turns going to the hallway payphone to stretch and call home to let their wives know they were still waiting. By then, news reports on the radio and television were coming in with stories of a devastating storm of twenty-four tornados ripping across the Carolinas and Georgia, the full impact of which wouldn't be known until the next day. The unprecedented swath of destruction ultimately extinguished fifty-seven lives and injured more than a thousand others. It was a grim coincidence that underscored the lesson one juror later said she took from serving on the trial: that anything can happen, and somehow you must take care to leave your family prepared for sudden loss.

Finally, shortly before ten o'clock, the court clerk suddenly reappeared and the energy in the room seemed to jump. Responding to the change, Whipple and Johansen returned to their positions at the plaintiff's table, leaving Klein in the observer section of the courtroom. The bailiff entered and asked everyone to stand as Judge Roth emerged from his chambers, still arranging his robes.

Now the jury returned in a procession to their seats, though one man, a forty-five-year-old shipping worker they'd selected as foreman, remained standing with a sheet of paper in his hand. There wasn't time to read any hints of the decision in the jurors' faces, except it was obvious they were exhausted after deliberating for ten hours.

Judge Roth got right to it. "Ladies and gentlemen, have you arrived at a verdict?"

"We have, your honor," the foreman replied.

Whipple had lost count of the jury trials he'd handled in his then thirty-three years of practice. The verdict moment was always stressful, but for some reason this one was different. He found he was holding his breath.

"Would you hand the verdict to the clerk," the judge continued, as the clerk stepped toward the foreman and received the paper. It was now her job to read it aloud.

"We the jury, duly empaneled and sworn to try the above entitled cause, find *in favor* of the plaintiff Elizabeth Marina Andor and against the defendant in the sums of $150,000 general damages, and $11,275 special damages..." The clerk paused. The next sentence was the important part, what everyone was waiting for.

"And we *do* find that punitive damages should be assessed against United Airlines Inc., but *not* against Malburn A. McBroom. The amount of punitive damages is $750,000."

Whipple felt a wave of elation and relief wash over him, but tried to resist it because he knew it wasn't quite over.

"All right," Roth continued. "Ladies and gentlemen of the jury, in respect to the general damages of $150,000; was this unanimous? Did all of you vote in favor of that amount?"

"Yes, it was unanimous," the foreman replied.

"How about the $11,275 special damages?"

"That was also unanimous."

"Now with respect to the punitive damages against United Airlines; was that unanimous?"

"No, your honor, it was not."

Whipple stiffened. If at least nine had voted for the punitive damages, the verdict would hold, but if not the victory could be snatched away in the next few moments. The jury would have to be polled. As the clerk prepared to call the jurors' names, Whipple picked up his pencil and drew two columns on his legal pad, one labeled "yes" and the other "no."

"Alright," the judge intoned to the jury. "As your name is called, if you voted for the amount of $750,000, say yes. If you did not, say no."

As each name was called, Whipple made a hash mark in one of the columns. Within the first seven jurors there were already three no's against four yes's. He looked at the jurors who had voted no, recalling a little about them from their interviews at the beginning of the trial. One was the youngest man on the jury, the twenty-eight-year-old former music teacher getting started in the audiology equipment field. The next was probably the oldest man in the group at age seventy-nine, the retired house painter who owned a few rental properties. And finally, a secretary in her late forties. No time to analyze their opposition now. He would file it away for later reflection, though the woman was a surprise. He remembered she had three children.

Whipple felt his tension mount. There couldn't be any more no's for the verdict to stand, and even though the jury's decision had been read as *for* the punitive damages just minutes earlier, he knew that miscounts could occur and reveal themselves during the polling. His hand hovered over the columns as he listened, barely breathing, to the last voices, two men and three women.

"Yes. Yes. Yes. Yes. Yes."

Whipple's heart was pounding now as Roth studied his own notations for a moment and then looked up over his glasses.

"As I count it, the votes are nine to three, gentlemen."

Whipple and Johansen sat for a moment in a suspended haze, getting used to the idea that they had won, and only vaguely aware of the movement around them. Then reality snapped back on and they were congratulating each other as they gathered their files and briefcases. But when Whipple went back to share the moment with Bill Klein, he found his friend bent over in his seat. Klein looked up and smiled at him, but something was wrong.

Looking back on the night, Whipple has a hard time capturing what he was feeling about the victory because, in a bizarre spin, something far more important was suddenly unfolding, almost as if augured by the flock of devastating twisters touching down across the country.

"He told me he was so pleased with the result, and would have his wife Mary, who was standing by for the news, call Maria," Whipple recalls. "But he also said he had a terrific pain in his groin."

Whipple had handled enough medical lawsuits to know a lot about health issues, and was immediately alarmed. This wasn't to be ignored.

217

"I said to Bill, come on, we're going to the hospital righ now."

All thoughts of the trial vanished as he drove his old friend t Kaiser Permanente in north Portland. Mary met them there, an Whipple stayed while Klein was checked in and then settled in a roor awaiting examination before he finally allowed himself to go hom around midnight. And that was the last time he saw him.

"I learned the next day that Bill had an aortic aneurism," h says quietly. "It ruptured in the night."

Whipple pauses, shaking his head as he recalls his shock an disbelief, then finishes, "He bled to death."

Chapter 22

A Dedicated Opponent

"$900,000 Awarded Injured Child: Verdict on '78 Jet Crash Against United"

The newspaper headlines announcing the jury's unprecedented punitive damage award against United were little comfort in the ensuing days as Whipple helped Bill Klein's widow through her sudden loss—and navigated his own grief. He and Bill had been close friends, colleagues and fraternity brothers for more than thirty years. Bill's two sons had shared joint family vacations with his own children. He could hardly believe that Bill wasn't just a phone call away. or that the day's mail wouldn't bring some interesting newspaper clipping and a personal note from his friend's office in Vancouver.

Instead, the post brought messages of condolence. United's attorney Steve Rosen reached out with a handwritten note of sympathy on the loss of his close friend saying, "I will long remember Bill as a warm and generous man." Whipple was touched by the kindness from his opponent, and still has the letter.

Maria, too, was stunned at Bill's sudden death. It was as if United Flight 173 had somehow claimed yet another victim. But she and Lisa were eager to get home, back to family, and within days of the trial's end they were on their way.

As for the more than $900,000 the jury had awarded, it was an amount that would ensure a comfortable future for Lisa. It wasn't the

219

biggest verdict Whipple had ever handled as a litigator, but the jury, in keeping with his assessment of them, had grasped the evidence and been reasonable, not excessive in their award. And he was glad of that because the decision wouldn't be criticized or second-guessed on that account.

Indeed, he was impressed by the way the jury had followed their instructions and crafted their decision so that McBroom was held blameless for deliberate wrongdoing while United was held accountable. They had no trouble threading that needle, where all others had previously failed—or refused—including the NTSB, the FAA and, of course, the airline. Whipple knew McBroom had been mercilessly scapegoated since the accident. Now, maybe he would find some measure of peace.

The jury had packed the bulk of the damages in the punitive award of $750,000 against United, which emphasized their finding of wanton misconduct, but also stopped well short of their $10 million ceiling. Their message to United was therefore attenuated. It was clear they found evidence that United's maintenance practices were worthy of censure, and they wanted to send a signal to the airline to make improvements, but the modest penalty by corporate standards perhaps reflected the minority dissent among them, and certainly proved they hadn't "gone off the deep end" as juries are criticized for doing in some punitive damage cases.

Still, as Whipple says, "I wasn't surprised at the amount. I didn't expect the outer limits, and it was a big verdict in those days, especially with a conservative Multnomah County jury—and there weren't many punitive damage wins at that time."

To be sure, the unprecedented verdict was a blow for United, but the jury award for Lisa was widely seen as fair and just. Still, any lawyer knows that the end of a trial is not necessarily the *end*, as one common legal joke captures:

> "After a long and difficult court battle, a lawyer calls his corporate client to let him know the verdict.
>
> The client asks, "So how did it go?"
>
> And the lawyer replies, "Justice and right prevailed."
>
> The client doesn't hesitate. "Appeal immediately!"

Within two weeks, that's what happened. United filed a motion with the court asking Judge Roth to do one of two things: reverse the jury decision by removing the punitive damage verdict, or grant a new trial. Asking for a "judgment notwithstanding the verdict" (Judgment NOV) is a quick, cost-effective next step in a legal fight. If the judge is willing to take care of a 'verdict problem' with a stroke of the pen, then it's both a victory and another foundation laid. But it's also risky to ask a judge to turn about face on a ruling or on a verdict he's just duly overseen. It can be received as an irritating waste of time, especially after a lengthy trial. But United's attorneys stuck with the methodical, no-stone-unturned approach. Time and money were on their side.

In their sixteen-page motion for judgment NOV the attorneys, Crow and Rosen now deployed their list of defense placeholders: the requests for summary judgment, directed verdict, and mistrial, which they'd carefully built up during the trial, and knew they would need on the record. It was all there down to their numerous exceptions to the jury instructions. The buckshot strategy would give the judge plenty of legal items from which to pick and choose. It would take only one to do the trick.

And they had a hunch about which one it would be. During one of the sessions in the judge's chambers during the last days of trial, Judge Roth had said something that indicated he might be sympathetic to their position, and thus amenable to their Judgment NOV motion. The conversation had gone like this:

Crow had just moved again for mistrial and Judge Roth denied the mistrial motion, but offered them a note of comfort for later, saying,

"This is a case of admitted liability as far as damages. See, I don't have the same crucial thing on that issue [landing gear maintenance], and as I've listened to the evidence of this case, the *real* thrust of the case is the cockpit handling."

"We think so," Crow said, gratefully. There it was. The sympathetic phrase they needed and would later quote verbatim as a respectful reminder to the judge in their Judgement NOV arguments.

Roth kept going as if his message needed underlining, and signaling that—despite the constitutional rules against it—*he*, not the jury, would assess the evidence and do the deciding.

"That's the real thrust of the case," he repeated. "And I think *this* is what the evidence is, and the only reason I ever considered the element of punitive still remaining in the case."

Roth paused and then put a stamp on it while United's attorneys must have rejoiced.

"The rest of this stuff is routine," he continued. "It could be negligence, could not be negligence, but there's nothing that takes on the realm of ignoring the rights of the people as a commercial airline. But the real heart of this case is the cockpit problem."

That's *not* how the jury saw it. In fact it was just the opposite for them, which they clearly expressed in their verdict against United but not McBroom. Despite this clarity, the judge's focus remained on the "cockpit problem," and this was precisely what United's attorneys replayed later in the conclusion of their motion for judgment NOV, profoundly misrepresenting the jury decision:

"The jury found against the plaintiff on her claims for punitive damages *arising from the conduct of the crew*."

On that baffling basis, a month later, Roth granted United's motion for judgment NOV, vacating the jury verdict on punitive damages. He agreed with United that there wasn't sufficient evidence to support punitive damages against United *as a result of what happened in the cockpit*. As he had said earlier, "The rest of this stuff"—all the maintenance stuff the jury found so disturbing and on which they'd so explicitly based their verdict—was "routine," beside the point.

"Judge Strikes Down Punitive Award in Jet Crash"

A small news item two months later in *The Oregonian* on May 25, 1984 reported that the $750,000 punitive damages verdict awarded to Lisa had been overturned. She could keep the rest of the money ($161,425). United didn't have a problem with that. And really it wasn't about the general damages money at all. It was about the punitive damages. Whether it was $750 or $750,000, United would likely have fought the verdict because of the precedent, and the door it would open to other lawsuits in future air disasters.

The judgment was a blow, but not unexpected for Whipple and Johansen who were a bit more philosophical about the sudden reversal than Maria since they were familiar with the routine. As long as there was a chance to obtain a better result, United would figh every available battle.

They'd tried to prepare her for that—the certainty of an even tual appeal by United. But *this*, Judge Roth's swift, quiet actio throwing out the jury verdict barely after the ink was dry was differ ent for her, stunning. It was a betrayal. It was as if the trial hadn even mattered. All the hours, all the days in the courtroom, and th months and years that she and Lisa and the family had lived with th consequences of the plane crash, none of it mattered if he could eras in a few moments the justice that the jury had seen fit to give in th courtroom, along with any sense of closure it had brought her. How could that be? They had followed all the rules and won fair and square. She'd gone home with Lisa feeling some hope and looking forward to some rest and healing. For a little while at least, they and everyone who had suffered in the crash had prevailed, had held airlin decision-makers accountable for their actions.

Yet here it was again. A judge this time. Another decision hidden from view, that Maria had no control over. It was as if th plane crashed again.

Lisa's attorneys had mounted their opposition to United's mo tion in a short hearing before Judge Roth, arguing that evidence o United's aggravated misconduct was "abundant to support an awar of punitive damages," and warning that granting a motion for Judg ment NOV "impairs the constitutional right to a jury trial of the party prevailing before a jury."

But Roth's concentration remained stuck on the cockpit evi dence rather than the maintenance evidence, putting his thinking— contrary to the jury's—squarely in line with United on the question o punitive damages. It was as if the judge and jury had attended two different trials—which is one reason we rely on juries in the first place as Chief Justice Rehnquist had observed.

It's also why Oregon passed an amendment to its state Constitution in 1910[1] preventing courts from re-examining any fact tried by a jury when the verdict returned is based on legal evidence. According to Matthew Macario writing in the Temple Law Review in 1995, "The amendment eliminated the power of judges to set aside verdicts based on their own views of the evidence." Further, like the U.S. Constitution, it enshrined the primacy of the jury's fact-finding function, and affirmed that jury verdicts reflect the common sense of the community. The amendment, he notes, embodies the choice and right of the people of Oregon to be governed by their citizen peers. It also echoes the U.S. Supreme Court which re-affirmed this in 1942: "Courts are not free to reweigh the evidence and set aside the jury verdict merely because the jury could have drawn different inferences or conclusions or because judges feel that other results are more reasonable."

Notwithstanding this, Judge Roth went ahead and took care of United's jury verdict problem, at the same time noting that whichever way he ruled, "This case is going upstairs; no question about that."

For justice and right to *re*-prevail, Lisa's attorneys would have to take her case to the Oregon Appeals Court.

That took two more years.

---

[1] *"In actions at law, where the value in controversy shall exceed $750, the right of trial by jury shall be preserved, and no fact tried by a jury shall be otherwise re-examined in any court of this state, unless the court can affirmatively say there is no evidence to support the verdict."*

"Punitive Award for Jetliner Crash Reinstated"

On May 14, 1986 the Oregon Appeals Court, in a majority eight to two 'in banc' decision, upheld the jury's verdict for Lisa's $750,000 punitive damage claim. Legal observers recognized the decision as a major victory in the *Andor v United* case since not only did it confirm that the jury acted appropriately, it double-stamped their punitive damage verdict against the airline. No other lawsuit resulting from a scheduled airline crash had gotten that far on punitive damages. And hasn't since.

Writing for the Appeals Court majority, Judge Kurt Rossman almost immediately flagged the constitution problem in Judge Roth's ruling and sent a pointed reminder to the courts of Oregon saying it was well established that the choice to impose punitive damages was for the jury to decide as long as there is evidence to support the finding and the jury's instructions were sound. In this case, the Appeals Court said that the jury *had* acted according to their instructions— which United did not dispute in their appeal argument—and that there *was* evidence to support their award of punitive damages against *either or both* of the defendants.

The Appeals Court added as a premonitory caution,

"The Supreme Court and this court have periodically succumbed to the temptation to make an impermissible independent normative evaluation of the aggravatedness of a defendant's conduct in the guise of reviewing for evidentiary sufficiency. This is essentially what United asks us to do here...We decline to do so. Our function is to determine whether the evidence and the inferences taken at their strongest, rationally support the jury's finding; it is not our function

226

to make our own assessment of how defendants' conduct should be characterized." [2]

Whipple called Maria with the good news of the court victory, and she was happy but couldn't let herself get excited. She certainly hoped that the Appeals Court decision would put an end to things, but she wasn't so naïve anymore about judicial proceedings, and was under no illusion about United's dedication to continuing the fight. She was focused instead on her family, and two years distant from the drama and pain of the trial. As grateful as she was for this win, she really didn't want to pick that scab. She suspected that she'd be getting another phone call soon enough when United took their case "upstairs" to the next level. But as long as Whipple and Johansen felt confident in the prospects and were willing to stick with it, she would, too. All three felt that the case was even stronger now that eight Appeals Court judges had upheld and reinstated the jury verdict.

Getting a case reviewed by the Oregon Supreme Court isn't automatic and it isn't easy. According to a retired judge who served on the Appeals Court during the *Andor v United* case and later on the Oregon Supreme Court, it is up to the Supreme Court's discretion whether to review an Appeals Court decision. Not many petitions for review are granted in civil cases like Lisa's, especially when there is a clear majority of opinion among the lower court judges, as there was in *Andor v United*. If a petition is denied, the lower court's ruling stands as the final word.

Still, with nothing to lose and everything to gain, United mobilized an additional attorney, James Westwood, along with the high-

---

[2] *Andor v. United Airlines* 79 Or App 311 (1986)

profile Washington, D.C. law firm Shea & Gardner, and petitioned the Oregon Supreme Court for review on July 28, 1986, two months after the Appeals Court ruling.

It's difficult to understand why the Supreme Court even agreed to hear it given the eight to two Appeals Court decision. That was a question for the retired judge who later agreed it was puzzling since "an 'in banc' opinion carries weight." Then he paused and reflected, "But, there was a lot of money at stake and powerful law firms involved."

Asked recently about the Oregon Supreme Court decision, Whipple takes a moment. After more than half a century in the practice of law, he is not given to the imprecise language of feelings. But his store of allegories and ancient 'Chinese' proverbs is never out of reach. He settles back in his chair.

"Well, I was reminded of the story of the traveling salesman..." he begins. "He got off the train at 3:00 A.M. in a small Montana town in December. The temperature was below zero, the town had no hotel and all of the stores were closed. While walking around to keep warm, he noticed a light coming from a window in a saloon where four men were playing draw poker. He was invited into the game because new money is always welcome.

"After a few hands, the salesman drew a royal flush. When he reached for the pot he was told that George had beat him with a "Montana Squeegen," which consisted of a two of clubs, five of diamonds, six of spades, two of hearts and eight of clubs. He'd never heard of this, but because it was so cold outside, he continued to play.

"After a few more hands, he drew a Montana Squeegen. But when he reached for the pot he was told that Fred had him beat with a pair of twos. Now the salesman protested that if a Montana Squeegen beats a royal flush it should certainly beat a pair of twos. But he was told that under local rules there could only be one Montana Squeegen a night."

Whipple waits to let his listener explore the corners of the story's implications, and then hands over a photocopy of the Oregon Supreme Court opinion[3] written by Justice Hans Linde on June 23, 1987.

"I was incredulous," he says simply.

We must leave it to the legal minds to analyze all the subtleties and citations of the decision overturning the jury verdict and the Appeals Court decision. But one odd thing immediately stands out for someone, even a layperson, who has examined the trial transcripts: the realities have changed. Facts that were disputed during the trial and for the jury to decide—or plain not there—have become certainties in the Supreme Court's version, not because new information or physical evidence was discovered but because—like the good fellows at the poker table—they *say so*.

In this alternate Squeegen universe, conjured by a bit of selective omnipotence favoring United and dismissing the jury's job description and hard-won determination of the facts—and pertinence aside—the landing gear *was unquestionably* down and locked, it *was* safe to land on, McBroom *was* told of this, and the bungee *did* work after the bolt failed:

---

3 *Andor v. United Airlines* 303 Or 505 (1987).

"United's choice to deal with the corrosion in its hy draulic gear system by installing an alternative "bungee" (o spring) system to secure the landing gear in the down posi tion, rather than replacing the eyebolt assembly when i showed corrosion...was a deliberate management choice, an a fact-finder [juror] might conclude that it qualified for puni tive damages if the substituted system failed to work and th landing gear did not lock in place or buckled on landing. *Bu that did not happen. The pilot was advised that the gear wa down and safe for landing, and there is no evidence that i was not safe to land.*" (emphasis added)

This is a dizzying misstatement of the facts submitted in tes timony, not to mention a blatant choice of relevancy, which again wa for the jury alone to resolve—and which it properly did. The Suprem Court has re-crafted and re-selected the evidence thus creating an al together *different record* on which to base its own conclusions in th service of a different result:

"On this record," the Supreme Court writes, stating as much "a claim of intentional or "wanton" disregard of the plane's mechani cal safety cannot rest solely on the failure of the eyebolt."

The Supreme Court then fulfills the prophecy of the Appeal Court by "indulging in the temptation to make an impermissible eval uation of the aggravatedness of the defendant's conduct in the guis of reviewing for evidentiary sufficiency."

The opinion states,

"United's failure to replace the corroded parts before
they gave way was an insufficient basis for punitive damages...For punitive damages, some conscious disregard of or

highly irresponsible indifference to this human element in the decision on equipment is required....The Circuit Court [Judge Roth] correctly concluded that the evidence did not support the level of culpability expressed in the court's instructions to the jury."

But the jury *did* find evidence of this "conscious disregard" and "highly irresponsible indifference" in United's conduct (but *not* McBroom's), which they explicitly demonstrated in their verdict. And they perfectly understood in their instructions the "level of culpability" needed to award the level of punitive damages they did. Nevertheless, the Oregon Supreme Court insists there was "insufficient basis" for their verdict. The Oregon Constitution says there must *affirmatively be no evidence* for a jury verdict to be overruled.

In this perplexing realm of opinion transformed to fact and the judge-knows-better, juries, like eyebolts, are non-essential equipment and easily ignored. Once again, Rehnquist's words remind us that when our judicial system was founded, *"Those who favored juries believed that a jury would reach a result that a judge could not or would not reach."* They understood that juries, plain people acting as a time-limited group of deliberators, represented perhaps the fairest mechanism ever devised to determine and weigh evidence, champion public justice and counter the encroachments of the more powerful.

Unfortunately, the Supreme Court's *Andor* decision did nothing to sustain this ideal. Instead it laid an early paving stone on the path to judicial overreach and the weakening of the constitutional guarantee of trial by jury.

We're further down that path today in Oregon courts—and in courts across the nation. In May 2016, Oregon Supreme Court Justice

Martha Walters pushed back on her colleagues' decision to limit a jury award given to another child in a devastating medical malpractice case (Horton v. OHSU). The legislative cap the court majority allowed on the jury award left the child far short of the funds needed for lifelong medical expenses. Justice Walters didn't mince her words in her dissent to her colleagues, reminding them that our constitution ensures "that an individual who suffers personal injury will have legal remedy for that injury, and that a jury will determine the extent of that injury and the monetary sum necessary to restore it." Those two provisions, she went on to write, "define what we mean when we use the word justice, and they make jurors its defender." She concludes with, "Together they provide a constitutional structure that is designed to provide justice for all and a means to provide justice for all. Today, the majority [Oregon Supreme Court] does real damage to that structure and to the real people it is intended to protect."

Deja vu, Stewart Whipple would say.

At least one of the Supreme Court Justices who participated in the 1987 *Andor v United* review and reversal was also evidently troubled by the decision—or willing to be honest about it. Although he'd gone along with the court, the Justice passed Whipple a short time later in the hallway at a bar convention and offered these words of acknowledgment:

"We screwed you, Stu."

To this day, the gentleman in him prevents Whipple from revealing who that was. Instead he shrugs and says, "I appreciated the gesture. You always wonder if you could have done something differently, better. It told me they were after a result and they got it."

In a twist of irony, the Oregon Supreme Court's *Andor v United* decision not only ended Lisa's long quest for justice but has also fused into the framework for the application of punitive damages in other cases. Now an un-inspected bolt in the judicial gear we've got to land on, *Andor v United* is still being cited, often at some length, in a wide array of cases—thirty-three at last count—including Boy Scout and Catholic Church sex abuse trials (1989, 2010), a securities fraud case (1991), an unlawful trade practices lawsuit involving a furniture company (1990), a pesticide misapplication lawsuit (1991), a Honda all-terrain vehicle product liability case that went all the way to the U.S. Supreme Court (1993), a nail gun product liability suit (1997), a Stryker medical equipment injury lawsuit (2011), a wind turbine noise and vibration damage case (2016) to name just a few. [4]

Indeed, the Oregon Supreme Court's *Andor* decision is now considered the "gold standard" when it comes to establishing the legal conditions under which punitive damages can be sought, won or denied in Oregon courts. Paradoxically, Lisa Andor did not benefit from these standards, though she likely would have, had the Court respected its constitutional limits along with the jury's lawful determination of the facts of her case. Instead, this is all but forgotten along with the justice that the jury in the trial court and the judges of the Appeals Court rightfully delivered.

So it's tempting to wonder why, in the face of unlimited corporate resources and the legal sophistry of judges, we continue the

---

[4] *Wilson v..Tobiasson and Oregon Trail Council, Inc.; Jane Doe v. Archdiocese of Portland, Oregon; Badger v. Paulson Investment Co.; Honeywell v. Sterling Furniture Co.; Faber v. Asplundh Tree Expert; Oberg v. Honda Motor Co., Inc.; Lakin v. Senco Products, Inc.; Shoenborn v. Stryker Corp.; Williams v. Invenergy, LLC.*

ritual of impaneling citizen juries if their verdicts have so little chance of holding. To be sure, the jury in the *Andor v United* case did not take their role in the trial lightly. Although they went home to their lives and lost track of Lisa's case as it was shunted through the courts for the next four years, being part of the case was a watershed experience, and two of the jurors were recently dismayed to learn that all their work had been undone. Marlene said it confirmed her mistrust of the judicial system. "The judges have too much power when all these people come to a decision and one person can throw it out."

Another juror named Nancy was silent on the phone for a moment when she heard that their verdict was upheld by the Appeals Court and then overturned by the Oregon Supreme Court. When she began to speak, it wasn't difficult to hear the emotion in her voice.

"It's not fair. It's a shame, a terrible miscarriage of justice," she said. "You have a jury that spends all that time to listen and decide..." Nancy pauses, collecting her thoughts, and then sums up the modest aspirations that she and her fellow citizens worked so hard for, and believed they'd achieved.

"We did what was right," she says with conviction. "Our verdict wasn't just to help the little girl; it was to prevent what happened to her from happening to others, to make United pay better attention to safety."

So, all for naught? Maybe not. As Chicago attorney David Rapoport observes, The *Andor v United* case counts as "one of the high-water marks" in aviation punitive damage lawsuits given that the Appeals Court upheld the jury verdict and overturned the trial judge. Punitive damages lawsuits against airlines in the last twenty-five years have been attempted, he explains, but they most often have ended in settlements or summary judgments in favor of the airlines.

"Courts have been in my opinion too quick to rule that evidence won't support a punitive damage claim," Rapoport says, adding that legislation across the nation restricting punitive damages has increased dramatically in recent years. Still, he notes, the threat of punitive damages is "a meaningful player in aviation accident litigation," and "critical to supporting the rights of families after an air disaster."

"It's unfortunate that the jury's decision in the Andor case didn't carry," Rapoport says. "But it did trigger a higher level of attention."

Ditto that, says Ralph Nader in his assertion that "your lawsuits are good for America." The Andor case may not have delivered the justice that Lisa deserved, but it made you and me a little safer.

The most widely publicized improvement—and the one always associated with the crash of United Flight 173—is the development of Crew Resource Management (CRM) techniques, first in the cockpit and later in maintenance centers, and now in many industries beyond aviation where effective teamwork and communication in high-risk decision-making is critical. To be sure, CRM practices have improved airline—and public—safety in ways that are hard to quantify since it's impossible to know precisely how many disasters *haven't* happened as a result. But statistics certainly indicate that aviation accidents and fatal errors occur far less frequently now.

More broadly speaking, CRM skills including collaboration, situational awareness, and being assertive and clear with superiors are useful wherever people in organizations interact. Today, it's even easy to imagine a time when most employees will be trained to use some version of the CRM "alarm" script as a standard formula to call out and defend against everything from safety and ethics lapses to sexual harassment in the workplace. The key words—"I'm concerned, I'm uncomfortable, I'm scared, this is unsafe or unacceptable"—would put everyone on notice that a dangerous or unwelcome behavior is on the record and must stop.

Less well known—or publicly heralded—was United's belated response to the eyebolt and fuel gauge problems on its DC-8s. The specter of punitive damages did finally convince the company to upgrade these systems and communicate better with their pilots about fuel management. So, it's a tool that works—at least in a focused way when the truth is allowed to come to light and money is at stake.

The prospect of punitive damages, and the very close call that *Andor v United* represented for the aviation industry, would have given many of the airlines pause to consider the impact of such a precedent. Defense attorneys are still paying close attention. In 2006 the law firm of Nelson Mullins published a white paper in the *In-House Defense Quarterly* warning that the possibility of a punitive damage victory in airline litigation "is no longer a remote possibility...The plaintiffs' bar has not yet 'rung the bell' against a major air carrier with punitive damages...However, courts are increasingly willing to issue findings of willful, wanton, reckless or grossly negligent conduct against the airline defendant...[and] juries are capable of doing the same."

A key worry, the authors write, is in the area of— yep—maintenance. They express concern over a 2004 study by Purdue University Department of Aviation Technology that claims, "flying is becoming less safe and maintenance errors are playing an increasing role in the reduced operation level of safety." In short, the attorneys write

"Air carriers are becoming increasingly exposed to potential punitive success."

With that in mind, the airlines should be doing the math and deciding that safety is less costly than cost-cutting in the maintenance department or anywhere that the safety of passengers must come first.

But just to make sure that an ounce of prevention *still is* worth a pound of cure, consumer and civil justice advocates advise the public to guard the power of punitive damages, and to be aware and beware of the "assault by a thousand cuts" that Ralph Nader calls the frequently overlooked, seemingly innocuous state and federal legislative attacks on tort law which limit people's protections and access to the courts, weaken penalties for corporate wrongdoing, debilitate the role of the jury, diminish judicial accountability, and allow corporations to write off the cost of their misconduct.

Protecting the constitutional right to trial by jury is fundamental to this cause. Individuals should be loathe to sign it away in Terms of Use agreements that force them into arbitration in case of injury and deny them access to a jury trial. Likewise, as Abraham Lincoln believed, any citizen can and must support this constitutional right by welcoming what he called the "highest duty" to serve as a juror. In other words, alert, active participation is vital to upholding our founders' conviction that, guided by a constitution, ordinary people, unschooled in the law, provide a kind of civic wisdom and social control which is essential to the preservation of justice and democracy.

This ideal formed the hope and the foundation of Lisa's case. Maybe it's also partly why her parents—her mother from Italy and father from Communist Hungary—were drawn to become full citizens of this land, too soon their final resting place.

Chapter 23

The Kindness of Strangers

It would be a kind of birthday party—or rebirth-day party.

It was already dark, and a cold rain was falling, as Aimee Ford Conner dashed inside the First Congregational Church in Portland's Park Blocks, her six-month-old son on one hip and a dish for the potluck on the other. It was only four-thirty and the event wasn't to begin until six o'clock, but she wanted to make sure that everything was ready in the fellowship hall. A pianist was coming who needed to set up, she wanted to check on the coffee delivery, meet the volunteers, and see that all the guests would have a chair and name badges, and serving pieces to go with the dishes they, too, were bringing—and enough Kleenex—lots of little details to think about, which was good because she was so nervous.

The Christmas decorations were still up in the big stone church, a festive note for a gathering that was likely to run the gamut of emotions. It was Monday, December 28, 1998, the twentieth anniversary of the crash of United Flight 173.

Two decades had passed, but Aimee, now thirty-seven, married and a first-time mother, was still haunted by the experience. Indeed, things had only gotten worse instead of better as the years went by and she couldn't understand why.

At first, she thought the crash had barely affected her. She was seventeen, then. She had it handled. Her ankle injury was minor and quickly healed. Within days of the accident, she'd even gotten back on an airplane—a very bumpy little one at that—and flown back to her boarding school at the north end of Lake Chelan. Curiously, she had a ball on that flight—the last one she ever enjoyed. She realized later that she'd still been in shock.

She graduated from high school a few months later and took the modest settlement money she'd received from United's insurance company and went to Europe to sort her life out and think about her future.

Years passed. She returned to Portland and became a nurse, deciding to devote herself to hospice. There was something familiar and compelling about working with people at the end of life and coming to terms with their past.

Although she'd been raised by Scandinavian Lutherans in the upper Midwest, Aimee was now a Quaker, and it was at a Quaker meeting that she met Peter, the man she would marry.

She had a rewarding career, a wonderful husband, and now her first son. But there was also a growing darkness in her heart that made her increasingly fearful. At first it was just the flying. It had gotten very hard to make visits home to Minnesota because she was now seized with panic about the plane ride. She tried Valium and hypnosis, and once drank a pitcher of gin and tonic before the flight in order to get through it; and then nothing worked anymore. Finally, in 1985, seven years after the accident, she had to admit that her flying days were over. It was an inconvenience, but understandable given her crash history, she told herself. Problem solved, she thought.

But from there, other things got more difficult to manage, especially in the winter, in December as the date of the accident drew near. Each year she was drawn to the crash site on December 28. In the beginning, going there was both comforting and incredibly eerie because she could still see the deep gouges in the ground like an inscription where the jet had plowed into the earth. She could close her eyes and imagine it all happening again—or *still* happening—the sudden darkness and utter silence before the roar of the impact. It was as if time, itself, was compressed here in this place, and the barrier between *now* and *then* was thinner, more like a veil that she could almost see through, even be pulled through.

For a few years, not much changed at 157th and Burnside except that the blackberry brambles regained possession of the empty lots on both sides of the thoroughfare, and scrub slowly covered the rain-filled impressions of the doomed aircraft. Then she arrived one December to find an apartment complex occupying the north-side lot where the plane had come to rest. Not long before, the MAX light rail line had been built straight up the middle of Burnside.

But the south-side lot remained vacant, the last reminder of the way things were the night of the crash. Apart from that, nothing even hinted that an airliner had fallen from the sky. No sign, no trace. It was all erased, as if it hadn't happened.

That bothered her. Sure, the newspapers ran a few where-are-they-now stories on the first, then third, then tenth anniversaries of the crash, but these momentary reminders, scanned over breakfast along with the sports and weather pages, didn't satisfy, didn't really connect anyone, didn't offer a chance to have a conversation about it beyond one's own kitchen table. She wasn't sure why that mattered, but it did.

And that's when Aimee began to think that somehow remembering *with* others was critical to shedding some light on the private shadows that always seemed to be there these days, tugging at the edges of her every thought and making it so hard to do the simplest things.

It's ridiculous! she would scold herself when her thoughts snapped again and again to the crash. *That was ages ago and you were hardly even hurt. Just get over it!*

It didn't make sense to her yet, but there was a part of her that was beginning to acknowledge that she wasn't fine, that the crash *had* affected her in ways she was only just starting to understand. She wondered if others felt the same. Twenty years is a long time, maybe long enough to get past the raw impact of such an experience. Maybe in a group, gathered together in a safe place, people like her would be willing to share their own soft painful spots, and it would help.

Sometimes when an idea takes hold it just feels right, and things begin to fall into place as if to help make it happen. Still, the first challenge was to find and contact people. She turned to the Internet. That's how she re-found Nancy Eldert, the woman she'd been sitting next to in the plane when it went down. They'd been in touch with each other for a while after the accident, but then drifted apart as their lives changed and got busy.

Nancy, now a teacher in Eugene, Oregon, wasn't so sure about the idea of a reunion at first. Why dredge up the past? What would they talk about? But when in the course of their conversation they realized they were both plagued by a terror of flying and even ashamed of it, they knew others might be quietly enduring the very same problems, that they all shared a common bond. So Nancy jumped on board.

These were the days before widespread social media, so Aimee did what so many with a story to tell had done before her. She reached out to Margie Boulé, a popular columnist for The Oregonian who specialized in writing about life events and the community, and was known for the deeply personal tales people entrusted to her to share. It was a perfect fit.

Aimee had thought maybe twenty or thirty people might be interested in knowing about the gathering she was organizing. She hoped that a few fellow survivors and their families along with the families of the ten who died in the crash would be able to come. She also wanted to include the neighbors and emergency workers who responded to the disaster. They, too, shared a bond with the passengers on that life-altering night.

She also wanted it to be private, safe, respectful. This wasn't to be an opportunity for the pubic to gawk as they had in crowds the night of the crash and for days after. Yes, they, too, remembered the accident, but it was more as curious onlookers recalling a piece of Portland history. The reunion she had in mind would offer a different kind of remembering. It might be a chance to heal.

Boulé wrote a column about the accident and the idea of a twentieth anniversary reunion. It was as if someone struck a match. Very quickly it was apparent that the space Aimee was thinking of renting for the event was too small. She switched venues to accommodate the nearly two hundred people who would ultimately come.

The outpouring of interest took Aimee by surprise, and as she made arrangements and spoke to people who wanted to participate she realized that indeed she wasn't alone in experiencing shadows from the accident. So she took a chance and invited a therapist from the Veteran's Administration who specialized in post-traumatic stress disorder (PTSD), a diagnosis that was by then more widely recognized in a broader range of trauma settings outside military combat. He would say a few words and provide information and resources for anyone who might need it. And she needed guidance about how to manage a gathering that might awaken long suppressed emotions. Her hospice training and experience would certainly help, but it was very difficult to predict how things would go in such a large and diverse group.

There was one more wild card: the pilot, Malburn McBroom. What about him? Boulé had asked her one day. He was still in Colorado. Did Aimee want to contact him if Boulé helped pave the way? His daughter lived in Seattle.

The question made Aimee's heart pound. She had to admit to herself that during the years since the accident, the bitterness she felt sometimes when she had bad days had centered on him and his mistakes. It was his fault the plane had crashed, his fault that her life was now filled with anxieties she couldn't control or banish. How could she open the door to this man, the source of her suffering? And what about the others who were coming to the reunion? Maybe they harbored similar feelings and would be upset and offended if he were there. She wanted the gathering to be a healing experience, not something painful.

And yet, part of her also knew that he of *all* people must attend the reunion—if he was willing, if he could bring himself to face them. She felt that any healing would come from forgiveness and reconciliation, which would only be possible face to face with the man whom many felt had brought them to this place.

It took a few days to untangle her feelings. Then McBroom's daughter, Carrie phoned Aimee conveying her support and saying that the crash had affected them all, that she and her siblings had 'lost' their dad afterward. His burden of guilt, the loss of his career, the legal issues and the drinking that had followed had walled him off from his family. Once a talkative storyteller, he had gone quiet and his health was increasingly fragile. She didn't know if he would come; she would encourage him, but he would have to get the invitation from Aimee.

So Aimee summoned her courage and called him.

The voice on the line sounded tired, sad, nothing like the commanding tone of a flight captain. To be sure, McBroom *was* tired. Now seventy-two, he'd been undergoing rounds of chemotherapy for prostate cancer. He was hesitant. He'd spent years trying to put the experience behind him, but it had simply grown into a dark, heavy presence that woke him at night and sucked the light from his life.

Aimee knew in an instant that he should come, and she tried to shape her words to express the heartfelt invitation her call to him meant. She told him that the gathering was for sharing and compassion.

But the idea of walking into a room full of people who had suffered because of him must have sounded awful. It would bring back so many memories of the crash, the lawsuits and depositions and his time in court, especially facing the family of young Lisa Andor. And he had a conflict near the date of the reunion. Still, he told her he would think about it and let her know.

Aimee reviewed her lists and made last minute checks of her preparations. Radio and TV stations, and a variety of newspapers had contacted her asking to attend the reunion, and although she felt it was important to have coverage of the event, she didn't want reporters interfering with the opportunities for the people coming to share their stories with each other in a safe setting. She arranged to have the journalists gather in the library room next to the fellowship hall so that those who wished to could speak separately with the press.

And then it was time. People arrived carrying covered dishes and scrapbooks. They paused at the reception table and picked out color-coded name tags: white for survivors and their families, red for rescue personnel, and blue for neighbors. There was a tentative eagerness in their eyes as they scanned each other's badges. Some wearing white name tags had written the airplane seat number they'd been in next to their name.

The printed program listed Mike Maxwell from the V.A. hospital and Margie Boulé as the two main speakers, with opening remarks by Aimee who planned to introduce the evening's open-ended purpose with an invitation to enjoy the food everyone had brought, followed by a gentle encouragement to share the memories, stories and conversation that had brought them together. But the room was already a breathless clamor with people talking, exclaiming and hugging.

Aimee stepped to the wooden lectern in a calf-length blue dress, and the din of voices began to subside. The sight of so many people seated at the round tables before her was overwhelming. Anticipation and waves of emotion summoned Aimee's tears as she prepared to greet them. She asked for a moment of silence in memory of the ten who hadn't survived, and a hush fell over the crowd.

The silence focused and steadied her for the important introduction she had to make next, a surprise, someone she felt was very brave. As the gathering began to murmur again, she took a breath, her heart filling her throat. There was a brief pause as the name she spoke —Captain Malburn McBroom—sank in, and a small, wizened man in a leather bomber jacket and jeans threaded his way slowly through the crowd toward her. Then the room erupted in applause. McBroom was stunned as people rose from their chairs clapping—for *him*.

245

Why? McBroom struggled to find words to express the swirl of grief and astonishment inside him. The last time he'd addressed these people was from the cockpit of the jet he was about to crash land. Ten people had died, dozens more were injured. And yet here were so many of his passengers and their families standing with a message of forgiveness and gratitude for their survival. McBroom couldn't speak through his tears. He had come from a sense of duty and responsibility to these people in the hope that his presence might give them some closure, some peace—but he suddenly realized that it went both ways.

In the hours that followed, people took turns at the microphone with their memories, and then approached McBroom one by one to take his hand and thank him for their lives. It was hard for him to accept their gratitude in the shadow of the ones who died, and he repeated again and again, "But what about the ten?"

And so, when the sons of Ray Waetjen stood before him still heartbroken from their loss and yet offering forgiveness, the sorrow visibly shook him. "I'm so sorry," was all he could say to them, and later to the still grief-stricken father of Gwen Griffith.

It was a sorrow he bore physically, as many noted including Boulé who wrote later in her story about the evening, "Clearly the guilt, the responsibility, the shame have hurt Malburn McBroom's heart. You can tell by looking at him that he has spent twenty years walking in the ruins of his memories."

Yet, it was as if each hand that touched his lifted a palm-full of the burden he had carried alone for so long. After the gathering marked by much weeping, his daughter Carrie told Boulé that on the drive back to Seattle later that night, for the first time since the crash, McBroom kept her company, telling her stories the whole way.

Experts say that processing a traumatic event happens over a very long period of time—even a lifetime. Al Siebert, an author and coach specializing in survivor issues, accompanied Mike Maxwell from the VA to the reunion. He provided handouts and brief counseling during the evening to help people better understand what they were going through, and noted later in a letter to Aimee that he had seen a few people that night who were clearly still experiencing strong signs of PTSD even after twenty years. As Siebert explained in one of his handouts entitled *Telling Your Survivor Story*, recovering from emotional trauma is a journey of personal transformation that everyone must take at their own speed and in their own way—if they manage it at all.

He wrote, "Anyone who survives a highly distressing experience will never be the same again. Some survivors remain emotionally wounded for life. They relive and re-experience distressing moments over and over. They often dwell on fears about what could happen to them again or to others."

But many people, he adds, do recover fairly well with help from family and friends, and some even go a step further becoming what he called "heroic survivors." These individuals find the wherewithal to engage themselves in a multi-step, transformational process in which they are first able to "integrate the traumatic experience into their public identity and make the experience a defining part of their life story." And second, "They talk or write about it in a way that has an inspiring effect on others."

Coincidentally, another researcher was delving at the time into similar survivor and recovery issues specifically connected with commercial aviation accidents, including United Flight 173. In her

2001 doctoral dissertation entitled, *Impact: A Study of Flight Atten*
dant Survivors of Air Disasters, psychologist Carol Herberger Pollard
interviewed many flight attendants who had been involved in famous
aviation accidents, among them two who were in the Portland crash.

At the time of her research, both women were still employed
by United and still processing their experience. Pollard changed their
names in her work to protect their identities. She wrote that "Alice"
said she was transformed and made stronger by the accident. She
credited this to her deep religious faith to which she had rededicated
her life. Because of her belief that the accident was a kind of destiny
for her, she accepted what had happened and felt she had not been
traumatized by it, especially since she had been spared from seeing
the images of death. She said she was grateful for the senior flight at
tendants who flew down from Seattle to be with her and her col
leagues after the crash while they waited several days to be inter
viewed by the NTSB.

Pollard's interview with "Denise," on the other hand, revealed
a far more troubled recovery. Denise did witness the death and de
struction of the crash first hand. She described having to be medicated
in order to continue flying, which left her zombie-like. For five years
she had nightmares, didn't talk about being in the accident; as she put
it, "I left the planet emotionally."

Then after a period of difficult emotional and physical mani
festations of her suppressed distress, she sought out a therapist and
began to transform the experience. "I was a victim, and then I got
some therapy and became a survivor. Survivors are not walking
ghosts," she said. "Let them speak, talk to them."

At the time of her interview, Denise had taken the further
steps needed to become a "heroic survivor." She saw the accident as

248

part of her and as a catalyst that brought purpose, change and strength to her life which she could use to help others. She became a leader in a crew resource management training program focused on safety-related communications and empowerment for cabin crews. She also felt strongly that survivors like her had an important role to play for others as a support and resource when disasters and trauma struck, and should not be ignored by the airline. She had offered to help after United's Sioux City disaster, but was refused. Because of that and her own experience after the crash—the airline never held a memorial for the victims of Flight 173—she felt that the corporate environment could not be counted upon to take care of the airline employee, especially after an air disaster.

Unfortunately, even though Aimee had contacted United asking that the four surviving flight attendants be informed of the reunion in Portland and invited, none of the women came. She learned later from one of them who called her after reading about it in a newspaper that they had never been told. Throughout the evening of the reunion, McBroom repeatedly credited the flight attendants for the emergency preparations and response which he believed saved so many lives.

For the survivors and families of Flight 173 the twenty-year anniversary gathering was part of their recovery process, and to be sure it was a vital part of it. Many arrived with blame in their hearts, unanswered questions, unexplained fears and anxieties and feelings of isolation. They left knowing that they weren't alone, a first big step toward healing.

The cards and notes Aimee received for weeks after the event are a record of this and of the gratitude people felt. Fellow passenger Lynn Egli wrote, "It meant a lot to me to be able to meet and talk with others from the flight. The reunion stimulated my 'reprocessing' the events, my feelings and their meaning in my life…I particularly appreciate the forgiveness and acceptance extended to Captain McBroom by the group there that night."

Some letters took up where the reunion left off adding or reiterating bits of information people deemed important enough to preserve in writing. One woman was grateful to have been able to tell the family of Ray Waetjen, fatally re-seated to the first class section, that they had spent a pleasant time chatting together before he had requested the move in order to make the connection in Portland on his way to Prineville to visit his son.

Fay Saxton sent a note recounting that he had caught a fellow passenger jumping from the downed aircraft, a woman named Diane Gray who pleaded, "God save my baby!" as she landed in his arms. He never saw the baby, which bothered him for twenty years, until the reunion when he met Diane again and learned that she was six months pregnant at the time. "I finally knew where the baby was!" he wrote. Diane gave birth to a daughter who had just had her own first child.

But there were some absences at the reunion. A few of the survivors said they couldn't come because they could no longer travel as result of ongoing anxiety issues from the crash. Others had moved on in their lives and simply chose not to dwell on the painful events of the accident. As Cheryl Lewis explained, she got some excellent therapy afterward and made a decision to focus on the positive in her life. "I definitely had an angel on my shoulder that night," she said, deeply grateful that she and her children were unhurt. She adds that her philosophy now is to "Live for today, forget the past, look forward to the future and love my family."

Nobody from the crew came except McBroom, nor did the families of Forrest Mendenhall and Joan Wheeler. McBroom's co-pilot, Roderick Beebe, who continued to fly until 1992, died of Parkinson's disease just a week after the reunion at the age of sixty-five. Flight engineer Mendenhall's son Chris sent a letter to Aimee a month later saying he had been to Beebe's funeral, and though he hadn't attended the reunion, it was because of reading about it that he finally visited McBroom for the first time since the accident. He wrote:

"I must say that even though I wasn't there for the event, it has had the same effect here. I was able to find the courage in myself to finally meet Captain McBroom and his family. I wasn't going in anger or still being upset. I wanted Buddy to know that all was alright and there was nothing to forgive... I could very much tell that he carries the loss with him."

Chris, who grew up and became a pilot, then worked for the FAA and is now an air traffic controller, also wanted Aimee to know that he was grateful for her efforts and that she had made a difference for many people.

"I can't thank you enough for doing such a thing. The ripple effect from the reunion definitely had an effect on others. I feel like such a different person after all that has happened. I'll be honest here, I've done a lot of crying this last month, all of those emotions, feelings from that day twenty years ago came rushing back like a freight train. Except with a different effect. It feels as if a weight has been lifted off of me and life is anew."

Lisa Andor, then twenty-three and living in Tennessee, also did not attend the reunion. *The Oregonian* reporter Catherine Trevison spoke to her by phone a week or so before the gathering and wrote in an article that she had recently opened her own real estate business.

251

Lisa told Trevison that she wouldn't fly on December 28 and that partly because she had to wear leg braces growing up and miss school during the lawsuit she never felt like a normal child. Trevison quoted her saying, "I feel like I'm living for other people, especially my sisters," she said. "They never got a chance to be in cheerleading or go to college."

Noting Lisa's maturity beyond her years and strong sense of duty, the reporter wrote, "She believes she was saved for a purpose, and that purpose is to help others."

Nevertheless, it was too difficult at the time for Lisa to participate in the reunion. She explained to Aimee on the phone that she had spent so many years after the accident as the focus and face of the plane crash, the prospect of playing that role again was simply overwhelming. She didn't want the painful events of the past to take center stage again just as she was beginning to chart her own future.

But she was missed. Rob Bean was working in the ER as a respiratory therapist at Portland Adventist the night of the crash. He wrote a letter to Aimee after the reunion recalling the patients he saw that night: the Carson family whose seven-month old daughter Kimberly was thrown from the aircraft and landed barely injured in some blackberry bushes. And the "quiet, stoic" gentleman from Yugoslavia who lost his wife and baby daughter.

"And then there was Elizabeth…the sweet child with the badly broken leg. She had lost a lot of blood. I was mainly hoping to see Elizabeth at the reunion. Once she stabilized and was moved up to 5300, I would visit her often. The nurses would put her in a red wagon with her big cast on and I would pull her around the hospital. I remember her laughing and waving at the other people from the wagon."

He ended the letter saying, "I don't know if it would help her but I feel a special kinship with her. My concerns, thoughts and prayers have been with her over the years."

And there was another absence at the reunion: United. Although Aimee had reached out to them, not a word ever came from the airline.

Epilogue

It's a fifteen-minute drive from my house in southeast Portland to 157th and Burnside, the heart of the working class neighborhoods just shy of Gresham known locally as The Numbers. The last time I came to this intersection was in August 2013 with Aimee then fifty-two, who had agreed to accompany me and talk about her memories of the place where she'd crashed in a plane. I was just starting work writing the story of United Flight 173, and she and I were still getting to know each other having only met once before. But it was a meeting that surprised us both, as if destiny had a hand in it. It turned out her oldest child was attending the high school where I taught language arts. We had passed each other many times without knowing that our paths would soon intersect over another important part of her life—and ultimately mine.

We got off the MAX light rail together at the 160th Street Station and walked the three blocks to 157th under gray skies. In the late morning quiet I could tell she was on alert as she gingerly took in the surroundings like a medium waiting to be contacted, waiting for the images to strike. She had told me that it was difficult sometimes to come here, even though she often did in late December. She wasn't sure how it would be for her. She'd learned not to be too surprised at sudden, unbidden reactions to reminders of the night her airliner had fallen to earth. Indeed, she and her reactions were old friends now. They had marked and marred her life for years until finally in 2007 she had to give up her beloved but demanding work as a hospice nurse because she could no longer manage her debilitating symptoms of PTSD: the panic attacks, the depression, her inability to drive or even leave her house. She'd been on disability ever since as she struggled to heal and function.

Earlier, during our first meeting at a cafe, I'd been startled by her frankness about the problems she was having. She wanted me to understand that she was coping with a mental illness and felt seventy-five percent of her PTSD was directly due to the plane crash. Yet, she added, since the twentieth anniversary reunion, her bitterness had dissipated and she was doing her best to recover—an irony given how much she had done to help others recover by organizing the event.

As we approached the intersection the jet had blasted across, Aimee pointed to the apartment complex on the north side of Burnside. "That wasn't there," she said. "No MAX line either." Then we turned to a small, vacant bungalow covered in graffiti near the corner on the south side. "That's the house. I knocked on the door and told them my plane had crashed. I asked if I could use their phone to call my parents. It all seems so surreal now."

Next to the house, a large empty lot covered in sere, late-summer grass, and humps of dehydrated blackberry brambles drew Aimee's attention next. "That's where we hit first," she said descending a short embankment toward the middle of the property, no sign in sight of the house that was flattened there. I followed her, wondering how she was feeling, making notes of what I saw and trying to imagine what *she* saw.

She said there were times when she felt sad for her seventeen-year-old self and remembered coming here around ten years after the accident with a yellow rose she'd bought as a gift for that young woman. "A woo-woo moment," she said, laughing.

At the far end of the lot behind a little stand of trees, the scattered mess of a homeless camp came into view. We paused, not wanting to go closer, and stood, chatting for a while about the night of the crash. She remembered how dark it was before the TV crew arrived with their lights, and that it was cold, though she couldn't feel it much, or the pain in her ankle. She recalled wandering around dazed until she was taken to a church nearby with other passengers. Where *was* that church? she wondered. It couldn't have been far, but now she wasn't sure. It was hard to be sure of things.

Now, three years and a story-journey later, it's late January and I'm drawn back to the intersection, with my dad this time. He's never had much reason to drive by the spot, so hasn't seen the changes in person. His stack of photos of the crash from the trial still comprise most of the images, frozen in time, that might jump to mind.

At ninety-three, he's been retired from the Oregon State Bar for a year, but he still has other business to attend to at his office every day, so he's dressed as usual in his suit as we drive east on Stark Street past discount auto dealers, nail salons and peeling convenience stores. We turn left at 157th Avenue and head north following the path and last seconds of the doomed jet. At the corner of Burnside, we park and step out into the chill air. It's been raining for two solid months, but today, though still cloudy, there's a break in the weather. Wisely, Dad takes his umbrella anyway.

Not much has changed since my last visit. The little bungalow Aimee remembered visiting the night of the crash has been fixed up and is inhabited again. Out-of-season Christmas lights are still draped along the roof line, though turned off. Across the boulevard where the plane came to rest, the nondescript tan Windsor Court apartment complex built in 1990 has a new layer of bark mulch in the front landscaping, its driveway the only echo of the path McBroom followed as he wrestled the jet into the small, dark slot he was aiming for.

But the empty lot where the plane touched down on the south side of the street is curiously still vacant in an area where boxy, multi-family housing developments in beiges and browns have eaten unused lots of any size and many of the one-story ranches that comprised the neighborhood until very recently. How this property has remained undeveloped in the midst of this trend, and next to the light rail line, is baffling indeed.

On the phone later, the second-generation owner laughs and says she's still waiting for the city to keep a promise to rezone it. But she remembers the night of the crash, and coming with her father the next day to inspect the demolished, just-vacated rental house he owned there, and to look for an abandoned cat she never found.

Today, the lot looks very much the same as when Aimee and I visited three years before, except for a now distinct little path that winds from one corner at the street to the concealed clearing in the rear, indicating the regular traffic it gets from the folks still squatting there. The ground is muddy so Dad and I stand on the residential sidewalk imagining the flying behemoth hitting the ground in a shower of sparks, utility poles trailing it like pilot fish, and we marvel once again at how much of the plane remained in tact, how few people were lost.

"It's just amazing..." my dad says, taking in the scene in his mind and before our eyes. "...how he did it, that landing."

But our imaginations are our own, and nobody but those who lived through it would ever know that such a thing happened in this place. A generation has passed, and there's nothing, no sign to show that an airliner crashed here.

What would such a marker look like and where would it go? I muse aloud, scanning the worn suburban surroundings. Maybe a plaque could be put at the MAX light rail station a few blocks away so that people waiting for their train could learn about that night in 1978, and pay their respects to the memory of the people on United Flight 173, and to the crash that changed so much.

Perhaps a yellow rose might even appear there one day.

When I caught up with Aimee a week after my visit to the site with my father, she had news to share. She had nearly completed the training needed to reactivate her nurse's license and was preparing to go back to work part time. She was drawn to hospice work again, but had also developed an interest in working with incarcerated women, and was exploring job opportunities in that area, too. It seemed a perfect fit that someone emerging from years of work on her own recovery from trauma, might have something to offer to women whose histories likely included traumas of their own. She's also an active member of an online air crash survivor group—but still can't set foot on an airplane. Now, nearly forty years on, knowing what it means to suffer from a lifetime of PTSD, how it affected not just her but also her family, another generation, and also knowing now what was revealed in Lisa's trial about United's role in the accident, Aimee wonders only half joking if the statute of limitations has passed to file a lawsuit.

As of this writing, Lisa's aunt Maria still lives in the same house she did during the years of litigation. The three girls she raised have children of their own so she is busy being a grandmother. Her memories of the accident and the court case are still stressful if she allows herself to think about them. She kept the suitcase, still packed with trial documents, for decades, unable to look through it but equally unable to throw it away until 2014 when she decided it was time to close the chapter. Even then she couldn't bring herself to sort through and discard the papers so her husband and daughters did it for her. Asked about the final Supreme Court decision, she says simply, "The truth never came out."

Lisa still prefers to leave the crash and trial in the past. But questions come up now and then for her. She long wondered who pulled her from the wreckage, likely saving her life. She finally learned the names of the two flight attendants who found her and the sheriffs deputies who got her out when she posted her query on a blog page created by Matt Camp devoted to the United 173 accident.

In 2004, six years after he attended the twentieth reunion of United Flight 173, Malburn "Buddy" McBroom died at the age of seventy-seven from prostate and lung cancer. Though he never completely shed the guilt and remorse he felt about the accident, in his obituary his daughter, Carrie, noted that attending the reunion helped, it lightened his burden some. She was quoted, "I remember him saying he could do a better job of letting it go. It was easier to put it down."

As for United Airlines, a lot has happened since the accident. The company survived a bankruptcy in 2002 following the human and financial disaster of 9/11, and the nation's economic recession. Then, during a flurry of airline mergers, UAL bought Continental Airlines in 2010 making the combined pair the largest airline in the world by number of destinations served. In January 2016 the company reported record financial performance of $4.5 billion in net income for the previous year, and announced that it would buy forty new Boeing 737-700 aircraft.

But it hasn't been all smooth flying. Also in the news was the sudden departure in 2015 of United's president and CEO amid a federal corruption scandal, as well as a letter from the FAA to United outlining concerns that the company's internal safety practices indicated "systemic" hazards. The letter, according to the Wall Street Journal (WSJ April 10, 2015), cited violations of mandatory pilot qualification and scheduling requirements, and told the airline that it needed to develop an action plan to "mitigate the hazard."

United announced that plan nearly a year later in a replay of what happened after United Flight 173 went down. Once again, all the airline's pilots (12,000 now) were called in for extra training following a series of safety incidents including dangerously low fuel events and emergency maneuvers to avoid crashing.

Once again, the training focused on "human factors" issues like teaching crew members situational awareness, how to communicate with each other better in the cockpit, especially across seniority levels, and how to accurately manage fuel. United's deep experience in this area is handy at a time when remembering the lessons of the past is facing a challenge: The entire industry is undergoing a generational shift as older pilots retire and newer, less-experienced aviators take the helm.

At the same time, airline industry lobbyists have renewed their push in Washington, DC to roll back the FAA's mandatory 1,500 in-flight hours minimum requirement for newly-hired commercial pilots against strong objections from aviation safety advocates including the famous "Miracle on the Hudson" pilot Chesley "Sully" Sullenberger III. He testified before a senate subcommittee in April 2015 saying,

> "There are some in the industry who look upon safety improvements as a burden and a cost when they should be looking at them as the only way to keep their promise to do the very best they can to keep their passengers safe. [ ]As airline professionals, aviation regulators, and legislators, we must have the integrity and courage to reject the merely expedient and the barely adequate as not good enough. We must not allow profit motives to undermine our clear obligation to do what is right to ensure public safety."

But, again, hands-on flight training requirements, or retraining pilots in updated crew resource management (CRM) principles addresses only one piece of the system—albeit one of the most critical and visible. It's just as important that these lessons-learned extend to vital aircraft maintenance and repair operations, and that *maintenance resource management* (MRM) training also gets a refresher. This is especially urgent, but far more challenging now since airlines have turned to outsourcing maintenance operations to contractors here in the U.S. and abroad in places like El Salvador, Indonesia, Turkey and China.

According to a 2008 audit conducted by the Department of Transportation's Office of the Inspector General (OIG), United (a trailblazer in this area) and other airlines subcontract up to seventy percent of their repair and maintenance work to outside and offshore shops where labor costs are a fraction of those in their own facilities—what few are left.

261

What this means for regulatory and corporate oversight, not to mention information flow and accessibility between stakeholders like pilots—and security against terrorism—is still becoming clear. But one thing is certain: it adds layers of logistical complexity and distance, in other words, several hole-filled slices of swiss cheese, to an already intricate and now far-flung organizational system. And it's further aggravated by cross-cultural communication hurdles in foreign maintenance operations where workers often do not have the language skills to read English manuals and understand directions, or be assertive with superiors or inspectors about problems.

News investigations by Frontline (2011) and NPR (2009-10) have illuminated these and other alarming maintenance/repair out-sourcing issues, including inadequate FAA inspection coverage, or inspections that are forewarned, giving the shops time to prepare. Also documented were shops failing to check worker qualifications or security background, workers using unauthorized component parts, or assembling components incorrectly, and "pencil whipping" by super-visors, under pressure to rush planes back into service, who did not actually check that repair/maintenance work was done properly before signing off on it. Such practices, they warn, can and do produce ha-zards that play out regularly in non-fatal flight incidents, but may again yield deadly consequences.

Indeed, questions must be asked about the potentially lethal incidents that occur on commercial flights *every week* and may well originate in faulty maintenance, such as in-flight engine shutdowns and fires, fuel leaks, cargo doors left open, electrical and hydraulic system malfunctions and landing gear failures. In seventy-two United Airlines incident reports documented in 2016 by the website aeroin-side.com, the majority of fifty-one fell into the category detailed above. Only twenty-one were due to pilot error, or the result of an unforeseeable event like a bird strike or turbulence.

In one oddly resonant incident in October 2016, passengers on a United flight from Belfast to New Jersey spent a terrifying two hours after take-off when the plane's landing gear malfunctioned. Fully loaded with fuel for the transatlantic flight and unable to land, the pilot declared an emergency and circled, burning off fuel and trying to trouble shoot the problem before he was able to bring the aircraft in safely.

Things didn't go as well in Colombia when a flight carrying a beloved Brazilian soccer team crashed in November 2016 apparently due to fuel exhaustion killing most aboard, or for the Pakistan International Airlines flight a week later that suffered an engine shut-down and crashed in early December killing everyone.

In her recent book, *The Crash Detectives,* author Christine Negroni has suggested that a sudden in-flight depressurization might even explain the 2014 disappearance of Malaysian Airlines Flight 370. Maintenance mistake or worse?

It remains to be seen whether such incidents and news coverage here in the U.S. will encourage greater vigilance and spur a chronically underfunded FAA to insist on corrective measures or levy meaningful fines for infractions before another disaster occurs—or convince the airlines that eating away at safety margins doesn't make economic sense. Aviation attorneys on both sides are taking note and preparing for the expensive, long-haul legal battles like the Andor case that follow a crash.

In the meantime, like any airline passenger today, I'm used to the fact that the peanuts are gone and my suitcase costs extra money to take along, but I do expect the price of the ticket to include a vigorous and scrupulous commitment to safety while my life is literally in their hands. Still, as the Andor case and others show, there can be little doubt about the cost-benefit calculation airlines do as a business to spend only what they must on safety. As Stephan Barlay notes in his book, *The Final Call: Why Airline Disasters Continue to Happen*, "It's a daunting task not to let the art of the acceptable deteriorate into the dodger's art of what you can get away with."

While it's reassuring and even lulling to note that according to recent statistics the number of accidental air disasters is at an all-time low (versus the growing number of intentionally-caused disasters), John Goglia, a former NTSB official told NPR, "The absence of an accident doesn't mean you're safe. We should be monitoring and doing our job before there's an accident, not after."

In honor of all who were aboard United Flight 173, and of every other commercial flight that has crashed because of errors, negligence, and especially, deliberate cost-saving decisions:

Amen to that.

Acknowledgments

This project owes a lot to serendipities and supports that often struck me as uncanny. From the beginning, stray conversations, random encounters and unlikely coincidences seemed to pave the way for this story of the crash of United Flight 173 to be told. They often led, almost by design, to information and to people who could and did help me. While I don't pretend to understand how such synchronicities work, I am very grateful that they do!

My father, Stewart M. Whipple to whom this work is dedicated, represents both the genesis and the guide star for the project. His experience, wisdom and sense of humor were the steady coordinates I followed throughout the process of discovery and writing—though he never let me forget that the path was always mine to seek. I consider myself very lucky to have had the chance to share this journey with him.

I must also note that my sister, Doran was the one who made the obvious plain to me by suggesting that the story of United Flight 173 was a book whose time had come, before it was too late. She backed the proposal with an introduction to a writer friend and former flight attendant, Sharon Rockey, who in turn opened the door to many others, especially my aviation guru, Tom Cordell, whose constant help and connections have provided so much to my understanding and progress throughout the project.

I am also indebted to Aimee Ford Conner, who at the age of seventeen survived the crash, and later went on to organize the twenty-year reunion of passengers, families and emergency workers, which offered so many a chance to remember and heal from the experience—including the pilot blamed for the crash, Malburn McBroom Truly a heroic survivor, her memories, contacts, insights and generos ity have been invaluable assets during the research and writing.

Also, I am so grateful for the support I received from othe survivors of the accident and their families who were kind enough to speak with me about their experiences. In particular, I thank Chri Mendenhall. He lost his father, flight engineer Forrest "Frostie" Mendenhall, in the crash, and is now an aviation professional, him self. His perspectives and words of support were especially importan and moving, and meant everything to me.

Many thanks, as well, to the Evergreen Aviation Museum Emily Gottlieb at the Center for Justice and Democracy, the Lewi and Clark Law Library, Patrizia Nava at the Eugene McDermott Li brary University of Texas at Dallas, The Naval Air Museum Barber Point, Hawaii; consumer advocate Ralph Nader, trial attorneys Davic Rapoport and Greg Kafoury. Also Louie Csonaki, Carol Pollard, Gary Estes, Lisa Andor, Maria Affatigato, Matt Camp, Lukas Ketner for hi artistry, my agent M. Damian McNicholl for all his efforts and hi belief in this story; Andy Davies, a get-it-done creative genius, Davi Whipple, my cheering section and source of inspiration. Also the MFA program at Portland State University for the wonderful commu nity of writers who supported my early work on this book, and espe cially for the guidance and help of author Paul Collins whose profes sionalism, ability to listen and encourage, and flawless instincts repre sent everything one could hope for in a mentor. And to Lori Osmundsen with deepest gratitude for so much: Think. Do.

Selected Bibliography and Works Cited

The following is a list of some of the books, articles, documents, videos, and websites I found especially useful during the research and writing of this book.

"Accident Overview United Flight 173." *Lessons Learned*. Federal Aviation Administration, n.d. Web. Jan. 2015.

Aeronautical Radio, Inc. Transcript of Radio Communication. 29 Dec. 1978. Raw data. Plaintiff's Exhibit, Portland. ARINC Communication between UAL 173 and United Airlines Dispatch and Maintenance on Dec. 28, 1978.

"Air Disasters Season 4 Episode 8." *Focused on Failure*. Amazon.com. 27 July, 2014. Television.

"AirDisaster.Com: Investigation: United Airlines Flight 173."*AirDisaster.Com*. N.p., 1998. Web. June 2014.

"Are Planes Dangerously Over-engineered?" *Popular Mechanics*. N.p., 9 Aug. 2011. Web. Apr. 2014.

1977 ANNUAL REPORT, (1977): 1-33. Division of Public Safety Multnomah County, Oregon. Web. 19 Aug. 2015. <https://www.ncjrs.gov/pdffiles1/Digitization/48343N-CJRS.pdf>.

"ASN Aircraft Accident McDonnell Douglas DC-8-61 N8082U Portland International Airport, OR (PDX)." *Flight-safety.org*. Flight Safety Foundation, 1996. Web. May 2013.

Associated Press. "Couple Wins $125,000 for Crash." *Columbian* [Vancouver, WA] 16 Jan. 1983: n. pag. Print.

Associated Press. "Court Ruling Favors Airlines."

The Oregonian [Portland] 6 Jan. 1981: n. pag. Print.

Aubert, Garth. "Punitive Damages in Aviation Litigation." Aircraftbuilders,com. 2006. Web.

"Aviation Safety Network ASN Aviation Safety Database." *Aviation Safety Network ASN Aviation Safety Database*. Flight Safety Foundation, 2012. Web. 24 Mar. 2015.

Bailey, F. Lee, and John Greenya. *Cleared for the Approach: F. Lee Bailey in Defense of Flying*. Englewood Cliffs, NJ: Prentice-Hall, 1977. Print.

Barlay, Stephen. *"The Final Call: Why Airline Disasters Continue to Happen."* New York: Pantheon, 1990. Print.

Baron, Robert. "The Cockpit, the Cabin, and Social Psychology." (2005): n. pag. *Crew Resource Management (CRM)*. GOFIR Global Operators Flight Information Resource. Web. Mar. 2014.

Boule, Margie. "Flight 173 Reunion." *The Oregonian* [Portland] 1998-1999: n. pag. Print. Various columns published between November 22, 1998 and January 3, 1999.

Camp, Matt. "1978 Portland Oregon Plane Crash." Web log post. *: 1978 Portland, Oregon Plane Crash*. Matt_Camp.-com, 2007. Web. 28 Dec. 2014.

Carley, William M. "Danger Aloft." *The Wall Street Journal* 2 Nov. 1979: 1+. Print.

Cockpit Voice Recorder Transcript of a Sundstrand V557. 28 Dec. 1978. Raw data. United Flight 173, n.p

Cohen, Patricia. "When Company Is Fined, Taxpayers Often Share Bill." *The New York Times* [New York] 4 Feb.

2015, Business Day sec.: B1. Print.

Cox, Fred. "UA DC-8 Fleet Information." *UA DC-8 Fleet Information*. Fred Cox DC-8 Jet Collection, 2009. Web. Mar. 2014.

Cranston, Mark, and Dee Waldron. "Douglas DC-8 Digested." *Historic Jetliners Group: Douglas DC-8 History*. Historic Jetliners Group, 18 Nov. 2006. Web. Mar. 2013.

"DC-8 Flight Operating Manual." (1996): 1-26. *Wdars.com*. American International Airways. Web. 2014.

Diehl, Alan E. *Aeronautical Decision Making for Student and Private Pilots*. Washington, D.C.: U.S. Dept. of Transportation, Federal Aviation Administration, 1987. Print.

Diehl, Alan E. *Air Safety Investigators: Using Science to Save Lives One Crash at a Time*. Place of Publication Not Identified: Xlibris, 2013. Print.

Dietrich, Bill. "Ex-Pilot Presses for New DC-8 Safety Rules." *The Columbian* [Vancouver, WA] 5 Jan. 1981, sec. 2: n. pag. Print.

Dietrich, Bill. "Pilot of DC-8 Frustrated in Attempt to Get Answer From FAA." *Columbian* [Vancouver, WA] 19 Jan. 1981: n. pag. Print.

"Douglas DC-8." *Douglas DC-8*. AFC Aviation Friends Cologne/Bonn, 2010. Web. Mar. 2014. Worldwide DC-8 Inventory.

"Douglas DC-8-63 Jetliner Promo Film - 1967." *YouTube*. Classic Airliners & Vintage Pop Culture, 31 Oct. 2013. Web. Dec. 2013.

Elizabeth Marina Andor v. United Airlines. M. 28 Mar. 1984. Print. Case No. 830100133 - Deposition of Thaddeus Delaney "TD" Garrett.

Elizabeth Marina Andor v. United Airlines. Multnomah County Circuit Court. 28 Mar. 1984. Print. Case No. 830100133 - Deposition of Martha Fralick (Flight Attendant).

Elizabeth Marina Andor v. United Airlines. Multnomah County Circuit Court. 28 Mar. 1984. Print. Case No. 830100133 - Transcript of the Proceedings Vol. I -Vol. XII inclusive.

Elizabeth Marina Andor v. United Airlines. Multnomah County Circuit Court. 28 Mar. 1984. Print. Case No. 830100133: Deposition of Malburn A. McBroom (Pilot).

Elizabeth Marina Andor v. United Airlines. Multnomah County Circuit Court. 28 Mar. 1984. Print. Case No. 830100133 Deposition of Nancy King Pirotte (Flight Attendant).

Elott, John. "Mayday! The Ordeal of Flight 173." *Airliners* Jan.-Feb. 1998: 18+. Print.

Erickson, Steve. "Memories of Crash Still Hurt." *Oregonian* [Portland] 29 Dec. 1983, Sunrise ed.: A1. Print.

E.S. Grush & C.S. Saunby. "Fatalities Associated with Crash Induced Fuel Leakage and Fires." Ford interoffice memo PDF Web. Dec. 2004. www.autosafety.org

"Evening News." *Evening News*. KGW Channel 8. Portland, OR, 28 Dec. 1978. Television. Local News Coverage of United 173 Crash.

Fallows, James. "The Great Airline War." *Texas Monthly*

Dec. 1975: n. pag. Google Books. Web. 30 Sept. 2015.

Ford Conner, Aimee. "Flight 173 Reunion Correspondence." Saxton, Fay, Chris Mendenhall, Lynne Egli, Bob Bean, and Eleanor Ross. 1999. MS. Personal Collection, Portland, Oregon.

Gonzales, Laurence. "Airline Safety: A Special Report." *Playboy* n.d.: 140+. Print.

Gonzales, Laurence. *Flight 232: A Story of Disaster and Survival.* New York: W.W. Norton, 2014. Print. ISBN 978-0-393-24002-3.

Gonzales, Laurence. "The Final Flight of 232 Heavy." *Popular Mechanics* (2014): 71+. Web.

Gottlieb, Emily. "What You Need to Know About Punitive Damages." *Center for Justice & Democracy* 22 (2011): 1-16. www.centerjd.org. New York Law School, Sept. 2011. Web. 25 Aug. 2015. <https://centerjd.org/system/.../PunitiveDamagesWhitePaper2011.pdf>. White Paper.

Grogan, David. "As the Airlines Cut Costs to Keep Flying, Safety Expert John Galipault Warns They Could Be Risking Passengers' Lives." people.com. People Magazine, 17 Oct. 1983. Web. Feb. 2015.

Harris, Jr., Roy. "Disaster Dollars." *Wall Street Journal* 11 July 1980: 1+.Print.

Heller, Jean. "Ill-Fated Crew Never Warned of Gear Failures."*Oregonian/Newhouse News Service* [Portland] 22 Feb. 1981: A11. Print.

Heller, Jean. "Landing Gear Failure Problems Remain Unsolved."*Oregonian/Newhouse News Service* [Portland] 22

Feb. 1981: A10. Print.

Herburger Pollard, Carol, Ph.D. *Impact: A Study of Flight Attendant Survivors of Air Disasters*. Diss. California Institute of Integral Studies, 2001. San Francisco: n.p., 2001. Print. Page 171-183.

Hicks, James. "Lessons From the Cockpit:What Aviation Has Learned That We Must." American Society of Anesthesiologists, Jan. 2014. Web. Feb. 2014. ASA Newsletter Vol.78 Number 1.

Hill, Jim. "6 Lawsuits Unsettled From 1978 Airliner Crash." *Oregonian* [Portland] 1 June 1982: n. pag. Print.

Hiltzik, Michael. "Punitive Awards Uncharted Sea for Courts." *Oregonian/LA Times-Washington Post Service* [Portland] 22 Feb. 1984: A2. Print.

"Horton v. OHSU." *Justia Law*. Oregon Supreme Court Decision 359 Or 168 (2016), 5 May 2016. Web.

Houck, Jerry. *Metallurgist's Factual Report*. Rep. no. 79-31. Washington, D.C.: NTSB, 1979. Print. Re: United Airlines DC-8, #N8082V, NTSB No. 79-A-A006. Examination of piston rod and mating rod end from right main landing gear retract assembly.

Hubert, Ronan. "Crash Statistics." *B3A Aircraft Accidents Archives RSS*. B3A Bureau of Aircraft Accidents, 1990. Web. Feb. 2014.

"The Human Factors "Dirty Dozen"" - *SKYbrary Aviation Safety*. SKYbrary, 25 May 2016. Web.

In Re Conduct of Roth. NO. 9; SC 28223. Oregon Supreme Court. 2 June 1982. N.p., n.d. Web. 20 Aug. 2015.

Kao, Lillian S., and Eric J. Thomas. "Navigating Toward Improved Surgical Safety Using Aviation-Based Strategies." *Journal of Surgical Research* 145.2 (2008): 327-35. *Med.uth.edu*. Apr. 2008. Web. 2013.

King, James B., Elwood Driver, Francis McAdams, and Philip Hogue. "Aircraft Accident Report: United Airlines, Inc. McDonnell Douglas DC-8-61, Portland OR, Dec. 28, 1978." *National Transportation Safety Board* 79-7 NTSB.AAR (1979): 1-64. *Libraryonline.erau.edu*. US Government. Web. 2013.

KingRey, Ed. "Close-Up: United Airlines Flight 173 — A Controller's Account - AVweb Features Article." *AVweb.com*. N.p., 1999. Web. June 2013.

Kohn, Linda T., Janet Corrigan, and Molla S. Donaldson. *To Err Is Human: Building a Safer Health System*. Washington, D.C.: National Academy, 1999. Print.

Landsberg, Bruce. "*Safety Pilot Landmark Accident: Flameout*." AOPA, 1 Oct. 2016. Web. 15 Nov. 2016.

Leonard, M., S. Graham, and D. Bonacum. "*The Human Factor: The Critical Importance of Effective Teamwork and Communication in Providing Safe Care*." Qual Saf Health Care (2004): 85-90. Web. 14 Sept. 2015.

Linde, Hans. "Andor v. United Air Lines." Justia Law. *Oregon Supreme Court Decision 739 P.2d 18 (1987) 303 Or. 505*, 23 June 1987. Web.

Leon, Pablo Mendes De, and Emilie Aberson. *Air Transport Law and Policy in the 1990s: Controlling the Boom*. Dordrecht: Martinus Nijhoff, 1991. Print.

Love, Peter, "A Case of Pilot Error?" *The Oregonian* [Portland] 30 Aug. 1981, The Sunday Oregonian Magazine ed., Northwest sec.: 4-6. Print.

Mantia, Patty. "One Year Later: Crash Still Haunts Many." *The Oregonian* [Portland] 23 Dec. 1979, Sunday ed.: A1+. Print.

Marshall, David. "Crew Resource Management: Its History and Development."*Saferhealthcare.com*. N.p., 1999. Web. Jan. 2014.

Martinussen, Monica, and David R. Hunter. *Aviation Psychology and Human Factors*. Boca Raton: CRC/Taylor & Francis, 2010. Print.

McBroom, Malburn A. "Probable Cause Appeal." Letter to James B. King, Chair NTSB. 3 Aug. 1979. MS. Plaintiff's Exhibit, Portland, OR.

McCarthy, Dennis, and Rolla Crick. "DC-8 Crash Memories Still Vivid a Year Later." *Oregon Journal* [Portland] 22 Dec. 1979: 3. Print.

McDonnell Douglas. "DC-8 Service Bulletin No. 32-131." Letter to All DC-8 Operators. 27 Mar. 1968. MS. Plaintiff's Exhibit, Portland, OR. Replace Main Landing Gear Retract Cylinder Rod End Assemblies.

McDonnell Douglas. "Main Landing Gear Retract Cylinder Assemblies." Letter to All DC-8 Operators. 31 July 1967. MS. Plaintiff's Exhibit, Portland, OR. Ref: Piston & Eyebolt Corrosion Telex, 30 Dec. 1966.

McDonnell Douglas. "MLG Retract Cylinder Piston Rod End." Letter to All DC-8 Operators. 22 Oct. 1968. MS. Plaintiff's Exhibit, Portland, OR. Re: Service Bulletin No. 32-131.

Melugin Jr., C.R., comp. "Maintenance Inspection Notes for McDonnell Douglas DC-8 Series Aircraft." *ADVISORY CIRCULAR AC No. 20-78* (1972): n. pag. *FAA Document Library*. Department of Transportation FAA. Web. 2013.

"Milestones." *Association of Flight Attendants*. N.p., n.d. Web. Feb. 2014.

Mitchell, Jann. "New Life Ahead for Tot Who Lost Family in Jet Crash." *Oregon Journal* [Portland] 26 Jan. 1979: 24. Print.

Moore, Kevin-Michael. "The Crash of Flight 173." Web log post. Dead Memories Portland. Kevin-Michael Moore, 2010. Web. 2013.

Nader, Ralph. *In Pursuit of Justice: Collected Writings 2000-2003*. New York: Seven Stories, 2004. Print.

Nader, Ralph. "Suing For Justice: Your Lawsuits Are Good for America." *Harper's Magazine* Apr. 2016. Print.

Napert, Greg. "Landing Some Information: A Fresh Perspective on Why Landing Gear Need an Overhaul." *Aviation Pros.com*. N.p., Oct. 1999.

Nelson Mullins. "Punitive Damages in the Airline Case." *In-House Defense Quarterly* Fall (2006): n. pg. Nelson Mullins Riley& Scarborough, LLP. Defense Research Institute. Web. 24 Aug. 2015.<http://www.nelsonmullins.com/news/articles-and-speeches-print.cfm?id=95>.

News Staff. "Neighbor: 'God Almighty, He Was Like Son to Me." *The Columbian* [Vancouver, WA] 29 Dec. 1978: 1+. Print.

Novell, Robert. "History of a Great Airline Part 2." Weblog post. Robert Novell, 2 Aug. 2013. Web. Jan. 2014.

Nowlan, F. Stanley, and Howard F. Heap. "Reliability-Centered Maintenance." *United Airlines & Dept. of Defense Study* (1978): n. pag. Web. 2013.

NTSB Accident Investigation Deposition, 1-97 (1979) (testimony of Malburn Adair McBroom). Print. In the Matter of the Accident of United Airlines, December 28, 1978

O'Brien, Miles. "Flying Cheaper." *Frontline* Transcript. *PBS*, 18 Jan. 2011.

Okray, Randy, and Thomas Lubnau. *Crew Resource Management for the Fire Service*. Tulsa, OK: PennWell, 2004. Print.

The Oregonian [Portland] 29 Dec. 1978: 1. Print. Coverage of United Flight 173 Crash, Dec. 29, 1978 - Jan. 10, 1979. Various articles and Reporters.

Petzinger, Thomas. *Hard Landing: The Epic Contest for Power and Profits That Plunged the Airlines into Chaos*. New York: Times Business, 1995. Print.

Pilot Judgment Training and Evaluation Volume I. N.p.: n.p., 1982. Federal Aviation Administration. Web.
"Plane Crash Info." Web log post. *Plane Crash Info*. Richard Kebabjian, n.d. Web. 24 Mar. 2015.

Rapoport, David, and Michael Teich. "*The Erosion of Secrecy in Air Disaster Litigation* | Rapoport Law Offices, P.C. | Illinois, Wisconsin. Rapoport Law Offices, P.C. N.p., 2011. Web.

"Reliability Centered Maintenance (RCM)." *Reliability*

Centered Maintenance (RCM). Weibull.com & ReliaSoft
Corp., 1992. Web. Mar. 2013.

Richards, Leverette. "Second DC-8's Landing Gear
Fails." *The Oregonian* [Portland] 17 Jan. 1979: n. pag. Print.

Rossman, J. "Andor v. United Air Lines." *Justia Law*.
Oregon Appeals Court Decision 719 P.2d 492 (1986) 79
Or.App. 311, 14 May 1986. Web.

Sian, Benjamin, Michelle Robertson, and Jean Watson.
"Maintenance Resource Management Handbook." (n.d.):
1-110. *Libraryonline.erau.edu*. Federal Aviation Administration. Web. Feb. 2014.

Simmon, Jr., David A. "Model Airline Safety Program."
International Air Safety Seminar (1988): 1-16. *Flightsafety-
.org*. Flight Safety Foundation Digest. Web. Jan. 2015.

Starr, Myla. "We All 'Die a Little' in Any Crash."
Loveland Daily Reporter-Herald [Loveland, Colorado] 10
Jan. 1979: n. pag. Print.

Stich, Rodney. *The Unfriendly Skies: An Aviation Watergate*. Alamo, CA: Diablo Western, 1980. Print.

Sullenberger, Chesley, III. "My Testimony Today Before
the Senate Subcommittee on Aviation Operations, Safety, and
Security." Sully Sullenberger. N.p., 27 May 2015. Web.

"Survivor Recalls Deadly 1978 Portland Plane Crash."
Seattle Times [Seattle] 29 Dec. 2008: n. pag. Print. http://
www.seattletimes.com/seattle-news/survivor-recalls-
deadly-1978-portland-plane-crash/

Tenby, Henry. "Last Arrival and Departure of ATI DC-8-
62 N799AL." *Airlinehobby.com*. Airlinehobby.com, 12 May

2013. Web. Apr. 2014.

TheRealNews. "Breaking Through Power: Richard Newman on Educating the Public on the Importance of Tort Law." YouTube. YouTube, 16 Nov. 2016. Web.

Trevison, Catherine. "Air Safety Statistics Fail to Calm Passengers' Frazzled Nerves." *Oregonian* [Portland] 6 Feb. 2000, Sunrise ed.: A1. Print.

UAL Inc. Annual Report 1978. Rep. Chicago: UAL, 1979. Print. Trial Exhibit. Author's Collection.

UAL Inc 1979-1984, Annual Report Collection. Print. Folder number 43, Drawer number 36, History of Aviation Collection, Special Collections Department, Eugene McDermott Library, The University of Texas at Dallas.

Ulrich, Roberta. "Injury Trials Near in 1978 Jet Crash." *Oregonian/UPI* [Portland] 5 Jan. 1981: 4. Print.

United Airlines. Overhaul Manual: Landing Gear. 2 Jan. 1974. Raw data. Plaintiff's Exhibit, Portland, OR. Instructions: DC-8 Main Gear Actuating Cylinder - Piston Thread Repair.

United States. Department of Transportation. Civil Aeronautics Board. *UNITED AIR LINES, INC., DOUGLAS DC-8, N 8040U, STAPLETON AIRFIELD, DENVER, COLORADO, JULY 11, 1961. National Transportation Library.* Web. 2013.

United States. Department of Transportation. *NTSB Accident Report AAR79-17 American Airlines Flight 191.* Washington, D.C.: NTSB, n.d. *Libraryonline.erau.edu.* Web.

United States. National Transportation Safety Board.

Department of Transportation. *Accident Investigation Interview*. San Francisco: NTSB, 1979. Print. Interview with Leland Buhr, DC-8 Maintenance Controller, United Airlines.

United States. US Government Publishing Office. Department of Transportation. *ECFR: Electronic Code of Federal Regulations*. Part 43 ed. Vol. Title 14. N.p.: n.p., n.d. Aeronautics & Space. *GPO*. Web. Aviation: Maintenance, Preventive Maintenance, Rebuilding and Alteration.

USPIRG. "Report: Close Corporate Tax Loopholes." Subsidizing Bad Behavior. *United States Public Interest Research Group*, 3 Jan. 2013.Web. July 2016.

Viscusi, W. Kip. *The Blockbuster Punitive Damage Awards*. HARVARD JOHN M. OLIN CENTER FOR LAW, ECONOMICS, AND BUSINESS, Apr. 2004. Web. 24 Aug. 2015.

Welch, Bob. "Survivor Still Feels Impact after 30 Years." *The Register Guard (Eugene, OR)*. N.p., 28 Dec. 2008. Web. 31 Mar. 2015.

Williams Walsh, Mary. "Filing of Punitive Damage Claims Is Focus of Increasing Controversy." *Wall Street Journal* 12 Nov. 1984: 27+. Print.

"The Year 1978 From The People History." *What Happened in 1978 including Pop Culture, Prices, Events and Technology*. The People History, 2004. Web. Oct. 2013.

Young, JP. "Flight Deck Action: DC-8." *YouTube*. YouTube, 16 June 2013. Web. Apr.

Zwerdling, Daniel. "To Cut Costs, Airlines Send Repairs Abroad." NPR. 19 Oct. 2009. Web.

Crevice corrosion. Trial exhibit photo.

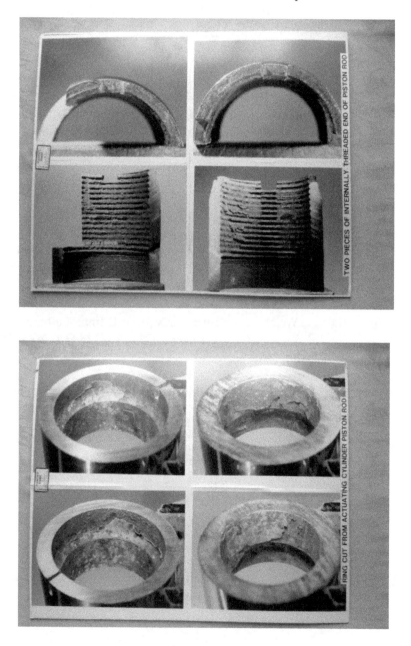

Landing gear of a DC-8. Trial exhibit photo.

The cockpit of DC-8 "Little Ami." Photo by the author.

Interior and exterior views of United Flight 173 after the crash. Photos from the author's collection of trial materials.

From the author's research collection.

Julie Whipple is a writer and educa-
tor living in Portland, Oregon. She
holds an MFA in creative writing with
an emphasis on nonfiction, and has
worked as a journalist in Kenya and
Tanzania where she was the East Africa
correspondent for the London-based,
weekly news magazine Africa Economic Digest. She also filed stories for the
London Observer, South Magazine, Radio France International and Deutsche
Welle among others. In the United
States, her work has been published in the Christian Science Monitor,
The Oregonian, the Portland Business Journal, and Portland Monthly
Magazine. She is the recipient of a Kellogg Award for Reporting and
holds professional memberships in the Authors Guild and PEN America.
This is her first book.

Photo by Andy Davies

Stewart M. Whipple at his desk in March, 2017.

CPSIA information can be obtained
at www.ICGtesting.com
Printed in the USA
LVHW08s2226300818
588617LV00012B/268/P

9 780692 070406